Bob Van Blaricom

TIME AND TIDE

A Nautical Memoir

TIME AND TIDE

A Nautical Memoir

Robert Van Blaricom

Lulu,Inc

2007

Printed in the United States of America
Book and cover design by Tinhorn@Dixie Press
Map courtesy of Latitude 38

Cataloging in Publication Data:
Van Blaricom, Robert
Time and Tide: a nautical memoir
1. Van Blaricom, Robert -- Biography   2.boats and boating
3. Voyages and travel   4. Sailing   I. Title
G540.V35 2007   910.45 – dc21

2nd Edition, 2007

To order additional copies of this book, contact:
Lulu, Inc.
www.lulu.com

DEDICATION

This book is dedicated to our granddaughter, Lacey, who has given us such joy in the past and hope for the future and without whose inspiration this account would not have been written.

ACKNOWLEDGEMENTS

The author gratefully acknowledges the invaluable help received from Robby Robinson for his kind assistance in solving some of the mysteries of the computers age and to John Sanford for guidance in the art of writing and for the photos on p. 306, p. 308 and the back cover. Thanks also to Suzie Knecht for her helpful suggestions and thanks to *Latitude 38* for the use of the map of the Northwest Passage. But most especially I am grateful to my wife, Jane, for her patience, understanding and encouragement.

"Believe me my young friend, there is nothing --- absolutely nothing --- half so much worth doing as simply messing about in boats"
                    ----"The Wind In The Willows", Kenneth Grahame

CONTENTS

The author at age three at Great Falls, Montana

INTRODUCTION

As a young boy living in the center of Montana, my idea of a body of water was the pond at a place we called "the springs" a short distance beyond the outskirts of town. My first memory recalls it being just a small swampy location at a low spot in the rolling prairie. A little later it was improved as a small WPA project during the depression and became a proper pond with a rock edging around it. We would sometimes build and launch a flimsy raft of scrap lumber and paddle around on it. Later my horizons expanded greatly when I became bold enough to ride my bicycle out to the banks of the broad Missouri River and gazed upon what seemed to me to be huge, dangerous and irresistibly intriguing waters. Then, at the age of 14, in a series of events which were unfortunate but at the same time liberating, I suddenly found myself with an endless expanse of salt water literally on my doorstep. I was immediately captivated by the boundless opportunity for adventure which lay before me. None of the other members of my family were particularly attracted to the sea, so why me?

As I try to explain to myself why I should try to answer this question by putting together the story of the sailing life that I have enjoyed, it becomes a little easier if I try to imagine who might bother to read the results. Hopefully it will be my friends who may charitably say they always wondered what made me tick. Also I hope my children and grandchildren (so far there is only one) will be pleased to have a record of some bits of family narrative which I have included. And finally, if any strangers pick up this volume, perhaps they will be amused by the way an interest can become an avocation and finally a virtual way of life. That may or may not be a good thing, but there are some things in life over which the poor individual has little or no control. My infatuation with the sea seems to be one of those things.

Thanks to my elder sister, Helen, who for religious reasons has traced the Van Blaricom family tree, I know something of my origins. It seems a certain Lubbert Gijsbertz*, who was born in the town of Blaricum, near Amsterdam, Netherlands together with his wife, Divertye, and their three sons sailed for America aboard the West India

---

*Because it was unwieldy to spell out the full patronymic which in this case is Gijbertzoon, it was common practice to abbreviate the written names by omitting the "oon" of "zoon" (son) and shortening "dochter" (daughter) to "dr". When spoken, the name would be pronounced in full.

Company ship, *de Eendract,* (Unity), on April 24, 1634. Lubbert was under contract to Kiliaen van Rensserlaer, the patroon of the area near present-day Albany NY, to work as the wagon maker or wheelwright for the colony. He arrived in Rensselaerwyck on July 20, 1634 (a speedy crossing, if the dates are correct) and was given land to live on with his family. In 1647, at the end of his contract, they moved to New Amsterdam. In 1654 Lubbert was given a Dutch patent for 50 mogens (about 100 acres) of land on Bergen Neck, south of present-day Jersey City. One year later, on Sept 15, 1655, he was killed in a very large Indian raid on the settlers in the area.

Jan Lubbertz, their third son and my direct ancestor, who had made the crossing from Holland at the age of 18 months, applied for a clerkship in the Secretary's office of the Director and Council of New Amsterdam in 1654 when he was 22. According to the records, he was granted a patent the same year for 25 mogens (about 50 acres) of land near his parents at Bergen Neck. In 1657 he was granted "small burgher" rights in New Amsterdam. The following year "Captain Jan" and others petitioned to re-occupy the family homes they had before the great Indian raid of 1655, a petition which was granted by the authorities in New Amsterdam on condition that they gather together in villages. Six years later, in 1688, England took control.

About this time, with English customs in the ascendancy, the patronymic form of surnames, in which the first name of the father became the last name of his children, began to be dropped in favor of the hereditary form used by the English. In 1706, or thereabouts, Van Blaricom became the surname of the third generation. Thus, the family of Pieter Janzoon and his wife, Jacomyntje, became Peter and Jacomina Van Blaricom (of the town of Blaricum).

Of greater import to the Van Blaricom clan and many of the other Dutch in the colonies (who were mostly in the New York and New Jersey area) was the fact that generally they were most emphatically not in favor of the American Revolution. Many of them emigrated to Canada at the outset of the fighting and other loyalist Dutch, including many who had fought with the British forces, joined them after the War. I had always believed that they emigrated voluntarily, but have since learned that the bitter feelings at the end of the hostilities caused them to be run out of the states virtually at the point of a gun. Fortunately, British ships for transport and a grant of land in Canada were available to all Loyalists. The Van Blaricoms joined the exodus in 1783 and settled in Ontario, especially around the Bay of Quinte and the town of Picton. From there they mostly spread across Canada and infiltrated the U.S. border in the western states.

My grandfather, Peter Van Blaricom, ran a small harness shop in the tiny town of Blackfoot, Idaho, a shop he kept open until his death in 1950, long after the use of horses in farm work had ended. He and my grandmother, Harriet Stander Van Blaricom had seven children including my father, Shelomi, and a brother named Solon, who was a family mystery until very recently. It seems Solon left home abruptly in 1924 at the age of 19 and was never heard from again. 73 years later in 1997, my little half-sister, Jan who lives in Oregon, phoned to tell us that she had received a phone call from a man named Harry Harris Jr. in the nearby town of Cottage Grove, Oregon, who informed her that he was apparently her cousin and that the Van Blaricoms were now the proud owners of a whole new branch of the family.

Harry Harris told the following account of how he found the Van Blaricom link: "None of us kids or our mother knew virtually anything about my father, Harry Sr.'s past. About all he had told us was that he was born in Blackfoot, Idaho, and graduated from high school there. Shortly before he passed away he told us the first names of his parents, brothers and sisters. We did not begin a serious genealogical search until a few years ago. The only other clues we had were the data on his insurance policy and a copy of his application for a social security number. On it he indicated that his father's name was Peter Harris and his mother's maiden name was Harriet Stander. We could find nothing in genealogical records matching the name Harris to the names Peter and Harriet.

When we turned up the fact that a school census for Brigham County, Idaho, had been compiled as a WPA project covering the years that my father had been in school, my brother-in-law and I went to Blackfoot, Idaho, to check this document which was in the county records. While looking through the census, not only for any Harris's but also for any parents names beginning with Peter, we found a Peter Van Blaricom. Included under this name was a list of all the kids in school that year. Some of these names matched those of Harry Sr.'s siblings including a Solon whose age matched Harry's. On a later listing for another year, the mother's name, Harriet, was also listed with Peter Van Blaricom. We were becoming convinced this had to be

Harry's family and Solon had to be my father, Harry Sr. From there it was easy to find a record of Peter and Harriet's marriage certificate which was in the town records and had Harriet's maiden name as Stander. This was all the confirmation we needed. Tracking down the rest of family was simple using the incredibly complete genealogical records of the Mormon Church."

At a reunion of the newly re-constituted Van Blaricom family, I asked Harry Jr. if he had learned why Solon had left home so suddenly with no job in mind and taking no personal effects. He said it was still a mystery but it might have been related to a terrible car-train collision which took place in the area about that time and which resulted in the death of several teenage boys. Harry Jr. said he recalls overhearing his father telling someone regretfully, "I should have been killed too". It is possible that he was the driver of the car and ran away to escape the guilt. It seems he found employment in eastern Washington with a farmer/beekeeper and lived there for some years before moving to central Oregon, getting married and raising a family. What a sad burden to carry through life!

My father, Shelomi, served in the US Army Signal Corps in World War I, but never got closer to France than Fort Riley, Kansas. Still he was very proud of his military service and later became State Commander of the American Legion in Montana in the 1930's. He and my mother Moselle, a school teacher, were married in Idaho after the war. After he worked in a local hardware store for a spell, they moved to Helena, Montana where he continued to work in hardware then started his own business assembling, selling and repairing radios. According to my sister, Helen, he even started the first radio station there so his customers would have something to listen to. In the late 1920's they moved to Great Falls, Montana on the high plateau of the northern plains, where my brother, Webster, and I were born and where he ran a tire store and later worked for Home Oil Company, a small refinery which sold a brand of gasoline called Silver Gas. One of its claims to fame was a deal they made with the Montana Highway Department wherein they would supply all the stop signs in the state provided they could put the word "Silver" above the word STOP and "Gas" below. The stuff was always called Silver Stop Gas by locals until a lawsuit brought by a ticketed stop sign runner put an end to the practice.

*My father, Shelomi (extreme left) shortly after WWI at work
in a hardware store in Helena, Montana*

Being born in 1930, I was very much a depression era child. In spite
of the hard times visible on all sides we were not greatly affected or so
it seemed to me. My father always had a good job, we lived in a modest but new house on a huge corner lot and my parents drove what I
considered a very nice car, a huge black Chrysler Royal sedan. We
lived rather close to the edge of town with the endless prairie nearby.
Enclosing the small city on two sides was the broad Missouri River
and the several dams which had tamed the huge waterfalls and rapids
which gave the city its name.

   We were a small family, just our parents, me, Webster, who we
called "Skip," and our big sister Helen, who was 11 years older than
me and always seemed like an adult to me as a youngster. Skip and I
were just 15 months different in age, he being the elder brother. Our
mother was a deeply religious woman who brought us up in the Mormon church.

*Me, my brother, Skip and our neighbor, Evelyn at
play at our house in Great Falls, Montana*

When I look back to those childhood days, images of the er-
ratic, extreme, even violent Montana weather come most readily to
mind. We played happily in the snow in what I would think of now as
brutally cold weather. And in the hot summers we spent long days in
the big open-air municipal pool or roaming the nearby open fields.
Thinking back on it, in those days, without much traffic, imagined
dangers, or a crowded population, it was amazing how much freedom
my brother and I had. We roamed on our bicycles freely all over the
city, down to the huge Missouri river and to outlying districts without
any concerns, it seemed to us, on the part of our parents. It seems incredible today, but I remember Mother and Dad leaving Skip and me
alone in the house to fend for ourselves while they enjoyed a week's
holiday. The place had a non-automatic gas water heater which required one to go down into the basement and light it with a match, and
if it wasn't turned off the tank would surely explode! I guess they
trusted us and as I recall, we were on better behavior than usual in
their absence. Capturing butterflies, listening to meadowlarks, killing

snakes, plinking bottles with our little .22 rifles were all part of our boyhood. Also fondly remembered were trips the length and breadth of Montana as Skip and I took turns accompanying our dad on his business trips for the oil company around the state.

My brother and I took turns taking trips around Montana with our father

A part of our upbringing was the expectation that one would earn money at some sort of job. As a result, both Skip and I sold magazines around the town including *Liberty, Saturday Evening Post, Colliers* and *Ladies Home Companion.* We received a small commission, of course, but also vouchers which could be exchanged for prized items like bb guns, and fishing gear. What I remember most from this enterprise was the enormous pressure out supervisors put on us to sell more magazines, the vicious dogs chasing me on my bicycle and the painful thawing-out process my hand and feet received after a winter circuit of my route. Later both Skip and I had newspaper routes in the morning as well as selling the evening paper on an assigned street corner. I had a particularly choice spot which was surrounded by bars and cocktail lounges which I always trolled for sales every twenty minutes or so.

When I was in junior high school, at the start of WWII, I worked during two summers on a 400 acre farm owned by a family acquaintance. My first assignment was to take care of a band of sheep which was kept on a large tract of public land. After some brief instruction, I was expected to saddle a horse, take a sheep dog and a lunch and ride several miles out to a corral where the sheep were kept overnight. After turning the sheep loose I was expected to more or less keep them together so that they could be rounded up and put back in the corral at the end of the day. Of course I had no idea how to do this, especially since the blasted sheep always wanted to go in different directions and crawl under the nearest barbed-wire fence. After nearly a day of shouting at the dog to help me, he disappeared in the direction of the farmhouse and refused to ever accompany me again. Since the horse was useless in my efforts to patrol the sheep, I was obliged to pursue them on foot and would run myself ragged until the end of the day. I was so tired after riding home and putting the horse away that I could hardly eat and sleep. Mercifully, after about three weeks the sheep were moved to a fenced pasture and I was able to work on other projects including weeding crops, haying, and doing the endless chores like milking and animal feeding. I can honestly say that after working on that farm, I knew what hard work was all about.

But these were not all perfect times. I grew up during the two pivotal eras of the 20th century, the Great Depression and the 2nd World War, both of which had a profound effect on my outlook and future life. Early in the War my parents separated for reasons which I never fully understood but I think were at least partly related to my mother's religious zeal and our father's distain for church in any form. My dad left Montana for California and interesting war work in the new shipyard in Sausalito. My sister had finished college and married by this time, and my mother, in increasingly poor health, struggled on with two young boys. We moved to Rexburg, Idaho when I was 13 so that my mother could have help from her family. In 1945 she died of Hodgkin's disease at age 49 in the care of my grandparents, while Skip and I lived with our aunt and uncle nearby. It was surely, the low point in our lives.

About this time while living in the solidly Mormon area of central Idaho, in the midst of good people but ardent believers and surrounded by church rituals on many days of the week, I began to feel smothered. My outlook wasn't improved when I began to question some of the preposterous stories upon which the Mormon Church was based. I also knew all about the pressure to proselytize which was put on young men in the church in the form of a two-year spell of missionary work. It was an obligation to promote a religion I increasingly doubted and I wanted no part of it. I was ready for escape.

A family photo taken at Rexburg, Idaho in 1944, shortly before my mother's death. (L toR) Me, mother, cousin LaRue, sister Helen, aunt Neta and uncle Clyde Cottle brother Skip, grandparents Roxie and Alfred Webster

I had enjoyed a good childhood in Montana and Idaho and fondly remember the times I spent in the great outdoors of the West. I was smaller than the other boys my age and had bad eyesight so I was always the last to be chosen for sports and consequently had a rather poor opinion of my abilities as compared with my schoolmates. Still, I was a reasonably good student and had no real difficulties that I can remember. When the time came to make an abrupt change in my life in a new location, I welcomed it.

My unnamed 10' skiff sailing on Raccoon Strait

CHAPTER 1

AN UNNAMED SKIFF

In the fall of 1945, after the death of our mother, my brother, being older and more enterprising than I, ventured out to California to find and reunite with our father. Not knowing exactly where my dad was, Skip went to a private investigator in San Francisco for help in locating him. Never was a mystery solved so easily – he simply opened a phone book and gave Skip the number! A few weeks later at the end of a long train ride crowded with returning service men, I joined them in Tiburon, Marin County, where my father had rented a flat in a duplex on the shore of Raccoon Strait. We were both of high school age at this time and were soon enrolled in Tamalpais High School. Our father had remarried, and May, our new stepmother, gamely took on a pair of teenage boys.

Marin County was a revelation. Spread out from the green slopes of Mount Tamalpais was a panorama of lovely rolling hills dotted with cozy towns tucked in the valleys and all encircled with exciting bays and waterways. I was stunned by the greenery, interesting buildings and novel sights like the Golden Gate Bridge, San Quentin, and the islands in the Bay. Tall eucalyptus trees. Ferryboats. Fog horns and ships hooting in the night. I was dazzled.

Also amazing was our new high school. My concept of a high school was a two or three story brick building. Here was something closer to a small liberal arts college campus with a variety of tasteful buildings arranged on a gently sloping hillside. Canvas covered walkways connected the buildings and the whole setting was landscaped and tended by a group of Italian gardeners whose specialty was colorful gardenia bushes. Montana was never like this!

*My new stepmother, May, gamely took on a pair of teen age boys. That's me
on the left with a friend and the Lyford Tower, an old toll gate behind*

     Our new home was perched on the steep shoreline of Lyford
Cove next to an interesting stone tower which had originally been a
toll gate for a large picnic area named "Lyford's Hygeia", popular with
San Francisco folks who came to Tiburon on weekends via ferryboat.
Our building even had a dock extending out into the Bay with a pair of
davits on each side for boats to be hoisted clear of the water. The view
from the flat was spectacular, especially for me who had never seen
salt water before. Directly opposite was the wooded mass of Angel
Island with an active quarantine hospital and a wharf for the quarantine boat to take the inspecting doctors out to check arriving ships for
sick and infected passengers. Out of sight on the Island to the left and
right were Army installations. In fact the whole island was crawling
with Army personnel, none of whom were probably doing much since
the war was most definitely over.

     To the west was the stunning view of the Golden Gate Bridge
and San Francisco and to the east was the more distant, but interesting
view of Oakland, Berkeley and Richmond with its vast but now idle
complex of wartime shipyards. The Bay itself was bustling with activity with the constant arrival and movement of warship and military

cargo vessels. Near at hand, Raccoon Strait was churned by destroy-ers, submarines and smaller vessels on their way to be stripped and laid up or scrapped after their war service. There was always the un-mistakable throb of GM 6-71 diesel engines in the air from the picket boats, landing craft and ship's gigs who passed up and down the Straits, many of which were performing the vital duty of hauling sail-ors to Hooper's Bar, the Harbor Light Tavern and Sam's Anchor Café and Bar in downtown Tiburon. And on top of all this was the frequent railroad-car barge traffic from the Northwestern Pacific rail terminus in Tiburon to San Francisco and the East Bay. In those days even the tankers from the Richmond refinery used Raccoon Strait. It was such a great scene!

Another fascinating scene was the active railroad shops, switch yard and barge loading dock of the Northwestern railroad in downtown Tiburon. In fact, Tiburon consisted of not much more that a short rowdy main street and the railroad yard with its large roundhouse ca-pable of holding 10 locomotives and big shop buildings. At the time, most of the locomotives were steam engines. A short train of passen-ger cars was assembled daily for the run to Eureka but mostly the rail traffic consisted of box cars and open lumber cars bringing timber down from the Mendocino coast in four trains each day. Barges, some self-propelled and some breasted (with the tug alongside) by tugboats shuttled between Tiburon and San Francisco, Oakland and Richmond, each carrying about 20 freight cars.

Tiburon was most definitely a railroad town. The neighboring town of Belvedere was entirely different being a fashionable residen-tial community with nice houses, a yacht club and a small golf course. It had always been an exclusive place and there was no mistaking the social division between residents of the two towns. As high school kids, we all rode the same school bus to Tamalpais High School in Mill Valley, but even in this situation there was a certain separation between the kids from the two towns. The rest of the Tiburon penin-sula was almost entirely taken up by three dairy farms; all owned by Portuguese originally from the Azores Islands. I sometimes rode in the truck to school with my friend Joe Avila whose father owned the dairy where Reed School now sits. He would drop off the large milk cans at a depot on the way to school.

Tiburon Boulevard with Mount Tamalpais in the background in 1945

Environmentalists today would have been horrified if they had seen the enormous oil slicks which drifted around in those days. The Bay and the shores were covered with all kinds of flotsam and jetsam (mostly jetsam) from the decommissioning of ships. It was paradise! My pals and I quickly learned how to reap the harvest. In borrowed rowboats we salvaged lifeboat rations, battle lanterns, life raft survival kits, oars, and especially boathooks. We had a standing offer of $1 for a hardwood boat hook with a galvanized head and $2 for one with a bronze head from Mr. Randolph, the owner of the local hardware store. We learned that the best pickings were usually to be found in the oil slicks where things seemed to accumulate. One can imagine the unholy mess we sometimes made of ourselves and our borrowed boats when the pickings were really good.

The rowboats we usually used belonged to the generous Mr. Randolph, who had a waterfront home nearby on Lyford Cove. One of the boats was a huge, heavy working skiff and the other a small, slim 10-footer best suited for one person. When there were two or three of us boys, we usually borrowed the larger boat. The tidal currents were always a big factor in these salvage forays because of our slow speed. If things were right, we would sometimes ride the flood tide several miles out to the US Navy Net Depot on the east side of the Tiburon peninsula, where ships were being de-commissioned and where there was an enormous trash pile and lots of stuff on the adjacent beaches. If our timing was good, by the time we had our cargo the ebb would have started and we would have an easy row home.

The Net Depot got its name from the fact that, among other things, it was the place where the huge anti-submarine net, which closed the Golden Gate during the War, was built and maintained. The Depot was also a Navy hard-hat diving school. Adjacent to the north, at the present-day site of a county waterfront park, was a large submarine base with sub tenders anchored offshore with rafts of subs alongside. Plenty of stuff there too. Of course all of this area was in a restricted zone, clearly marked by buoys, but in the euphoria of the end of the War no one seemed to mind a few boys poking around in a rowboat.

Our other great hunting ground was Angel Island with its many beaches. Being a large Army facility, it was also off limits which made it all the better. It was always a race to arrive at a cove and scour the beach before the guards in jeeps showed up to run us off. I honestly don't think the GI's on guard duty looked on their work as much more than interesting entertainment. One afternoon our cat-and-mouse game really paid off when we found a wooden rowboat in the sand. It had a hole stove in one side and lots of other minor damage but it was good enough for us. It couldn't be towed so we loaded the whole thing in the big skiff and pulled slowly home. Earlier, I had bought the small skiff from Mr. Randolph, so now my friend Loren Plum and I each had a boat.

Unlike the boat we had salvaged from the beach, the 10' skiff I owned was a beauty, or at least I thought so. In a talkative moment one day, Mr. Randolph had suggested that he probably really didn't need two rowboats. When pressed a bit, he said he might sell the small skiff for about $30. I immediately ran home, borrowed the money from my stepmother, May, and ran back before he could change his mind. The boat was built of redwood, not normally used in boatbuilding because of its soft, porous nature, and consequently weighed more than desirable. But it was nicely painted and slipped along well with a pair of long ash oars. I soon had it hanging proudly at the end of our dock.

I knew nothing of sailing at the time, but I was fascinated by the variety of sailboats I saw lying at moorings off the two yacht clubs in Tiburon and Belvedere. Big and small, on the weekends they were to be seen everywhere on the Bay. At first I couldn't even distinguish the difference in their rigs, but I soon learned. Since it wasn't likely that I would be invited to crew on one, I decided to try to convert my skiff into a sailboat. Luckily, a neighbor in Lyford Cove, a Scotchman named Mr. Ross, who just happened to be a shipwright at the Moore Drydock in Alameda, took an interest in me and offered to help with the project. He built a hardwood centerboard case and showed me about where in the boat to cut the slot and how to install it. I made a centerboard (actually a daggerboard) and a rudder from plywood and from a huge oak boathook I had found floating in the Bay, I made a mast. A boom, a tiller, and a small deck with a hole for the mast completed the woodwork. Next I sewed a sail from a pair of US Navy mattress covers (fart sacks in navy-talk) and I was in business, except I had only a vague idea of how to actually sail.

Step one, of course, was to lower the boat into the water, then paddle it to the rocky beach and pull it ashore. Next the mast was stepped, the boom attached and the sail slides fitted to the mast track. Step three was to shove the boat off the beach, hop aboard and attempt to more or less simultaneously hoist the sail, put down the centerboard, fit the rudder into its gudgeons and sheet in the sail, all while trying to keep from drifting back onto the rocks. Needless to say, it didn't always work out that way! When I was able to get the whole act together and actually begin sailing, I learned the next lesson: boats heel over and when there is no deck, water, lots of it, comes over the gunwale and into the boat. I tried tacking a strip of canvas between the edge of the boat and the nearby stringer, but it didn't help much. The solution, I learned, was to keep an eagle eye on the wind on the water, be quick as a cat in releasing the mainsheet and be nimble as a monkey in getting my body weight out to windward. After a few near-disasters I slowly, very slowly, began to master the art of sailing.

As my confidence and skill improved I joyously tacked and reached across Raccoon Strait, sailed down to Belvedere Cove and beyond. I made friends with Tom, the son of a quarantine doctor at Hospital Cove, who had a similar sailboat converted from a rowboat. My friend, Loren, also converted his salvaged boat into a sailing skiff. It was all great fun, then, one day I came as near to losing my life as I have ever done.

On a beautiful Sunday, sailing by myself, I ventured to the waters beyond the Navy Net Depot. There was a fine breeze of just the right strength to make good speed in perfect safety. Suddenly the wind stopped and I realized that I was being swept into the restricted area by the fast-running ebb tide. Soon to my horror I saw that the current, which was running at about 4 knots, was taking me directly down onto a huge barge moored to a big cylindrical mooring buoy. There was no time to attempt to row out of the way and before I knew it, my boat came up broadside against the buoy and instantly began to be sucked under it. As the boat filled with water and slid underwater, I jumped for the flat top of the buoy and managed to scramble aboard. The last I saw of my boat was the image of its hull, on its side, heading under the bow of the 200 foot long barge. It didn't take much imagination to know that if I had followed it, I would have been history. I had bad dreams about it for years.

At the time the main thing that was worrying me was how was I going to get off that buoy and how much trouble would I be in for sailing in the restricted area. Being Sunday, there were sailors hanging out on the wharf who had seen my difficulty. Soon a few of them had jumped in a picket boat and skillfully maneuvered alongside the buoy to retrieve me. To my surprise, they then went downstream of the barge and put a towline on my boat. The mast was broken, the oars were lost and the little foredeck was uprooted but they had my boat! Then they towed it all the way to Tiburon and tied up at the dock at Sam's Café and Bar. How lucky can you get!

* * * *

I was determined to get a better boat, something more like the trim, swift sloops I saw at the yacht clubs. As a first step, I joined the Corinthian Yacht Club as a junior member and then started looking. I spotted an ad for a 14' keel sloop for the affordable price of $125 and made an appointment to look it over. It was sitting on the dock at Sausalito and in spite of its park-bench green color it looked fine to me.

What I didn't realize was that its seams were all gaping open from months, perhaps years, of drying out. The seller had the use of a little motorboat and offered to tow the boat over to Tiburon, so we closed the deal and launched the sloop with the hand-cranked hoist on the wharf.

On the tow to Tiburon I bailed frantically to keep the level of water down and wondered what I had gotten myself into. I wasn't fully a member of the Corinthian yet so I had arranged to rent a mooring nearby. I tied to the mooring and continued to bail as the seller waved a cheery goodbye and motored away. I had been assured that wood boats need only a few hours to "take up" and stop leaking as the seams swell shut. It didn't happen. By evening I was exhausted, discouraged and disgusted with myself for being such a fool. What really worried me was the fact that being a boat with heavy chunk of iron on the bottom of the keel, it would surely sink if enough water leaked in. In the end I got ashore and went home to spend the night worrying about my new boat on its way to the bottom. To my surprise, when I rowed out to the mooring in the morning she was full of water and awash but still floating…just barely. Obviously she had the bare minimum of ballast.

Soon my membership in the Corinthian Yacht Club was official. I hoisted the boat (she never did get a name) onto the dock and began learning the unending process of fixing, maintaining and improving a sailboat. I was shown how to caulk her seams and how to install proper hoisting gear. I built a cradle with wheels for moving the boat to the hoist, re-covered her deck with new canvas and replaced the awful green paint with white. When she was ready to sail I set forth only to discover that she was awfully tender (tippy) from lack of ballast, not too fast and badly in need of a better suit of sails. And if that wasn't enough, in a moment of boldness, I invited a nice girl I was hoping to impress with my new yacht out for a sail. I had made careful preparations by having the boat nicely scrubbed, the sails in place and the boat ready to go at the float when we arrived at the Club in my folks car (with my stepmother as chauffeur). As we got nicely underway and headed out of the cove, a gust of wind hit the boat, a rigging wire snapped and the mast fell over the side in two pieces. We paddled the boat back to the yacht club, put it up on the dock and caught a ride back to Mill Valley. My already shaky self confidence around girls took a giant hit that day!

Another unnamed boat, my somewhat troublesome 14' sloop on the deck of the Corinthian Yacht Club in Tiburon, 1947

There was still one more even bigger disaster in store for me with that boat. After repairing the mast, I had the boat operational once more. One afternoon a friend of my brother who was, as far as I knew, a capable sailor, asked if he could borrow the boat for a couple of hours after school so that he and a pal could do a bit of sailing. I somewhat reluctantly said OK and got the sloop ready for them. I told them to just tie it up to the Club float when they came back and I would put it up on the dock the next day. The following day I got a call from the harbormaster at Berkeley who told me that my boat had drifted onto the old Berkeley Pier and that he had rescued it and towed it into the marina. I soon learned that the two boys who had borrowed it had run out of wind and drifted with the tide way up the Bay. As evening approached a strong gust of wind capsized the boat and put them in the water. Fortunately the boat didn't sink altogether so they had something to hold on to, but the cold water of San Francisco Bay soon began to take its toll. On a weekday evening there were very few boats out on the Bay, but just before sunset and just as they were about to give up, a motorboat spotted them and took them aboard and got them to medical care. The boat, of course, was left to drift. I borrowed a boat trailer and brought the boat back but as I don't think I ever sailed it again.

Although the little sloop was not a great success, something very good came from it. Shortly after I bought the boat we moved from Tiburon to Mill Valley. Our landlord informed us that he was putting the building up for sale for $18,000, a price which my father considered absolutely outrageous. Never mind that it was two units of waterfront property in one of the most desirable locations imaginable. I was not too happy about exchanging our exciting access to the Bay for a nice but ordinary little house surrounded by more houses and land. Another complication to add to my unhappiness was the need to take a bus or catch a ride to get to my boat at the Corinthian Yacht Club in Tiburon, about five miles away.

As mentioned earlier, my sloop badly needed a new and better suit of sails. I was aware that there was a small sail loft on Hill Street in Mill Valley. The sailmaker was an elderly Dane named Captain "Cap" Ferdinandsen, a genuine square-rig ship sailor of the old school. He was also the skipper of the Mill Valley Sea Scouts. Looking ahead, I joined the Sea Scouts and started hanging around the Mill Valley Sail Loft after school. Cap Ferdinandsen was a wonderfully friendly man who took a special interest in young fellows like me who were genuinely interested in rigging, marlinspike seamanship and sailmaking. He had made his loft by expanding the detached garage in back of his house. To increase the area of the wooden floor he had built a hinged section which he lowered over the concrete floor when the loft was in use. Upon closing up shop in the evening he would always announce, "Time to take a reef in the floor" as he heaved on the tackle that swung the floor up against the wall. The shop had a couple of ancient but excellent Singer zigzag sewing machines, and a wooden sailmakers bench with holes in the end for various fids and marlinspikes and a bin underneath for sail needles, marlin, waxed sewing twine, beeswax and that indispensable item, the sailmaker's palm, for pushing needles through heavy canvass. The loft also had racks for sailcloth and coils of Italian hemp boltrope which reeked of Stockholm tar. I can still imagine that wonderful smell to this day.

At work in Cap Ferdinandsen's small sail loft in Mill Valley

Since I knew nothing, Cap suggested I start by making a suit of sails for my boat under his supervision. Exactly what I had in mind! We used ordinary cotton duck which was not the high quality Wamsutta Egyptian cotton sailcloth in use in those days, but plenty good enough for me. Cap showed me how to put the false seams in the cloth, cut the curves in the edges (roaches) to give the sail its shape, then sew on the multiple layers at the corners (doublings) and then sew on the reinforced edge (tabling). Finally in the case of the mainsail I was taught how to adjust and sew on the boltrope, and for the jib, how to splice the eyes in the wire rope luff and sew it in. All this together with the details of hand work to finish the sails was a grand education. Eventually I knew enough to be really useful around the loft and was hired at a very modest rate to work regularly after school and on Saturdays and vacations. I loved the job. The skills I learned at this little sail loft have remained useful to me for the rest of my sailing life.

The Mill Valley Sea Scouts as an organization had been more or less dormant until Cap Ferdinandsen came along about 1947. It seems the previous skipper, a crusty old timer named "Cappy" Robinson, had used the old Sea Scout vessel, a converted lifeboat named *Tamalsea*, pretty much as his personal yacht without much regard for the boys. Finally, a truck accidentally dumped a load of steel pipe off the wharf and into the boat, sending it to the bottom and Cappy Robinson into retirement. This was a blessing because now Cap Ferdinandsen could make a fresh start.

About this time a very large old schooner named *Eloise* was sold at an estate auction to the owner of a little cigar store in San Rafael. As I recall, his name was Mr. Riley. The schooner was built about 1910 and had a colorful history including service as a mail boat in the Aleutian Islands in World War I. In 1924 she was entered in an ocean race from San Francisco to Tahiti along with three other schooners. Apparently she damaged and lost her centerboard just outside the Golden Gate but sailed on and finished the race anyway. Later she was acquired by a famous old yachtsman named John C. Piver who had been commodore of the San Francisco Yacht Club in 1930-1932. He had tarted up the boat to look like a proper yacht and used it on the Bay in the pre-WWII years. By the time of Piver's death it was showing its age badly, but was a wonderful old classic. She was 81' long and gaff rigged with topmasts on both masts. Being a centerboarder, she had a shallow draft and was powered by an ancient 3-cylinder, air start, Atlas diesel engine with a marvelous assortment of oil cups and push rods on the outside. She also had a full-size, claw-foot bathtub in the owner's cabin. With her vastly complicated rigging and broad decks, she was the perfect Sea Scout ship.

The new owner of *Eloise* had not much money and absolutely no experience, so when Cap Ferdinandsen approached him and told him he had a group of boys eager to be crew and could get plenty of rope, canvas and other supplies for free from the US Navy, he readily accepted. Since she was berthed in Lowrie's Harbor in the shallow waters of the San Rafael Canal, her shoal draft was a real asset. The arrangement held for only a few years before the schooner was sold, but it was wonderful fun while it lasted. One of my lasting impressions, which clearly showed the advanced age of the boat, was to sit on the bow and watch the stern moving in opposite directions when sailing in rough water! There were some interesting and instructive work days and some exciting days on the Bay. It was especially nice to see old Cap Ferdinandsen in his element piloting the big schooner to and from her moorings, showing the boys how to handle the sails and the gear, how to steer and how to become real sailors.

The 81' schooner, Eloise, in her heyday before WWII. She became the perfect ship for the Mill Valley Sea Scouts under Cap Ferdinandsen.

Eventually I left the Sea Scouts and the Mill Valley Sail Loft and went off to school at College of Marin then the University of California at Berkeley. Cap Ferdinandsen was apparently not making a go of it at the little sail loft and when his wife became ill, he closed the loft, sold the house and moved to Florida. The *Eloise* was sold and renamed *Gallant Lady* (mistake #1). She then tried to go to sea (mistake #2) on a voyage to the South Seas with a bunch of dreamers who had pooled their money. She got a few miles past the Golden Gate when, with the whole crew deathly seasick and the hull leaking badly, she was towed into Monterey Bay and the cruise abandoned. Eventually she managed to sail to Southern California where she was later wrecked on a beach.

Tai Fung, a 45'gaff-headed yawl on San Francisco Bay

CHAPTER 2

TAI FUNG

One day before the little Mill Valley Sail Loft closed up, an order came in for us to make up a set of deck covers for a 45' sailboat named *Tai Fung* in San Rafael. The boat belonged to an elderly gentleman named Maurice St. Gaudens, the son of the famed sculptor, Augustus St. Gaudens who designed the US gold "double eagle" $20 gold coin in the 1905. I did most of the measuring and sewing of the covers and when I took them up to the boat for fitting he asked me if I would like a job on Saturdays working on the boat. I readily accepted.

Tai Fung ("Big wind" or "Typhoon" in Chinese) was a yawl with a gaff-rigged mainsail and a Bermuda-rigged mizzen. She was constructed of teak and was entirely varnished except for the cabin top. Designed by D. M. Callas, she had been built in Southern California in 1927. She was a beauty even with her rather homely-looking canvas "dog house" over the front of the cockpit. In spite of her antique rig, she had a reputation for being quite a fast sailer and had been raced regularly on the Bay for many years. I liked the boat immediately and happily took up my new job each weekend, sanding, varnishing, scrubbing and polishing all the brass in sight including the wide trim around the portholes. Within a few months, however, in the late summer of 1948, she was sold to Bradley (Doc) Richardson, an optometrist from Santa Rosa who took me along with the boat, an arrangement which was fine with me. For years thereafter, the deal was that I would work on Saturdays for my very modest pay and on Sundays we would go sailing.

Doc was a slim, dapper man who drove down from Santa Rosa in his Cadillac each Saturday, arriving exactly at 1:00 PM after spending the morning in his office. He sported a pencil thin mustache, much in favor in those days by such figures as Errol Flynn and William Powell. He always came wearing his double-breasted suit which he exchanged for a pair of faded blue yachting trousers and a red wool shirt after depositing his small automatic pistol in a drawer in the forward cabin, a habit which later proved fortuitous in a comic but potentially tragic incident.

A number of years later, on a weekend when I was not around, Doc and another couple went from Sausalito to Tiburon by car to have dinner at the Corinthian Yacht Club. When he returned after dark he was astonished to see *Tai Fung* partially out of the slip with the mooring lines cast off and all the sails hoisted. The man aboard was trying desperately to push the boat out of the slip, a difficult task because it was being forced by the sails against the pilings. Doc was furious, of course, and raged at the man to get off his boat, throw him a line, and other demands. I am sure he would have used his pistol on him except, fortunately, it was locked up below in the cabin. The police soon arrived and arrested the villain who turned out to be a recently released inmate of the insane asylum whose name was Mr. Friendly. The newspapers and the wire services gleefully picked up the story of "The Friendly Act of Piracy" complete with Doc's name and spread it all across the country. This made him even more furious!

Doc had never owned a sailboat before, but had read a great deal about sailing. He also knew a lot about navigation, including celestial navigation. Of course, I didn't know a heck of a lot either about sailing bigger boats, so it was a learning experience for both of us. *Tai Fung* was moved to a berth at Godfredsen's Boatyard at the shallow upper end of the San Rafael Canal, not exactly the ideal place for a boat drawing 7½ feet of water and a long way to go to get to open sailing water. Eventually Doc joined the Corinthian Yacht Club and got a berth at the Sausalito Yacht Harbor, a big improvement. By the spring of 1949 Doc was planning a month-long sailing trip down the coast as far as San Diego.

In June we set forth under the Golden Gate Bridge on our way on our first ocean voyage. Aboard with Doc and me was Doc's brother, Bruce, a college engineering teacher and my friend, Harland Peterson. We were all in for a big surprise when the sunny run down the coast turned out to be a cold, windy, foggy, scary, seasick-making endurance contest which I will never forget.

Not knowing any better, we headed out the main ship channel intending to go the eleven miles out to the San Francisco Lightship before heading south. As we were motorsailing with our sails barely full, punching almost directly into the wind, we were amazed (and humbled) to see the beautiful big 80' M class sloop, *Windward*, on her way to the start of the Transpac Race in L.A, come slashing past us with the crew cheering at each tack, as she smartly bore off around Seal Rocks and zoomed off to the south over the shallows along Ocean Beach. Not long after that our jib, which had been shaking badly, split from side to side. We turned around and retreated to the Bay.

The next day after getting the jib sewn up we tried again, this time taking the short cut along the beach. By afternoon the sky was solidly overcast, the wind was blowing very strong and the sea was plenty rough. We managed to get the big gaff mainsail down and furled, then carried on under jib and mizzen. After dark it got windier and rougher still. About midnight the jib, which had a boom on its foot and slammed back and forth as we ran downwind, ripped again so we sailed the rest of the night under just the mizzen, the worst possible sail to carry when running before the wind. I recall the heaving dark masses of water against the even darker sky and the flashes of white from the breaking crests. Fortunately, we were well offshore because we had only a vague idea of where we were. It was inky dark, the compass light in the binnacle cast only a dim yellow glow which barely illuminated the tiny figures on the old-fashioned, flat-card compass, and our steering was probably about as straight as a snake as we slid down the face of the steep waves. And that was only part of our problem.

Although I seemed to be more or less immune, the rest of the crew was seasick by varying degrees. Harland was moderately sick, Doc was barely functioning between trips to the rail and his brother Bruce was hoping death would mercifully come soon. Added to all this was the frightening moan of the wind in the rigging, the violent rolling of the boat, the sodden state of our clothes, the damp cold of the wind and the fear which comes with the unknown. Added all together, it was a night to remember (or forget).

After a seemingly endless night, a cheerless, grey dawn slowly, very slowly, opened to show us a windy broken sea, a darkly overcast sky and no land anywhere in sight. We had been towing a taffrail log which recorded our distance run, but we had no way of knowing how far offshore we were, so Doc set a course to take us toward the land. Hour after hour went by until in the late afternoon we made out the sight of the coastal mountains and finally identified what we presumed to be Point Piedras Blancas, an assumption that was reinforced by the obvious color of the large white rocks. We rounded the point and to our immense relief sailed into the smooth water of San Simeon Cove and dropped the anchor. The main thought going through my mind was how in hell are we ever going to get back up this coast again against all this wind and rough water?

Doc Richardson at the helm on our rough trip to southern California in 1949

The next morning we were off again running before the wind and sea. Two events occurred that day which remain in my mind. About noon we sailed through an unbelievably large school of alba-core tuna. It was a churning mass of large fish which seemed to stretch for miles. I had seen newsreels of tuna fishermen using poles and unbarbed hooks to pull huge tuna aboard their boat as fast as they could re-cast their lines. This was exactly the same situation except there was not a fishboat in sight. We were astonished but had neither the equipment nor the energy to try to catch a fish.

Later that night, long after dark, as we were approaching Point Arguello, a dangerous landmark which juts out several miles from the shoreline, we spotted a flashing light well off on our port side which seemed to match the characteristic of the lighthouse on the Point. Doc even went so far as to get out a stopwatch to time the interval of the flashes. Convinced that we had strayed too far out to sea and that we needed to go to the left to approach and round the Point, we altered course. By a blessed miracle, the horizon was reasonably clear and as we neared the shore we saw that the Point was way off to our right and what we had been following was actually an aero beacon on top of an inland hill! Many years later I learned of a famous incident which took place on September 8, 1923 when a squadron of seven US Navy destroyers, with great loss of life, piled up on the same piece of shore we had been headed for!

By dawn we had rounded Point Conception and our ordeal was over. We were now in the smooth seas and gentle winds of Southern California. As soon as he could set foot on land when we stopped in the pleasant little harbor at Santa Barbara, Bruce departed on the SP Coast Daylight train for home. We stayed for a day or two then headed for Santa Cruz Island. As I recall we saw no other boats during our stay in several of the coves and anchorages. We then headed for the big commercial port of San Pedro to be near the start of the '49 Transpac Race to Hawaii which we wanted to observe. At the time there were simply no other yacht harbors or marinas along the entire coast between Santa Barbara and San Diego except Newport Beach.

We found a berth at the California Yacht Anchorage next to Humphrey Bogart's famous yawl, *Santana*. He wasn't around, of course, but we were much impressed by his professional hand, Swenson, who kept the yacht in gleaming condition. Also in the harbor, living aboard his little 26' Seabird yawl was the famous circum-navigator, Harry Pigeon who had sailed around the globe in his 36'yawl, *Islander*, in 1925. He was a charming little old man who insisted we come aboard and meet his wife. He had a carton or two of his book "Around the World Single-handed" and, naturally, we all came away with an autographed copy.

Since arriving in San Pedro Harbor, Doc had been reminiscing about a time many years ago when he lived in LA as a young man and regularly went to a famous burlesque theater in the city. He described the absolutely lovely girls in the show, and since he had no doubt it was still in existence, he insisted Harland and I come along to see it. We took the electric Red Train from San Pedro to downtown Los Angeles and by golly, found the theater. It was in a rather seedy part of the city which perfectly matched the tone of the show. The "girls" were not so lovely and the raunchy comedians were worse. I think time had taken its toll on Doc's memory because he never mentioned it again.

On July 4th we motored out to the starting area of the LA to Honolulu, Transpac Race, off the Los Angeles Harbor breakwater. The fleet of 24 yachts including a number of big schooners, seemed incredibly exciting as they slowly maneuvered in the light airs, then, as the starting gun sounded, filled away and headed for the distant and exotic port of Honolulu, 2400 miles away. At the time, the idea of actually sailing to Hawaii seemed to me to be the most adventurous and desirable event which could possibly ever happen to me.

We sailed to Catalina Island where we spent a few days at various anchorages especially enjoying our time on a mooring at Avalon. The steamers, SS *Avalon* and *SS Santa Catalina,* arrived daily with a deckload of visitors who tossed coins for the young local swimmers to dive for. I recall a booth directly in front of the pier where disembarking passengers could get an instant suntan sprayed on their hide. And then there was the Casino, an architectural wonder which had a movie palace on the lower floor and a ballroom with a big band on the upper floor. Of special interest to me were the flying fish tour boats which took passengers out at night. They had powerful searchlights which brought the flying fish to the surface and into flight by the thousands. Later when we left and motored (mostly) to San Diego, we saw innumerable large flying fish who leaped into the air and glided away from us as we moved along. Sadly, in recent sailing trips in Southern California waters, I have seen no flying fish at all.

San Diego, which had yet to build the huge complex of yachting facilities we see today, was a busy commercial and military port but a bit of disappointment as we anchored off the waterfront and rolled in the wash of ships and tugboats. I suppose I was also depressed about the thought of starting back home and tackling the windy coast up to San Francisco. We stopped in Newport Beach where we spent several miserable days digging out the deck seam compound and replacing it in anticipation of the rough seas going north. Then it was on to Santa Barbara for a brief fuel stop and off for the dreaded Point Conception. To my amazement and vast relief, we made steady progress up the coast, mostly with the help of the big Universal Superfour gas engine. We got stalled for a long windy afternoon off Point Sur but otherwise had no great difficulty and at last sailed under the Golden Gate Bridge at the end of my first ocean cruise.

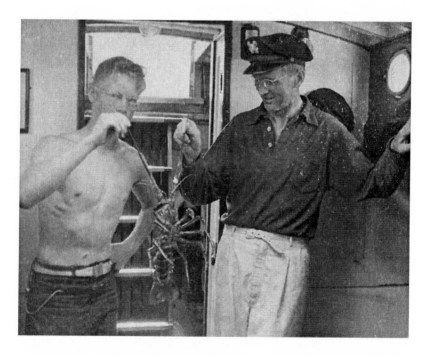

Doc and I with a langouste we caught during a cruise to Santa Cruz Island

During the next two years we sailed around the Bay on Sundays, raced in the handicap regattas, with lots of excitement but only modest success, and each summer made a month-long cruise to Southern California which more or less followed the pattern of the initial cruise but without the anxiety and drama of the first trip. During the spring of 1951, just prior to our usual trip down the coast, I broached the subject of a possible voyage to Hawaii following year. As an inducement I offered to make a (badly needed) suit of sails for *Tai Fung* during the remainder of the summer after our return. This was possible because I had suggested that Doc buy one of Cap Ferdinandsen's sewing machines when he went out of business. Doc said he would think about it during the week. The next Saturday, to my delight he said OK! He had lined up a trusted, retired optometrist friend to run his practice during the trip and had received permission from the Santa Rosa High School principal (another old friend) for me to use the gymnasium floor as a sail loft when school was closed for the summer.

After our return from Southern California I moved into a back bedroom at Doc's house in Santa Rosa and spent two months making sails. Following a trip to San Francisco to the ancient Simpson & Fisher sail loft (which had been making sails since the days of square-rigged ships) on Steuart Street near the waterfront to buy canvas and fittings, I started in on the big gaff mainsail. After this was finished I went to work on a new jib and a mizzen. For downwind running I made a pair of twin staysails and finally, made a stout storm trysail with extra reinforcing on all the corners and a strong boltrope all the way around. It was a very busy time with me working well into the evening almost every day. However I was so excited about actually sailing to Hawaii that I enjoyed every minute of it.

During the months prior to our voyage we worked on the boat making many little improvements; we modified the stove so that it would gimbal (stay level), made new deck cushions stuffed with war surplus kapok (which always stayed wet) and installed a medium-wave marine radio (with a range of only about 50 miles). Missing was any kind of life raft, depth sounder, decent windlass, bow or stern pulpits, lee cloths for the bunks, or electric running lights. Available in abundance was enthusiasm, trepidation and naiveté.

*   *   *   *

In mid-June 1952 we set sail from Sausalito with a crew consisting of Doc, me, a strapping 15 year old high school student from Mill Valley named Phil Price and a 19 year old college youth from Santa Barbara named Dick Keiding. Neither Phil nor Dick had any appreciable sailing expertise and certainly no ocean voyaging experience but we were aboard a well designed and strongly built boat and were setting out on a lengthy but not particularly difficult voyage (if all went well) so our confidence was high and our spirits soared as we hoisted full sail on a fine, sunny Sunday morning and headed out under the Golden Gate Bridge with Honolulu 2200 miles ahead.

A fresh breeze held as we made a long tack out the Gate which took us close to Point Bonita, the outermost headland of the Bay entrance. As we came about we saw a group of waving friends at the lighthouse to cheer us on our way. I don't know about the others, but it was a very emotional moment for me, with my mind filled with thoughts about the unknown challenge which lay ahead of us. We fell off on the starboard tack which took us down the coast and as the wind became light, we put on our big overlapping genoa jib. In the late afternoon we came about and stood offshore and into a dense fog. All night we sailed slowly through the fog and light drizzle and sometime in the wee hours slid by the Farallon Islands. We heard its foghorn but never caught a glimpse of its rocky shores or its powerful lighthouse on the top of the island. Once past the island we breathed a little easier.

For the next three days we sailed in a variety of breezes, all headwinds and generally not strong enough for us to sail decently. The boat rolled, the sails slatted, and the long heavy gaff at the top of the mainsail swung back and forth putting a heavy strain on the rigging and our nerves. At this time we had not yet gotten our sea legs so none of us were very hungry, although Doc was the only one who actually "fed the fishes". We all felt very tired and weak I suppose from lack of sufficient food and sleep. At this time I was the only one doing any cooking since Doc was doing the navigating and the boys were not yet up to the cooking chores. We were standing the traditional 4-on and 4-off watch system with two on watch at all times, not a very restful routine. Our foul weather gear was green navy surplus which only pretended to be waterproof and when on watch but not steering, we lay on the sodden cockpit cushions. The air was cold especially at night.

Our salvation was the ugly canvas shelter over the companionway and bridgedeck.

Before dawn on about the fourth day the wind was beginning to moan in the rigging, the sea was rising and the long, heavy boom was starting to dip and drag in the sea. We managed to douse the mainsail in the dark with some difficulty and carried on under jib and mizzen. Later in the morning we set the storm trysail at my urging, mostly I think to try it out rather from any real necessity. It was the only taste of nasty weather we encountered on the entire trip. About this time I was beginning to realize that *Tai Fung* was certainly not the ideal boat for the trip. The biggest problem was the old fashioned gaff rig with its long boom and heavy gaff which were the devil to handle, especially when the boat was rolling (which was just about always). We had no winch or tackle to help with reefing the big mainsail, a difficulty which became starkly clear when we tried to shorten sail in the dark. Also, the problem of the long boom dragging in the sea when we rolled or heeled in the wind was unnerving and quite dangerous since it tended to make the boat very difficult to steer.

During the pre-dawn hours of the 6th day we encountered a rather violent squall. After it passed, the wind suddenly began to come out of the northeast and was much warmer. We had entered the trade winds! The following days were sunny and bright with little puffy clouds overhead and a steady wind blowing from starboard quarter. At this point it was becoming very difficult to use the big gaff mainsail but we soon found that a good sail combination was to use the large genoa jib to leeward together with one of the twin staysails on a pole to windward, plus the mizzen.

One day near the half way point of our voyage we spotted what appeared to be a sail ahead but which turned out to be the superstructure of US Coast Guard weather ship NAN on station in mid-ocean. To our surprise and excitement she changed course and steamed toward us. As she passed alongside we shouted a radio frequency to them and they responded immediately. After receiving our assurances that we were fine, the captain offered to notify Doc's wife of the encounter and give her the news of our good health and safety. It was to be the only vessel we saw on the passage.

By this time we were well into the routine of shipboard life and well (maybe too well) acquainted with each other. Doc had his little foibles including a lot of worrying about the weather and the state of the sea. He was cheerful enough but not possessing much of a sense of humor, a factor which set a rather somber tone aboard the boat. He was also a rather bigoted and cynical man, making light hearted conversation difficult. I knew all of this at the outset, having been around him for years, but I think the other boys were a little subdued by his nature. Phil Price was a jewel. He quickly picked up the essence of sailing and was eager to learn as much as he could of seamanship and rigging. Although rather quiet, he was very amiable and a pleasure to share a watch with. Best of all, he really enjoyed learning to cook aboard the boat. Dick Kieding was quite reserved and also an excellent shipmate. For some reason, which I will never understand, Doc was not as friendly with him as I would have expected. Dick had good judgment about how to handle unexpected situations when on watch and was completely reliable. While not a great cook, he cheerfully did his share. I don't know how the others viewed me, but I was having a wonderful time. In spite of the long night watches, the days flew by and I reveled in the life at sea.

In the final week of the trip the sea had become marvelously deep blue. The waves formed by the fresh trade winds were high, up to about 15', steep and crowned with white caps and typically were very regular and well spaced. It was great sailing, sliding down the faces of the waves although we were always haunted by the fact that before too long we would have to sail back against these same seas. The wind had become very steady in force and direction, day and night. Since the wind was now blowing from right aft we decided to make another effort to use both of our twin staysails together. Previously when we had tried, we found that the wind would spill from one sail to the other and cause them to flop wildly. After studying the situation for a while, I tried setting one of the sails a little ahead of the other. As if by a miracle, they both went steadily to work and pulled like a team of mules.

From that moment on, the voyage became a real lazy-man's vacation. There was nothing to do but eat, sleep and steer the boat. I was surprised, however, to find that these three activities nearly filled up the day. We were carrying a sufficiently small amount of sail so that when the occasional squall came along we simply charged through the water at a great rate ahead of the blast, which seldom lasted more than ten or fifteen minutes. A small amount of rain would fall and then in a few minutes things would be completely back to normal. We sailed along without touching a sheet for days on end.

During the last few days the crew began to prefix every sentence with "When we get to Honolulu......", but I found that I did not have a great desire to make port as I had expected. Each day seemed to me to be nearly the perfect fulfillment of my wish to sail over the face of the ocean. I would have been content to have the trip continue indefinitely.

After 17 days at sea we sail down the Molokai Channel toward Diamond Head

On July 8th we were coasting along the Islands, about 60 miles offshore. The clouds were so thick that we didn't sight the land until the following day as we sailed down the channel between Molokai and Oahu. By noon we made out the unmistakable shape of Diamond Head and soon were off the shoreline of Honolulu. A magical moment! I was thrilled that I had actually lived the experience of making a transoceanic passage with all its anxieties, excitement, boredom, thrills and new understanding of voyaging under sail. And now the prospect of sailing through the Hawaiian Islands was an additional bonus.

Tai Fung's crew on arrival in Honolulu (L toR) Dick Kieding, Phil Price, Doc Richardson and me

We had a bit of a problem getting our engine to start and run smoothly after being idle for a couple of weeks. Doc removed and cleaned the carburetor (the gunk in the iron gas tanks had no doubt been well shaken up) and after we were confident that it would keep going, we followed a launch into the cut through the reef to the harbor. In those days it was necessary to first enter the Kewalo Fish Harbor, and then follow a long, narrow, poorly marked channel between the reef and the beach, which led to the Ala Wai Yacht Harbor. The harbormaster, a weatherbeaten but friendly character named Chick Allen, showed us a berth amongst the small collection of cruising sailboats, local "sampan-style" fishing boats and ramshackle houseboats tied to the single dock in the basin.

The little yacht basin was an interesting place. All along the wooden pier were Chinese fishermen sitting on little stools as they tended their several lines attached to springy wires stuck into the timber planks. On the top of the wires were bright red balls of fluff to alert them to nibbling fish and in wicker baskets alongside were the little mullet fish they had caught. It all seemed to require enormous patience for such a meager result. On the shore was "Mama-San's" café, an open pavilion with a few tables and a counter where we could buy snacks and meals. Here, five cents would buy a huge slice of fresh pineapple and ten cents would buy a scoop of ice cream in a half a papaya. A tiny boatyard with a rickety marine railway constituted the remainder of the facilities. Beyond the dusty empty lots surrounding the harbor and across the street was the Superette (nicknamed the Robberette by Doc), a small mom & pop grocery store. Although we were on the edge of the Waikiki district, there was not a high-rise building to be seen.

We had made the passage to Honolulu in 17 days. This was not bad time for a cruising boat and caused more than a little favorable comment. Although the Transpac Race attracted a fleet of yachts to the Islands on odd-numbered years, it was fairly unusual for a cruising sailboat to make the voyage in those days. To our knowledge, the only other boat to make the trip in 1952 was a little red schooner from San Diego named *Buccaneer*. We were interviewed by a reporter and were impressed to see the article and photo of *Tai Fung* in the paper the next day. On the afternoon of our arrival a man stopped us on the dock and asked if we were from the boat which had sailed in. When we said yes, he replied, "I thought so because you all look like a bunch of milk bottles". At that point we knew we would have to work on our suntans.

Doc moved ashore into a small hotel where he was soon joined by his wife, Betty, and Mrs. Kerrigan, a friend of the Richardsons. The plan was to stay in Honolulu for about a week then sail to the other islands. But first we needed to look after the boat because the varnished hull and all the trim had taken quite a beating on the trip over. While Doc and the ladies toured the Island, Phil, Dick and I set to work and in three days we had the job done, working from 6 AM to

11 AM , a schedule which allowed us to look around a bit and enjoy the sights. In this, we were helped by an introduction to an enterprising man named Earl Thacker who owned property and businesses throughout the Islands, including the Gray Line Tour buses in Honolulu. In addition to free passes on the buses, this generous man instructed a driver to deliver milk and eggs to the boat each morning from a dairy farm he owned on the outskirts of the city.

Tai Fung's varnished hull took a beating so we immediately set to work

After a big struggle to get the ladies and their unstowable suitcases arranged in the forward cabin, we set off to sail directly to the south coast of the "Big Island." It was then that we realized that we had made a serious tactical error in our cruise planning. Not knowing any better, we had simply headed for Honolulu because that was the glamorous place where the racing boats went. What we didn't know was that to get to all the other islands except Kauai, we would have to brave the strong easterly trade winds. As soon as we got out from under the lee of Diamond Head, we quickly encountered the strong winds and steep seas which are common in the channels between the Islands.

We had hoped to keep in the lee of Molokai and Maui and out of at least some of the worst of the rough water but in vain. The afternoon and night turned into a nightmare of flying spray, the boat steeply heeled over, decks awash, pounding thumps of the bow, deck leaks and seasick passengers as we were forced off the wind and ended up passing to the south of Lanai.

The next morning we were in relatively smooth water and able to get close to Maui with the help of the motor. Looking for any kind of harbor, we headed for Lahina's tiny enclosed basin. As we sailed through the narrow channel through the reef we got a severe scare when *Tai Fung's* keel hit the bottom. A group of observers on shore frantically shouted and waved directions to us as the swell lifted and dropped us on the coral. We managed to get free and into deeper water, then rounded the end of the little breakwater. Inside was a miniature harbor, scarcely big enough for us, but offering perfect shelter in an exotic setting. Our neighbors were a handful of small, active sampan fishing boats, while ashore was a public square with an ancient courthouse and a gigantic, spreading banyan tree. Opposite the harbor entrance was the old fashioned Pioneer Hotel, which looked like something out of Somerset Maugham's tale, *Rain*. Doc and the ladies moved into the hotel.

Lahaina was a sleepy little pineapple and sugar cane plantation town. We soon met Verity and Al Collins who managed the Pioneer Sugar Mill and Ethelva and Bill Troy who was in charge of the large pineapple company. By the best of good fortune, it happened that the Troy family had three attractive and vivacious daughters about our age and a spare jeep for us to use. The five days we spent at Lahaina were a grand whirlwind of tours, picnics, and beach parties. Our time there was easily the highlight of our time in the Islands.

To our great relief, we sailed without too much difficulty to the Island of Hawaii where we spent time anchored off the little stone pier at Kailua watching cattle, bellowing and mooing, while being loaded by belly sling onto small inter-island cargo boats. From there we went on to the ideal anchorage of Kealakekua. Here we visited the spot where Captain Cook met his fate at the hands of early Hawaiians who had come to the conclusion that he wasn't a God after all. Also, here we arranged for a ride to the Kilauea Crater of Mauna Loa Volcano which was in a spectacular state of eruption. Our next destination was island of Molokai where we stopped at Kaunakakai and spent an extra day at yet another of Earl Thacker's properties, a cattle ranch where he offered us horseback riding and wonderful ranch cooking.

In Lahaina, Maui we were escorted by a bevy of friendly natives.

As we returned to Honolulu across the normally windy channel between Molokai and Oahu, we encountered a very rare day of calm but with a huge oily swell running. As we neared Waikiki Beach we noticed a misty haze over the shoreline caused by enormous breakers on the beach. A patrolling Coast Guard vessel warned us not to attempt to enter the yacht harbor but to go into the commercial harbor instead. We tied up at one of the large ship piers and spent the night without incident. The next morning we checked with the Port office and were told that it was safe to go to the yacht harbor so we proceeded to the entrance buoy and started in. Just as we were fully committed and approaching the critical gap in the reef, we noticed that it was breaking very heavily on the reef ahead of us. Then, to our horror we saw a pair of huge swells behind us beginning to steepen and build in height. Everyone except Doc and I jumped below. He was at the wheel concentrating on keeping the boat straight in the middle of the channel as I watched astern. The breakers grew in height until the faces of the waves were nearly vertical and the sun shone through the top of the crests. They caught up with us as we were about half-way through the channel then broke like thunder on the reef on each side of the cut. I kept telling Doc, "Don't look back! Just keep steering!" Luckily they never broke in the channel and Doc was able to keep *Tai Fung* running straight and true as she accelerated ahead and surfed at frightening speed. It was a hairy experience to say the very least especially in light of the wreck of a 50' motor cruiser at that very spot the previous morning with five persons aboard (they survived).

The final leg of our Island cruise took us to Kauai where we stopped at the little commercial port of Nahwiliwili, enjoyed tours of the island courtesy of the generous Mr. Thacker then sailed on to lovely Hanalei Bay, surely the prettiest anchorage in Hawaii. We spent several days there in solitude, enjoying the spectacular setting and bracing our nerves for the 2500 mile voyage back to California. It was now a little after mid-August and high time to get underway if I was to make the fall semester at Cal Berkeley.

The well-known strategy for sailing back to the Coast was to sail north as close to the northeast trade wind as possible, cross the wide area of calm known as the "Pacific High" keeping on a northerly heading, then after picking up the westerly wind north of the high, come barreling onto the coast on a broad reach or run. Of course back in 1952 we had no meaningful weather information for the area we were headed for nor any means of getting any en route, so when the scheduled day of departure arrived, we simply raised the anchor and got underway, close- hauled on the starboard tack.

The trade winds were apparently down a peg as we left the Islands because we did not have the great difficulty with strong winds and rough seas that we had expected and each day after the first two or three, the breeze became less. In fact, it was very nice sailing. We quickly fell back into our routine of four-hour watches off and on, with Doc doing the navigating and the boys doing the cooking. I had a smattering of knowledge about celestial navigation from my surveying classes at the College of Marin. Also I learned a bit from an astronomy class there taught by Roger Strout, a Blue Water Medal recipient who had sailed his yawl, *Igdrasil,* around the world in the mid-1930's.

Doc was a very precise navigator who kept meticulous notes and had an excellent grasp of the theory. He was more than willing to show me his methods and help me become a good navigator too. Since there was a spare sextant aboard, both of us would take sights and work out our position at least a couple of times a day. It was one of the most enjoyable aspects of the voyage for me.

By the end of the first week, as the breeze grew lighter, we knew that we were definitely beginning to enter the area of the Pacific High. Within a few more days we were mostly becalmed in a dead smooth sea without the slightest sign of a wave or a swell. The weather was absolutely lovely with cool temperatures, clear skies and wonderful star-filled nights. The only trouble was we weren't getting anywhere. We had a fair amount of gas in the tanks and two large containers of gas on deck but were reluctant to use much of it because there was no telling how long the calms would last. As a result we struggled to use every vagrant puff of wind by day or night. Occasionally we would motor for a few hours until a little zephyr would come along, then we would go back to nursing the boat along under sail. It was a great temptation, but we didn't dare to head directly for San Francisco under power because we knew we would be out of gas long before we got out of the High. So we slowly, very slowly kept working our way north.

At last when we reached latitude 45 degrees (the latitude of Portland, Oregon) we started to feel some wind from the west. Within a day or so we were bowling along making great time but in overcast weather with a real chill in the air. On one occasion, for a two day spell we were seeing a truly huge swell overtaking us from astern. This had a very ominous feel to it even though the wind was steady and of moderate velocity. Our fears were not helped by Doc's habit of frequently tapping the barometer and muttering, "I think we're in for a big buster!" As it happened, nothing came of it. The swell went away and we continued along with a generous but not excessive wind. In the wee hours of the 26th day we spotted the previously elusive lighthouse on the Farallon Islands and by early afternoon we passed under the Golden Gate Bridge at the end of our great adventure. What a summer it had been! Our voyage had been all that I had hoped it would be. I was tired after our long passage, of course, but at the same time excited and energized. I knew I had found my true interest in life.

*On the return trip we found many prized Japanese glass net floats
in the calms of the Pacific High*

I had missed the final date for registration for the fall semester of my junior year at Cal. With two years of civil engineering behind me I had no trouble finding a job with PG&E on one of their survey crews. I was a chainman on a three man crew working on the alignment for a new power line in Lake County, the poison oak capitol of the world. Part of my job was to clear the brush (poison oak) along the line so that the instrument man could take his sights and allow us to measure the distance. The weather was nice, the work was interesting, and countryside was lovely but oh what misery I was in! Eventually, I actually became somewhat immune to the poisonous stuff. After Christmas we moved to the coast to survey a line near Point Arena, an area I liked even better. In spite of working for a man who I found out later was considered the most cantankerous party chief in the whole company, I got along fine and learned a lot. By February, 1953 it was time to go back to Berkeley for the spring semester.

My little break from college had its perils in those days since the Korean War was on and the military draft was fully in effect. I was very conscious of the war since my older brother, Skip, a US Navy medical corpsman had been transferred to the Marines (the Marines have no corpsmen of their own) after the start of he war in June 1950. I vividly recall coming home to Mill Valley in August to find my folks huddled around the radio listening to reports of the sinking of the Hospital ship, *Benevolence,* about four miles outside the Golden Gate in a collision with the freighter, *Mary Luckenbach,* in dense fog with much loss of life. It seems Skip had phoned them the previous day from Oak Knoll Hospital in Oakland where he was stationed, informing them that he would be would be shipping out shortly on a hospital ship for Korea. Naturally they assumed he was aboard. To our immense relief, we learned that his orders had been changed at the last minute and he was to go on an ordinary troop ship. This wasn't the end of it, however, because on arrival in Korea, Skip found himself with the 1st Marine Division, where in November he was in the middle of the huge Chinese counterattack at the Chosin Reservoir on the northern border of North Korea. Skip never talked about the desperate battle at all, but it must have been terrible. In the end he was evacuated from Hagaru-ri on one of the last flights out with badly frostbitten feet.

As it turned out, I needn't have worried about the draft. In the early spring I received a notice from the Draft Board to report to the Presidio for a medical examination and induction. When I inquired as to why my presence at Cal didn't qualify me for a deferment, I was told that I had already spent enough time in college. I was not terribly surprised by this answer since many students were being called up. I said goodbye to my parents and my friends and showed up at 6:00AM at the designated location in San Rafael. The Red Cross ladies were there at the bus stop with coffee and doughnuts, and soon we were lined up for the Army doc to have a look at us. I had always been very near sighted (myopic) so when it came time for me to read the eye chart on the wall I had to admit that without my glasses I could only manage to read the big E at the top of the chart. The doctor said the Army had no problem sending kids out to get killed but they really didn't like to commit murder. So he reclassified me as 4-f (medically unsuited) and in no time I was out on the street. I was disappointed for about one minute.

I had found a room with a pleasant family named the Balls who owned a big old Victorian house in Berkeley and was back into the routine of acquiring a civil engineering education. Like most engineering students, it was mostly all work and not much play. I was pretty much of a social klutz anyway, so being distracted by girls and parties was not a problem. I worked and studied hard during the week, trying to keep my weekends clear. I would head for Sausalito on Saturday mornings in my old '35 Ford sedan to work and sail on *Tai Fung* and earn my meager pay of $20. Surprisingly, it was almost enough to keep me going at Cal when supplemented by my savings from the PG&E job. I was very restless however, and my mind kept returning to the excitement and challenge of our sailing trip to Hawaii. I knew that, being an odd-numbered year, 1953 would have a Transpac Race to Honolulu, so I kept my eyes and ears open for a chance to go.

The 39' sloop, Mistress, entering Papeete, Tahiti harbor

CHAPTER 3

MISTRESS

In my weekly trips to the Sausalito Yacht Harbor and visits to the Corinthian Yacht Club to which both Doc Richardson and I belonged, I was always on the prowl for intelligence about what boats might be going in the next Transpac Race to Hawaii in 1953. Although I had never been in an ocean race and in fact had never even crewed on a serious, up-to-date racing boat, I was confident that given the chance, I could be a good crew. After all, I had sailed up and down the Coast several times, had sailed to Hawaii, could navigate, repair sails and even cook (sort of) at sea. And I was keen — more than keen — to go.

At last I heard a rumor that the *Mistress,* an old, pre-war Farallon Clipper sloop from our yacht club was signed up to go not only in the Transpac, but in the follow-up race from Honolulu to Tahiti. The boat was to be skippered by Pete Fromhagen, an expert sailor whom I knew slightly, so I wasted no time in visiting Pete's yacht brokerage office in San Rafael to make my pitch for being part of the crew. Pete listened patiently and said he would let me know. I wasn't encouraged much by his reaction to my plea and had almost given up hope, when to my surprise and joy he called me at Berkeley a couple of weeks later and said I was on.

It seems the boat had been sold by Pete to Walter Johnson, a 28 year-old fellow from a wealthy family who was new to sailing but eager to get into it in a big way. He had talked Pete into being skipper and put him in charge of getting the boat ready and lining up a crew leaving one spot open for his drinking buddy, Russ Larson, another novice to sailing who owned a muffler shop in Oakland. With me on board, Pete rounded out the crew of five by inviting Bill Garvie, a local boat builder.

Mistress was one of seven identical boats built in 1939 by Stephens Brothers Boatyard in Stockton. She was 39' long and was a sort of knockoff of the Sparkman & Stephens designed, 36' "Weekender" class which was popular on the East Coast. One of them, the *Gladys N*, had been built at the yard, so when the proposal to build a fleet of boats came along, the yard added three feet to the design and gave it the name of Farallon Clipper for a local flavor. The boats sold new for $4500 and were rather cheaply built, with a minimum of trim and canvas-covered plywood decks. *Mistress* had been raced very hard during her life and was beginning to show her age. Still, it looked pretty classy to me. Bill Garvie took a more critical view of her construction and immediately took steps to beef up her rig by installing a new set of chainplates for the lower shrouds among other jobs. In the end he took along a huge, heavy tool box. When questioned about it, he reckoned the right amount of tools to bring along for this vessel was enough to build a new boat.

The Marin County contingent of the crew, me, Pete Fromhagen and Bill Garvie

Pete Fromhagen was a very experienced sailor who had skippered racing yachts, including sleek 8-meter sloops, for years on the Bay. He was unusually even tempered and diplomatic in his ways and could have "charmed the birds out of the trees" as my mother used to say. He had done many things, but in recent years had run a small yacht brokerage in San Rafael. I was pretty much in awe of him and was anxious to learn as much as I could from him. Bill Garvie was an entirely different type, a big husky man who had a rather self-deprecating but humorous way about him. Although he had done little, if any, sailboat racing, he had an encyclopedic knowledge of wooden boat building, rigging and practical boat repair. He was always quick to find the best in people and was ever ready with a grin and a chuckle. It was impossible to not like him. Walter Johnson was more of an enigma. I had no idea what, if anything, he had done for a living. The only hint I ever got was a comment that he had tried being a businessman but quickly found out that it wasn't for him. He was a very jolly fellow who relished telling of his youthful escapades and adventures with women. Unlike Pete, Bill and me, he was married. His wife was a charming little woman named Hathily and he had two young sons, Walter, Jr. and Mark. The final member of the crew, Russ Larson, was somewhat more serious than his pal, Walter, but still a fun-loving guy. His knowledge of boats was just about nil, but he was a practical, mechanically minded man who quickly picked up plenty of sailing skills. He was also married, but without children. We were not exactly an Americas Cup class crew but were ready for the challenge of a couple of long distance ocean races in one of the simpler, smaller boats in the fleet.

Mistress had a waterline length of 28 feet which made her just barely able to qualify to race in the Transpac. She would be racing in Class C, the smallest, and theoretically, the slowest boats. In actuality however, if the bigger boats failed to get enough wind to sail up to their potential speed, the Class C boats would be favored to be among the overall winners. As it turned out, this is exactly what happened. The Transpac Race had been around since 1906 and had been run more or less continuously since the early 1930's making it (along with the Newport – Bermuda Race) one of the classic ocean races of the world. It was definitely a glamour event and we were excited to be a part of it.

The other race, from Honolulu to Tahiti, was a different story. A race to Tahiti had been carried out only once before, in 1924. That event had started in San Francisco and went 3800 miles directly to Tahiti. It had only four entries: *Mariner, Shawnee, Idalia,* and *Eloise,* all big schooners. The *Eloise* was the same boat we had in the Mill Valley Sea Scouts. The Honolulu – Tahiti race would be 2100 miles long but in some respects a much more difficult race than the original one because Papeete, Tahiti lies about 600 miles to the east of Honolulu and every inch of that 600 miles would have to be made against the prevailing wind and current, whereas the original race was entirely off the wind. Either people either didn't know what they were in for (like us) or they didn't care, because 15 of the total Transpac fleet of 32 boats signed up for the race.

First we had to get the boat fitted out and down to San Pedro by July 4th for the start of the race. *Mistress* had lots of sails but most of them were veterans of much hard use. We went to the new sailmaking firm of Larson & Sutter on the Embarcadero in San Francisco and ordered a mainsail of a new material called "dacron". To our knowledge it was the first one on the Bay. We also ordered a storm trysail of heavy cotton canvas, partly at my urging. I believe we may have also ordered a new nylon spinnaker and a nylon spinnaker staysail to be carried under the chute. Otherwise we didn't do much to alter the boat's equipment except hang a couple of big orange life saver rings on the stern pulpit which were required because of a near drowning of a crew in the previous race. It seems he fell overboard and survived for over 24 hours because he was such a skinny guy he was able to wiggle inside a small 18" life ring. In late June we shoved off from the Corinthian Yacht Club in Tiburon and headed out the Golden Gate.

As might be expected at that time of year, there was wind, and plenty of it, out on the ocean. We were tearing along under full sail and by the next morning were somewhere near Point Sur. Bill Garvie and Russ Larson were on deck in the early morning with Bill at the tiller. I was below getting some oatmeal going for breakfast while Walter and Pete were still catching up on sleep. The boat was sailing hard and going very fast when suddenly there was a tremendous crash on deck and the boat heeled far over on its side. The hatch boards were in so there was no water coming inside the boat but it was obvious that an enormous wave had come aboard. I think everyone had the same thought, "Wow. What's going on up on deck!" I slid the companionway hatch open and immediately saw that Bill had been washed overboard. He was skittering alongside the boat with his boot miraculously tangled up in the mainsheet! I don't remember exactly how, but he was able to get hold of the rail or something and managed, with a little help, to get himself aboard. Typically, his first words were, "Man! We better take a reef in that mainsail!"

Bill said afterward that he had heard the big wave coming and braced himself solidly in the cockpit and held on to the tiller with all of his strength. Bill is a very big strong fellow, but even so, he had been swept over the lifelines and into the sea. If he had not caught his boot up in the mainsheet, I think our chances of getting him back would have been pretty near zero, what with our speed and the rough sea at the time. Russ had been sitting on deck with his back against the end of the cabin house and had been simply plastered up against the boat by the wave. The wave had hit the stern pulpit with such force that it had carried away the life rings and had bent the pipe framework over. Needless to say, we were all very sobered by the incident.

Within a couple more days we arrived at Newport Beach and moored at the Villa Marina Hotel where Walter and Russ moved ashore. Our little shakedown trip down the coast had shown us that we had plenty of work to do before the start of the race. One of our first priorities was to replace the stove. The alcohol stove we had been using had consumed nearly a gallon of alcohol in our relatively short trip so we knew it was useless for the long passages ahead of us. It was replaced with a kerosene model. Next we had to make up a man-overboard pole with a lead weight at the bottom, a flag at the top and a float in the middle. We had all the ingredients including a long bamboo pole. Bill proceeded to melt a pig of lead in a saucepan on the galley stove. He carefully carried the hot, melted lead in the pan up the stairs and onto the float where he would pour it into the hollowed out end of the bamboo which had its other end stuck into the muddy bottom. It was a great plan except when he tilted the pan to make the pour, the pan turned upside down because the handle had become loose from all the heat. The molten lead hit the water with a big explosion and that was that. Eventually we recovered the lead (which had turned into a lovely, lace-like pattern in the water) and succeeded on the second try.

On July 3rd we sailed up to San Pedro to be ready for the start the next day. The boat was fully loaded with water and stores. Unfortunately the only sizable storage space for the groceries was under the bunks in the forward cabin. Their weight, together with Bill's big tool box and the anchor gear, put the bow down rather badly, but there wasn't much we could do about that. There were only four bunks in the boat so we were to use the "hot sack" system wherein the person coming off watch would use the warm bunk of his replacement, when all five of us were aboard. But none of this was on our mind as we spent the final night before the start in the anchorage off the old Los Angeles Yacht Club which was perched on the stone breakwater at the Fish Harbor basin in the middle of the Port.

The next morning we motored out to the starting area, shut off the engine and slowly maneuvered into position in the light breeze. As I recall we got a reasonably good start and sailed gently toward the west end of Catalina Island. It was a foretaste of what the 1953 Transpac Race was to be. We had light airs and sunny skies the entire way. I don't think the wind ever got over about 10 to 15 knots in the whole distance. The boat rolled, the sails slatted, the spinnaker jerked from side to side and the crew sweated under the shade of a little makeshift awning we hung over a rope stretched from the mast to the backstay. It was a big anticlimax after our exciting ride down the coast and a bit of a let-down after the thrill of my first long ocean passage on *Tai Fung*.

Actually the light winds worked in our favor since the bigger boats just couldn't get up to speed without strong winds, so on a handicap basis we were doing fine. We had to check in by radio every morning at roll call and our daily positions, on a corrected time basis (with the time allowance or handicap figured in) began to show us in a very good position. At last, after 16 days, 7 hours we crossed the finish line to come in 2nd in our class and in 8th place overall amongst the 32 boats in the fleet. Not bad, we thought for a plain little boat

On the way over there was plenty of time to spend talking and a very big topic of conversation -- especially between Walter and his pal, Russ -- was about all the wild times they planned to have in Honolulu with the local girls, especially since such activity had been forestalled with the arrival of their wives during our stay in Newport Beach. In those days the Transpac fleet was moored stern-to the quay at the Kewalo Basin. In order to make the mooring process easy, a little towboat met contenders outside the harbor and escorted them in.

At the last minute it would tie alongside and "breast" the boat stern-first into place. As they were getting set up, one of the crew on the towboat whispered to Pete that a couple of wives were waiting on the dock for our arrival. Pete tipped off Bill and me to this information and we all watched for the inevitable reaction. There was a large, cheering crowd on the quay to greet us as our mooring lines were thrown ashore. Walter and Russ were all smiles and eager anticipation until they caught sight of their wives in the crowd, then did some of the best double takes I have ever seen.

Mistress being moved into her berth in the Kewalo Basin,
Honolulu after the 1953 Transpac Race

The scene at the Kewalo basin was wonderfully colorful and dramatic, with all the boats moored side-by-side in plain view for the whole city to see. Only a couple of boats away from us was the gargantuan, 161' schooner, *Goodwill,* with a crew so large they were dubbed "we the people". She had spinnaker poles so big they had to be wheeled up the deck on rubber tired dollys, and the clew of the spinnaker had to be released, when being taken down, by a small explosive charge. She had been taken out of retirement and completely fitted out at vast expense at the Douglas Aircraft Corporation in Burbank. It was to be her only race, and a few years later she left her bones on Sacramento Reef off Baja California, Mexico with the loss of all hands including the owner.

Each boat was assigned a Honolulu family as hosts who went all-out to show us a wonderful time. In fact, the next 10 days or so were a blur of activity with endless parties, excursions and visits aboard boats. Walter and Russ disappeared ashore with their wives. Pete and Bill quickly found amorous girlfriends and I happily enjoyed the whole hectic atmosphere. Bill took up an affair with a well known sailor and yacht broker (now departed) named Peggy Slater, a wonderfully flamboyant gal of generous proportions with flaming red hair. One day Bill returned to the boat with a big smile on his face and a continuous chuckle. When we asked what was so funny, he said he just had a tryst with Peggy in her luxurious hotel room which was furnished with a wall-sized mirror. At the height of the scene he had looked over at the mirror and couldn't resist laughing at the sight of two badly overweight lovers in action.

A few days before the start of the race to Tahiti, we moved *Mistress* down to the yacht basin and made a feeble effort to get organized for the next race. It didn't help that Walter decided that he really wanted a bigger, better boat and was negotiating to purchase the lovely 60' schooner, *Dirigo II.* Naturally, we in the crew were wildly in favor of this idea, but at the last moment when a deal couldn't be struck, we had to face the fact that we were going to have to sail on *Mistress.*

On the afternoon before the start of the race we dashed off to a nearby grocery store and began to load up a train of shopping carts with an enormous load of food. Since we had all been invited to a dinner party that night, we made a deal with the Chinese owner of the store to forgo any talk of a discount for our large order if he would agree to strip the paper labels from the cans and mark them with a grease pencil. We returned to the store long after closing hours and found a very disgruntled owner and staff. He angrily said, "I never do again. Too much trouble!" At this point we noticed that a typical marking on a can of tuna would read: "Chicken of The Sea, whole chunk tuna". By about 1:00 AM we had the stores aboard and more or less stowed.

On July 29th the race from Honolulu, Hawaii to Papeete, Tahiti was due to start at 12:00 noon. We were scarcely in shape to sail anywhere and it seems neither was anyone else. Of the 15 original contenders who had signed up for the race, there were only two others besides us, still game to go. One was a slender 55' yawl named *Silhouette* the other was sturdy 61' ketch named *Chiriqui,* both considerably larger and faster than us. Their crews were just as partied-out and hung over as ours so at an impromptu meeting on the dock a compromise was reached. Silhouette was to give us a time allowance of 2 days, 1 hour and *Chiriqui* was to give us an allowance of 2 days, 6 hours so it was agreed (reluctantly by us) that they would start exactly two days after us. We wondered if they would actually do it.

We hurriedly threw off the mooring lines and got out to the little starting line which had been set up outside the yacht basin. At exactly noon a tiny saluting cannon was fired and we were on our way with Tahiti 2100 miles ahead. A fresh wind was blowing, as usual, and soon we were off Diamond Head. Pete asked if I had filled the water tank. When I said no, he quickly asked the others and received the same reply. There was no other choice but to turn around and sail back to the harbor and up to the fuel dock for water. Luckily we were able to tack right up to the dock because, having started the race, we could not use our motor. Amazingly, while we were filling the water tank, the owner of *Dirigo II* came by and he and Walter resumed their negotiations for purchase of the schooner. Of course nothing happened in the few minutes it took to fill up and get away again. As we passed Diamond Head again we noted that we had lost a little over an hour. Not a good way to get started. We found out a little later that water was not the only thing we had forgotten.

The easterly trade winds were blowing strong and a rough sea was running as we tried to work our way to windward. The obvious strategy, which had been strongly advised to us by the few experienced sailors in Honolulu who had made the sail to Tahiti, was to sail close-hauled on the port tack for as long as it took because once we crossed the doldrums and entered the southeast trade winds, we would be lucky to lay a course for Tahiti. In other words, we were in for a long, very rough ride. Poor old *Mistress* slammed and bucked and threw spray over the boat while those off watch huddled below in the stifling heat with the hatches and portholes tightly closed. The boat was badly trimmed down by the bow with a ton of stores aboard. The deck leaked, the mast shook and the strain on the rigging combined with the noise of the pounding made it almost impossible to relax. On deck it was worse; since this was well before the age of spray dodgers and autopilots, the helmsman simply had to endure the constant drenching of the spray. There was so much water on deck that eventually it worked its way between the deck canvas and the plywood so that walking on deck resembled walking on a clam bed with water squirting up from the little holes in the canvas.

The 2200 mile, 20 ½ day trip was a hard beat to windward

None of us were feeling wonderful, but not long after the start, poor Pete simply wedged himself into a bunk in the forward cabin and became utterly *hors'de combat.* No food, no water, simply inert misery for several days.   As skipper and navigator, he didn't normally stand watches anyway, so the rest of the crew carried on.   It was quickly apparent, however, that we had a major problem.   We simply did not have a way to reduce our sail area to match the strong winds since we had only a single reef in the mainsail and no headsail smaller than an overlapping genoa jib.   We tried every combination we could think of including sailing without a jib and without a mainsail.   Finally we settled on sailing with the jib and the storm trysail which wasn't too bad except the trysail was quite baggy and didn't allow us to point very high into the wind.   It was all very discouraging, especially because we were never able to contact anyone in Honolulu on the radio to find out if the other two competitors had ever actually started the race.   We were sure they hadn't.

We struggled on.   We had no refrigeration, of course, and with the wild motion in the galley, our *cuisine* became rudimentary to say the least.   Another problem was the salt-water sores on our bottoms from sitting in the cockpit for hours in wet, salty clothing.   We came to the conclusion that the only effective treatment was to expose our butts to the sunshine whenever possible.   I wish I had a photograph of the sight of several of us receiving the solar treatment each day by lying across the cabin top with our shockingly untanned *derrieres* facing the sun.   Another problem became apparent when we saw Pete making a chart of the Pacific Ocean on a blank sheet, carefully plotting in the islands and reefs between us and Tahiti using data from the Pilot Book.   It seems we had neglected to buy a chart.   There weren't all that many islands and reefs to hit along our course but we had no assurance that all of them were mentioned in the Pilot Book.   As it turned out, we actually sailed within sight of the palm trees on tiny Caroline Atoll.

Another bit of foolishness took place when we crossed the Equator.   Following nautical tradition, Russ, Bill and I were subjected to a visit and interrogation by King Neptune with appropriate punishment for our sins.   During the ceremony we hove-to (stopped the boat) so we could all participate.   Afterwards we celebrated with a tot of rum and went for a swim which ended with the realization that we were all in the water at the same time with no one on deck to maneuver the boat if it decided to sail away.   One final bit of tribulation was the discovery that the seacock on the head had apparently become defective and was impossible to completely shut off. This meant the person on watch had to pump the head at least every 15 minutes or else the cabin floor would become flooded.

We took time out for an Equator crossing ceremony

In spite of our endless struggles to windward, by the time we were nearing Tahiti we realized that we still were not able to lay a course to the island. It was apparent a change in the weather was coming, however, and one day the sky became heavily overcast and the wind swung into the west. We abruptly headed due east and ran swiftly for a full day to gain as much longitude as we possibly could. Finally, however, our fine wind turned into a moderate gale, forcing Pete to order us to drop all sail and lash the tiller to leeward. Thus we lay a-hull all night with the boat riding quite easily in the trough of the seas. Except for the occasional loud thump of a crest hitting the windward side of the boat, we were fine. It was the first time I had seen this maneuver and was very impressed. By the next morning, the wind was much abated and back in its usual southeasterly direction.

One day later, in the early morning we were within sight of Moorea. As we sailed past the island we spotted a sailboat close inshore which we soon identified as *Silhouette*. We had struggled so long and hard to make our passage that we jumped to the conclusion that she had probably arrived at least a week ahead of us and was probably on a little cruise to another island while waiting for our arrival. Tahiti was soon in full view and we noticed that *Silhouette* certainly seemed to be in racing trim toward the finish line. We both tacked for the finish at the Papeete harbor entrance with *Silhouette* finally passing us and crossing the line about 15 minutes ahead. With the remainder of our 1-hour time allowance still in hand however, we beat her on corrected time by 45 minutes. Our passage had taken a little over 20 days. *Chiriqui* came in the following afternoon. After having blown out all of her sails in our gale, she had run off to Bora Bora and enlisted all of the local women to hand-sew them back together. Since we had easily saved our time allowance on her, *Mistress* was the winner.

Tacking to the finish line with a competitor in sight

As we approached the town quay at Papeete a spry little man in a jaunty uniform jumped; aboard from a launch. He was the harbor pilot and immediately took command, ordering us about with directions on where to drop anchor, how much scope to veer, when to cast the stern lines ashore, etc. all with crisp commands suitable for an ocean liner. A large, welcoming crowd lined the shore including, we were quick to notice, many lovely girls. A photographer came aboard along with several officials from the race committee and the government. It was obvious that a much larger fleet of yachts had been expected but no one seemed disappointed. A jolly man named Guy de Friesel introduced himself with the news that he was our official host and immediately swept us off the boat for drinks and lunch at a small establishment across the street named the Hotel Stewart which served as the impromptu location of the Tahiti Yacht Club.

The scene along the waterfront was exotic, quaint and right out of a National Geographic article on the South Seas. *Mistress* was moored stern first to the rock quay with her stern lines led to ancient cannons sunk into the ground to serve as mooring bollards. A wide grassy strip with many palm trees lay between the shore and the narrow main street. Fronting the street was a ramshackle but picturesque collection of two story wooden buildings which seemed to contain mostly small Chinese businesses. The traffic which moved quietly along the street was largely pedestrian but mixed in with the few autos was a fascinating parade of bicycles, many powered by tiny French *Solex* motors mounted in front of the handlebars. Purring along on many of these machines was a lovely *vahine,* clad in a colorful *parau.* For a young, virgin college kid just in from an arduous ocean voyage, it was almost too much.

To get to Tahiti in 1953 was not easy. One either took a ship on a leisurely schedule from Los Angeles or San Francisco or came by air on a twice weekly flight from Fiji on a British-built Sutherland flying boat which stopped overnight at Penrhyn in the Cook Islands. Travel amongst the Society Islands was solely via bug-infested copra schooner. Along the quay in Papeete there were only the three race boats plus two or three cruising boats and a huge dismasted schooner named *Te Vega.* A large open-market for fresh food was a block away and just down the street was a popular bar called Quinn's, famed for it's unisex bathroom which consisted of a concrete room with water running down the lower portion of one wall (for the men) and a hole in the floor (for the ladies). One day soon after our arrival we were all invited for an afternoon swimming party and picnic. We still hadn't cleaned up the interior of the boat so we hired a local Tahitian to scrub out the boat in our absence. We connected a hose to a tap on shore for him to use, showed him the soap and scrubbers and went on our way. When we returned several hours later we were shocked to see the boat way down below her waterline and looking ready to sink. Our man was still below in his shorts happily splashing and scrubbing away and with the hose still running full-on with the water up to the bunks!

A lovely vahine welcomes the winners of the Honolulu – Tahiti Race
(L toR) Russ Larson, Walter Johnson, Bill Garvie, me, Pete Fromhagen

With our voyage back in mind, I was determined to remedy our need to be able to shorten canvas in stronger winds. Step one was to make provision for a second reef in the mainsail, which I did by spreading the sail on the grass astern of the boat and hand-sewing the necessary modifications. Next I learned that the owner of *Chiriqui* had purchased the only bolt of sailcloth on the island and made a deal with him. He would give me the canvass if I would make him a small mizzen for his boat, leaving enough cloth for me to make a small jib for our boat. I found the island sailmaker who had an ancient straight-stitch Singer machine at his small house and who agreed to sew the panels together. I forget exactly how, but I also obtained the use of the Mormon Church recreation hall to use as a sail loft. I started by laying out and roughly cutting the cloths for the sails. Then I would stack them on the old rental bicycle I had and pedal them over to the sail-maker. When he had sewn them together, I would take them back to the church hall and cut the final shape of the sail, prepare the edge re-inforcement, cut and mark the corner reinforcements and pedal the whole works back to the sailmaker for sewing. Finally I would go back to the hall and sew on the boltropes and finish the sails. It seems surprising to me now, but I made both sails in less than a week. Of course, as things turned out, the weather was so nice on the way back we never needed to shorten sail at all!

In between all this was an almost endless round of activity and entertainment. One day three young men took Pete, Bill and me on a trip around the perimeter of the Tahiti on their Harley-Davidson mo-torcycles. On another day the City of Papeete hosted a huge outdoor luau with endless beer, food, singing and dancing. Finally the Gov-ernment held a prize-giving reception and dinner party at the Gover-nor's mansion. We received a gold medal from the Yacht Club of France as first prize. *Silhouette* was awarded an exquisite small outrig-ger canoe, which I understand still hangs from the ceiling of the New-port Harbor Yacht Club. *Chiriqui* received a suitable prize too, but I cannot remember what it was. It seems incredible, but we were only in Tahiti for about ten days. But what a time it was! I was completely in love with the people, the music and the whole magical scene. Pete was under the spell of the island too. Bill had fallen for a Tahitian lovely and was vowing to get home, finish his partly-built sailboat in record time and return directly. Walter and Russ took the flying boat home leaving the three of us to sail *Mistress* back to California.

It was now almost the first of September and we were a very long way from San Francisco. Not only was I certain to miss the start of the Fall semester at Cal, we were going to be sailing home from Hawaii quite late in the season and could likely get hit with stormy weather, especially as we neared the Coast. The best thing we could do was to get organized and get started for home as soon as possible.

As soon as we had put stores and water aboard we headed for the island of Moorea, about 20 miles north of Tahiti. We threaded our way through the reef and anchored in Papatoi Bay (now called Opunohu Bay), the most scenic spot imaginable with spire-shaped

"Tiger Tooth Mountain" at its head. That evening we were invited to dinner at the home of the Kellum family, Americans who had arrived by yacht in the mid-1930s and never left. It was a wonderful place, but the next day we were on our way toward the Tuamotu Islands. By late afternoon of the second day we were sailing eastward along the southern shore of Rangiroa Atoll with the intention of heading north as soon as we had cleared the eastern end of the low-lying island. Unfortunately, it became dark long before we had reached the point where we were safe to turn the corner. The currents run strongly between the atolls and with only the afternoon sun sight to guide us, we held our breath as we tacked northward in the heavy darkness. Either our navigation was good or we were lucky because we heard no breakers in the night and sunrise found us with a clear horizon.

Our destination was Ahe Atoll but after sailing most of the way around the island and not spotting the entrance, we sailed off to the nearby atoll of Manihi where we easily entered the reef and moored to the rock wharf at the village. Near the boat was a large rock-lined pool with a pair of huge sharks swimming inside. I was horrified to think what would happen to the any of the many children playing nearby if they fell into the pool, until in a little while we saw some of them inside riding around on the sharks' backs. We were told later that the sharks were a completely harmless type. The villagers were friendly and the setting was idyllic but the next day we were off to Takaroa Atoll.

Here we were surprised to see another sailboat tied up to the stone wharf, the first boat we had seen since leaving Tahiti. She was a rather boxy looking, gaff-rigged ketch named *Mandalay* with the owner, "Pebble" Rockefeller and his friend Bob Grant aboard. After getting acquainted, Pebble got me aside and inquired discretely how we were fixed for toilet paper. It seems they were getting dangerously low and feared they wouldn't be near a store for some time. I told him I would check. After inventorying our stock including noting the number of sheets on each roll, I made a guess at my own daily usage and checked with the crew. Pete's consumption seemed to agree with mine but when I approached Bill he warned me off by saying, "Don't try to figure my needs. I wrap it around my hand." Nevertheless, we gave a few rolls to *Mandalay* and wished them well.

Takaroa was the perfect South Sea island with a tidy village of palm thatch houses connected with little pathways, swept clean and edged with stones. A wide lagoon of perfect blue sparkled beyond the palm trees. Sailing outrigger canoes and charming little gaff-rigged sloops which hauled fishermen and cargoes of copra from the distant *motus* could be seen at the wharf and in the distance plying the breadth of the lagoon. In the evening villagers would wander down to the wharf and more likely than not we would hear the strum of guitar music. This was not an easy place to sail away from but sail we did.

On the way back to Hawaii we admired a copra sloop in Takaroa Atoll

The 16-day sail to Hilo was about as good as it can get. With the trade winds and the current now in our favor, we broad reached and ran day after day with the hatches and port holes wide open under full sail including the spinnaker most of the time. It was a great time for reflecting on our wonderful time in Tahiti. Somehow all of our tribulations in getting there were entirely forgotten. The only small cloud on the horizon, in my mind, was the thought of getting *Mistress* back to California so late in the season.

We checked in and spent a day in Hilo then sailed for Maui and tied up in the little basin at Lahaina. We stayed only a couple of days then sailed for Honolulu where we were surprised with the news that *Mistress* had been sold as part payment on Walter Johnson's new boat, the 72' schooner, *Nordlys.* We were told the old owner of *Nordlys* (now the new owner of M*istress*), Ted Enoch, was en route to Honolulu to do a bit of Island cruising. Pete and Bill packed up and flew home but since I had already missed my semester at Cal, I decided to stick around, partly to see what would happen and partly because I loved the scene around the Ala Wai Yacht Harbor.

Ted Enoch arrived in a few days. He was a small, rather effeminate man with a very likable personality. His favorite attire was a natty white, terrycloth, jumpsuit which perfectly matched his personality. He said he was anxious to sail on a tour of the Islands but first wanted to have the interior of the boat painted (it needed it badly), a job I readily agreed to do. A week later we were joined by Peggy Slater who had brokered the sale of *Nordlys* and *Mistress* and who, as part of the deal, had promised to accompany Ted on a cruise of the Hawaiian Islands. This was good news as I gotten to know her quite well from our earlier stay in Honolulu following the Transpac Race and was very fond of her. She was a wonderfully effervescent, big gal who had an endless fund of stories from her long sailing career and who, I knew, would be a grand shipmate.

Ted had an interesting group of local Hawaiian friends who were his constant companions and who were quite musically talented. It was decided that it would be best to depart in the evening so that we would possibly have the benefit of lighter winds after dark and so that we would make a landfall on Maui in daylight. We all went out to dinner at a small café then down to the boat for a drink and some Hawaiian songs under the moonlight in the cockpit. After singing the Tahitian farewell song, *Maruru a vau,* we shoved off into the dark, windy waters of the Molokai Channel.

As soon as we got out from under the lee of Diamond Head, it was slam, bang, and flying spray all over again as we bucked into the notoriously rough seas in the channel. I was under a bit of stress as I was the only one aboard who had sailed on the boat and knew how everything worked. At some point in the night Peggy came on deck and mentioned quietly that something seemed to be wrong with the head. Well, she was certainly right. When I went below to investigate, I quickly saw that the combination of the wild motion below and Peggy's hefty weight had been too much for the toilet's anchor bolts and hoses, and the whole works was now adrift in the head compartment. It was not a pretty scene but there was no other option than to get out the tools and go to work.

We stopped at Lahaina, Maui then went on to the Big Island to visit Kailua and Kealakakua Bay. We spent a day at the huge Parker Ranch, drove to the top of Mauna Kea volcano, saw the lush Hamakua Coast and in general had a wonderful time. With Ted's and Peggy's connections in Hawaii, I was lucky to meet some interesting local people and to have a chance to look behind the scenes in the Islands. After two weeks we were on our way back to Honolulu, where I packed my duffel bag and flew back to California with a few dollars in my pocket from the paint job on *Mistress* and a whole lot of memories.

Nordlys, a 72' schooner underway in the 1954 San Diego – Acapulco Race

CHAPTER 4

NORDLYS

I arrived back in California near the end of October 1953, well beyond any hope of picking up the fall semester at Cal. I was, of course, very interested in what was going on with Walter Johnson's new acquisition, the 72' schooner *Nordlys*. I knew the boat and had even spent an evening aboard her in June 1949 following our ignominious retreat from the sea on the first day of our attempt to sail to Southern California on *Tai Fung*. After ripping our jib while trying to beat out to the Lightship, we sailed back into the Bay and anchored off the Corinthian Yacht Club in Tiburon. Nearby at anchor was a handsome big schooner whose owner, Omar Darr, came over to our boat to inquire if we would be interested in baby-sitting his boat while he and his wife, Harriett, went out to dinner. He explained that he never left the boat unattended. The schooner was *Nordlys* and she was a beauty.

When we readily agreed to watch his boat, Omar invited us to come over a bit early, take a look at the boat and have a drink. While we were relaxing in the spacious saloon he explained that he and his wife had just sailed up from Tahiti and wondered if we would like to see some of the portraits of Harriett that had been done by a relatively unknown artist in Tahiti named Letag. I had heard of Letag because I had seen a window display in a photo portrait studio shop advertising striking portraits painted on black velvet from photos for the reasonable price of $125. Later in Papeete I heard his name mentioned and saw some paintingsof his of Tahitian women. Harriett Darr was an absolutely beautiful woman with dark hair and an olive complexion. When she demurely held up life-size painting after painting on black velvet, mostly semi-nude, I was floored. I had never seen anything so lovely. Ever since that time I had connected *Nordlys* with that wonderful evening.

I phoned Walter who told me that Nordlys was in Alameda at the W.F. Stone Boat Works where she had been surveyed and had some work done in preparation for a two year cruise of the South Pacific with his family. The first leg of the cruise would be to enter the 2nd biennial San Diego to Acapulco Race in January 1954. He offered me a job for a couple of months helping to get the boat ready and a chance to crew on the trip down the Coast and in the race. It all sounded perfect, so I immediately agreed and proceeded to move aboard and get busy.

Nordlys (northern lights) was a big, sturdy cruising schooner, 72' long with wide teak decks, a long bowsprit and a lofty rig with a bermuda mainsail and a gaff foresail. She was designed by Ford, Paine & Roue and built on the East Coast in 1935. I was told she was originally owned by Chester Bowles, the head of the Office of Price Administration in WWII. It had been requisitioned by the US Navy during the war for submarine patrol duty on the Eastern seaboard (there was still some of the wartime wiring on the boat when I came aboard). Omar Darr had bought her after the war in Annapolis in 1949 then sailed her to the South Pacific and used her as a charter boat for several years hauling passengers between Honolulu and Tahiti. Ted Enoch, the previous owner, had kept her in very nice condition at Lido Isle in Newport Beach harbor although I don't believe he used her for anything other than local cruising to Catalina Island.

Knowing that she would be in the tropics for the next two years, I set to work to cover up some of the varnish before it got eaten up by the sun and salt water. The boat had about 150'of wide varnished caprail which I knew would never survive, so I gave it a good coat of varnish then painted the whole thing with teak brown paint. I was sure I was doing the right thing and even old Lester Stone, the boatyard owner, came by one day to agree with me, but I caught hell from Ted Enoch, the former owner, when he saw the boat in Newport Beach with its beautiful rails covered with that awful shade of paint.

There was plenty for me to do aboard in getting the schooner ready for sea. I replaced the flooring in the galley, sketched up a pair of stowage racks for slickers for the yard to build, and similarly designed a crib for the aft cabin for the baby which would be aboard, installed a track for the spinnaker pole and on and on. I loved every minute of it.

It was decided that we would depart for the trip down the coast on December 15th and of course, there was a terrific rush of last minute jobs as departure day approached. One of the final jobs I had to do was to stow a huge amount of disposable, paper diapers for the baby, which ended up being crammed into the lazarette, in the very tail end of the boat. By the time I left the boat a few months later, they had turned into a big swollen mass from deck leaks and were eventually heaved overboard.

Hathily Johnson and her three boys sailed to Newport Beach with us.
After the race they cruised aboard to the South Pacific.

We were having a wonderful run of fine weather and on a bright sunny morning we cast off and headed down the Oakland Estuary. Aboard were Walter and Hathily Johnson and their two young boys, Walter Jr. and Mark plus the new toddler. Also aboard was a college girl/baby sitter named Daryl Broderick, Walter's old buddy, Russ Larson and me — not much of a crew for a big schooner on a winter passage. We had barely begun the voyage when the ebb tide combined with an inattentive drawbridge tender almost caused us to crash into the unopened Park Street Bridge. Once past that drama, we hoisted sail and rode a brisk north wind down the coast to Newport Beach where we temporarily berthed *Nordlys* in her old slip in front of Ted Enoch's luxury apartment.

While sailing with Ted on our little Hawaiian cruise on *Mistress,* he had frequently told me about his prized parrot, Henry. The bird was apparently a bit of a character and very talkative. Ted said he enjoyed taking him to bars and parties where he was always the center of attention. One day, Ted came by the boat and asked if I would be willing to keep and eye on Henry, filling his seed and water dish every day while he went on a little cruise to Catalina on a friend's boat for several days. He gave me the key to his apartment and showed me where everything was and went on his way. Three days later I was at the top of the mainmast in a bosun's chair doing some rigging job. From my fine view of Newport Bay, I saw Ted's boat coming up the harbor. In a horrible moment I realized I had forgotten all about poor Henry! Without even bothering to lower myself to the deck, I slid down the rigging and ran up to the apartment fully expecting Henry to be lying on his back with his legs up. To my vast relief he was very much alive but mad as hell. I quickly filled his water and seed dishes, put fresh newspaper in the cage and ran back to *Nordlys.* I think Henry must have told Ted about my dereliction of duty because Ted never spoke to me again.

The schooner remained at Lido Isle for a few weeks where I remained aboard by myself, still a paid hand, working hard on getting the boat ready for the Acapulco race and for the big cruise to the South Seas. The marina where she was berthed was filled with magnificent yachts, both power and sail. A gorgeous big schooner with two paid hands aboard was my next door neighbor. They quickly took me in hand and showed me some of the ropes of the professional yachting world. On my first trip to the chandlery, they told me with a wink, "Be sure I got your "10%". It had never occurred to me that a boat supply store or shipyard paid a kick-back to the paid hands.

About the middle of January we sailed to San Diego and tied up at the San Diego Yacht Club in preparation for the Acapulco Race. Peggy Slater had been invited by Walter to be our guest skipper. She had put together a racing crew consisting mostly of her sailing friends in Southern California. We were a crew of nine including Peggy, Walter and me. Our new crew were a very likable group included Bob

Dixon, a sailing legend from Newport Beach, Will and Inez Bell (she was to be the cook), Dr. Ed Wright, Bob Chandler, and Frank Powers (who was to be our navigator).

Frank Powers was a very interesting guy with movie star good looks who had sailed around the world with Irving Johnson on the brigantine, *Yankee* in 1949, and never stopped going to sea thereafter. I had gotten to know him when he sailed in the Honolulu - Tahiti race the previous year aboard *Chiriqui*. Like most of us, he had fallen in love with Tahiti and had married one of the best dancers on the island, a beauty named Augustine. Frank was a very quiet but extremely competent sailor and was, without doubt, the most popular person in the crew. A couple of years after the trip I saw his picture in the newspaper. It seems he and two other paid crew on a big ketch named *Kamalii* were hijacked by a gang of thugs in Honolulu who intended to take the boat to Thailand for a load of drugs. When well out to sea they ordered the three crew overboard but relented when they pleaded for a life raft. Luckily for Frank and his two friends, in spite of being way out of the shipping lanes, a cargo vessel came by within a few hours and rescued them and alerted the US Coast Guard, which promptly retook the yacht. The photo I saw in the paper showed Frank with a grin from ear to ear!

The day for the start of the race to Acapulco finally arrived. We were tied up on the outside of a float in front of the yacht club ready to get underway on a sunny, mild winter day. A very large spectator fleet was milling around waiting for the racing fleet to assemble. Just as we were about to cast off, a sloop with a sharp-pointed bow, powered with an outboard motor, lost control and stabbed us exactly where a porthole was located in the forward cabin. We were horrified, expecting at least to have to deal with a large round hole in the topsides. I jumped below to see the extent of the damage and was amazed to see that there was none. The glass was set back from the surface sufficiently so that instead of the bronze bow fitting of the sloop hitting the glass, it nicely pushed the whole brass porthole fitting inward. In fact, the porthole was lying intact on the bunk. The screws holding it in place were so rotten it had simply fallen in. I just needed to rotate the porthole slightly to get to fresh wood, insert new screws and we were good to go.

The fleet for the race amounted to 16 boats, as I recall, including an number of big schooners. The biggest was the 85' *Sea Drift*, complete with a piano in the saloon. *Constellation* and *Nordlys* were both about 72' long and looked pretty impressive, at least to me. The smallest boat was a little 32' sloop named *Flying Scotchman* which the Mexicans renamed *Escoces Volante* (flying highball) at the awards dinner in Acapulco. The start off Point Loma for the 2350 mile race was in the usual San Diego light airs so every one, including us, hung up "all the laundry" in order to catch every zephyr.

Nordlys roaring along in the strong winds early in the race

Gradually the breeze increased, and we carried a fine wind all the way down to Cabo San Lucas, across the Gulf and beyond to Cabo Corrientes on the mainland. At times we were going about as fast as a big heavy schooner could go. What a thrill it was! With all sail set including a big fisherman staysail between the masts and a huge spinnaker, we really plowed a furrow in the sea. I marveled at what a contrast it was to our struggle on little *Mistress,* against wind, waves and current. I recalled on the previous trip all my thoughts were focused on getting there, whereas now I was content to keep sailing every day without a thought about the end of the voyage. Being on a big boat with wide steady decks made all the difference. I became convinced that the bigger the boat, the better. That is, as long as I was not the one paying the bills.

Celebrating Frank Powers birthday in mid-race

When we reached Cabo Corrientes, with 80% of the distance behind us, we ran out of wind. Suddenly the breeze died, the air got hot and sticky, the sails collapsed and the sun beat unmercifully upon us. Worse, it meant that the race started all over again as the smaller boats caught up with the big ones and thereafter sailed almost as fast (or faster). It was very discouraging and in the end doomed the future of the Acapulco Races. Walter Johnson had ordered a big spinnaker from Larson & Sutter who now had their loft in Sausalito. Against the advice of Bill Larson, the old Swedish sailmaker who was Pete Sutter's partner, Pete Sutter recommended that they make it to one of their new radial top designs. This type later became their most successful design but for some reason it didn't work out well for *Nordlys*. Maybe it was too wide for its height or something, but when the wind got light it simply would not stay full. It just about drove everyone crazy with its flapping and sagging, and it certainly didn't help our flagging morale.

After 16 days we had almost reached the entrance to Acapulco Bay. We elected to enter via the *Boca Chica* (little mouth) which lay between the cliffs and a small island. Just as we reached the narrowest part of the passage, we all felt the boat shudder as though it had run aground or was bouncing along the bottom. We could plainly see that we were still moving however and in a few seconds the peculiar motion stopped. None of us had an explanation for the phenomenon, but when we entered the harbor a short while later and anchored, we were informed that the city had just experienced a severe earthquake. Years later, on October 17, 1989, I was going down the California coast aboard *Pastime*, a 41' sloop, when we experienced an almost identical sensation between Halfmoon Bay and Monterey. It was the shock wave of the Loma Prieta earthquake passing through the water. I felt smug in being to state with some certainty just what was happening.

Nordlys was one of the first boats to finish the race but was by no means among the winners because of our time handicap. We were greeted by a large welcoming committee that came out to our anchorage. The group included the usual port officials, customs and immigrations officers who quickly completed their paperwork in our saloon and enjoyed a drink of our best whiskey. Amongst the large group were a rather seedy little man and his young son who claimed to represent the local newspaper. I noticed that the camera he was carrying was a funny little Brownie Reflex which didn't look very professional. Sometime after the welcoming was over and everyone had left we realized that the reporter/photographer had slipped into the aft cabin and removed several hundred dollars from the bureau drawers! Still, we were all impressed by the genuinely sincere welcome we had received and looked forward to the festivities.

Each boat in the fleet was assigned a host family from among the members of the Club De Yates De Acapulco. They were a very wealthy and sophisticated group who lived in elegant homes around the spectacular waterfront. One of the hosts was the actress Dolores del Rio, a genuine sailing lady who kept a trim racing dinghy at the Club. Our host was a wonderful man named Juan Manual Salcedo who apparently owned large auto and tractor dealerships. Someone had once told me that there is no one as rich as a rich Mexican and I think they were right. Almost every one of the hosts put on an elabo-

rate and exciting party or dinner for everyone in the fleet. It was a
scene which I had never seen before (or since).

The race crew on arrival in Acapulco
(rear L to R) Frank Powers, Bob Dixon, Will and Inez Bell, Ed Wright, Peggy Slater
(front L to R) me, Bob Chandler, Walter Johnson

Other activities were happening too. Walter had put aboard
SCUBA diving equipment which was just becoming available. At the
time it was referred to as "Aqua Lung" gear. We even had a gas-
driven Cornelius compressor for filling our own tanks (it took a couple
of hours to fill one tank). None of us had ever had any instruction on
diving much less any kind of certification, if it even existed at the
time. A couple of our hosts knew about diving and offered to show us
how. We moved the boat over to a pretty little bay named Puerto
Marques, anchored in front of the house of the President of Mexico

and tried out our gear. Now that I know some of the hazards of diving, I wonder that we didn't explode our lungs or get the bends or worse.

On another occasion, the Yacht Club invited us all to come out to their outstation at Laguna Cayucas, a large lagoon north of Acapulco for dinghy racing and a picnic. The Club dinghy fleet consisted of 14' Lehman dinghies and it just happened that we had one aboard *Nordlys*. One of the Club members offered to haul our boat out there to give the races a bit of international flavor, I suppose. Our beat up old sailing dinghy didn't look like much amongst the well maintained Club fleet and it didn't sail all that well either but we had fun. One of the top sailors was Dolores del Rio, still in good form after her long retirement as a screen actress. At the time the Acapulco Yacht Club was a very modest little structure tucked between a couple of tall apartment buildings at the very head of the bay. It was much too small for the awards dinner, so the affair was held in a waterfront restaurant.

Immediately afterwards, the focus aboard the boat changed from the race to the forthcoming cruise to the South Pacific. The racing crew went home and soon it was time for me to depart as well if I was to arrive in time for the spring semester at Cal. I took a plane from Acapulco to Mexico City where I would stay overnight. On the flight we were served lunch which included two cups which I, being the sophisticated traveler, recognized as being the makings of *café au lait*, coffee and milk. When I poured them together and drank the mixture, I knew something was wrong because it was a very strange taste. By listening carefully to the other passengers, I was able to figure out that the cups I'd combined actually had contained root beer and potato soup.

Back at Berkeley I found a small basement apartment which I shared with a fellow civil engineering student for my final term at Cal before earning a Bachelor of Science degree. According to my counselor, I had the grades to continue on to get a Master of Science degree, but I was determined to get out of school and into the real world. I had been very lucky to be at Cal in the early 1950's. It was in a lull between the crowded times of the veterans in the late 40's and the baby boomers in the 60's. The school population was somewhere around 16,000, less than half of what it would become later. It was also very inexpensive. Tuition was free. The only cost was a student incidental fee of $32 per semester which included admission to all the football games, a subscription to the *Daily Cal,* and free medical care at the on-campus hospital.

Meals were cheap at the campus cafeteria. I practically lived on my favorite meal, corn fritters and syrup which cost about 35 cents, as I recall. My old '35 Ford sedan, which I used to get over to Sausalito or to my parents house in Mill Valley on weekends, was still running (barely). I carried on a correspondence with Daryl, the babysitter on *Nordlys*, and looked forward to graduation in June.

Ballerina, our 23' Maya class sloop in 1954

CHAPTER 5

BALLERINA

In June 1954 the great day arrived. Amongst the thousands in the huge Greek Theatre above the Berkeley campus, at the age of 24, I actually walked up and received my diploma, a B.S. in civil engineering. It had been a long road — six years altogether — partly because I chose to take a slightly smaller load of engineering units each term so I could take in a few electives and partly because I missed a couple of semesters with my sailing trips. I was elated to be done with the stress of classes, problem sets to be turned in and exams to be passed. On the other hand I could not escape the feeling that I had missed the classic college experience with all its supposed social life, lifelong contacts and enlightening intellectual events. It seemed to me that I had ground my way through the usual engineering preparation for a career (or job at least) and that was the end of it. Except for the wonderful times I had enjoyed during those years on my sailing adventures, the college experience was simply a period in my life which was over and soon forgotten.

The next step was to find a job which turned out to be very easy. The 1950's was a time of a great expansion of the nation's infrastructure and building in general. With my degree in civil and structural engineering in hand, it was simply a matter of walking in the door of any engineering/construction firm and going to work. Of course, getting a highly paid job was another matter. I started with International Engineering Co., the design subsidiary of Morrison-Knudsen Contractors who built big hydroelectric projects worldwide. Their office was just behind the Palace Hotel on New Montgomery Street in San Francisco and my pay was a magnificent $350 a month, payable on the last day of the month, a perfect way to learn fiscal discipline in the era before credit cards.

I lived at my parent's house in Mill Valley and aboard *Tai Fung* for a couple of months until I could get a bit of money in hand, then I looked for a more independent living setup. At that time a very popular housing arrangement in San Francisco was the "guest house". These were actually boarding houses, usually populated by young college graduates in the big old mansions in the Pacific Heights district. The usual arrangement was for a couple of people (same sex of course) to share a room and have breakfast and supper served six days a week. There was a guest house to suit any style.

A fellow engineer named Harold Anderson and I decided to check out several of them over the course of a few evenings after work and what a variety we found. One was like a proper British club with guys sitting around smoking pipes, having cocktails and reading the evening paper in front of the blazing fireplace. Another, The Mansion, had a grand circular staircase leading up to the elegant dining room with properly attired folks sitting for dinner and yet another named the Chateau Bleu was famed for its wild parties. Harold and I eventually settled on one of the smaller ones named the Bel Air on Franklin Street. It was formerly a lovely three story victorian house now gone slightly to seed, and had room for about sixteen guests in the various former bedrooms and slightly remodeled attic. The rent was $65 per month including meals and housekeeping service.

Harold and I had one of the larger rooms which had an adjoining bathroom which we shared with two girls, Jane and Ann, in the adjacent room. When we moved in the place was managed by a somewhat promiscuous lady who, to no ones great surprise, was soon replaced. The new management team consisted of a wonderful, large black woman named Mattie and her friend/partner, a cheerful man appropriately named Guest, who did the serving. It was like a big happy family. After dinner it was common for a large group of us to wander down to a peanuts-and-beer place called the Monkey Inn on Van Ness Ave. or down to a sing-along bar at North Beach named the Red Garter. I am not sure that guest houses like this even exist anymore in San Francisco. I suspect that the huge increase in the value of real estate has doomed them. The last time I drove by the old Bel Air, it looked like it had been re-converted back into its former elegance. It was a wonderful era while it lasted

Jane at the Bel Air guest house

One of the best aspects of the guest house life was that it was a splendid place to meet people of the opposite sex. Life there, for the most part, was quite proper but it was a chance for guys like me to get to know girls and see them before they had their makeup on in the morning. Not surprisingly, in the relatively short time I lived at the Bel Air, there were a number of romances and a couple of marriages. I became attracted to Jane Lindley, the strawberry blonde in the next room and soon invited her to join me sailing on various boats on the weekends. She had graduated from Pomona College and was working as a secretary at KPIX TV (her degree in English literature was not a good job ticket). She knew absolutely nothing about boats but was game to give it a try and I was delighted to show her what I knew. Besides, she was a pretty thing with plenty of intelligence and a nice sense of humor. In the early spring of 1955 I took Jane for her first sail on a 55' yawl named *Kialoa,* a beautiful boat with sleek lines and lots of varnish. I hoped that she would be suitably impressed. She seemed to enjoy herself and thereafter we were out sailing on the Bay on most weekends or at least somewhere around boats.

Kialoa (ex-Tasco) had been purchased recently by a couple of partners, Bill Clum and Ed Gilmore, with the intention of doing some ocean racing including the 1955 Transpac Race to Hawaii. Although the owners were experienced sailors, they had asked my old skipper,

Pete Fromhagen, to get the boat ready for the race and to be the Sailing Master. To my delight, Pete invited me to join the crew. During the spring and early summer we worked on the boat, went in several local ocean races, then in late June shoved off for Los Angeles for the start on July 4th. Prior to leaving I had moved out of the Bel Air and into a small studio apartment in Pacific Heights which I shared with Pete. At the same time, Jane and her roommate, Ann, got an apartment on Russian Hill above Chinatown.

We had an extraordinarily fast sail down the coast, almost coming to grief near Cape San Martin when, running at top speed under spinnaker in dense fog, we suddenly saw kelp streaming past the hull, a sure sign we were about to hit the rocks. Never was a boat gybed so fast! We survived that scare and two days later we were anchored off the California Yacht Club in San Pedro Harbor awaiting the start of the race on July 4th.

We had an excellent racing crew which included the legendary sailor, "Commodore" Tompkins who had sailed around Cape Horn on his father's schooner, *Wanderbird,* when he was 5 years old. Also aboard was a very likable young sailor and sailmaker named "Punky" Mitchell who had lots of experience in Bay racing. Unfortunately, he had a well known tendency toward seasickness, however, he wanted to sail in a Transpac so badly that he persuaded Pete to let him join the crew, a decision we were all to regret, especially Punky.

Unlike the race in 1993, two years before, this time we had plenty of breeze right from the start. By late afternoon we were off the west end of Catalina and by dark we were close reaching with all the wind we could handle. Before long, Punky was sick, very sick. It is one thing to be sick in a nice warm bedroom but quite another to be sick in a wildly pitching sailboat in a cold wind with icy spray soaking your clothing and chilling you to the bone. Poor Punky remained sick for the next week, almost halfway to Hawaii. He was not passively sick. He was *actively* sick with horrible groans and retching night and day with never a bit of food or a drop of water passing his lips as he lay helpless in his bunk. After several days we were afraid he would become dangerously dehydrated and might have to be transferred to the Coast Guard escort vessel. We were alert for any sign of vomiting of blood, a serious indicator of problems from seasickness. At the end of a week he seemed to be a bit better so we hauled him up to the cockpit like a rag doll and propped him up to sit in the sun. In another day he was ravenous and couldn't stop eating. Needless so say, it was Punky's last ocean race.

The 1955 Transpac Race crew on Kialoa
(rear L toR) Tony Sousa, Pete Fromhagen, Punky Mitchell, "Commodore" Tompkins
(front L to R) Bill Clum, Ed Gilmore, me, Joe Bitterlin

The race was fast and exciting and *Kialoa* sailed like a thoroughbred. The navigator was an old timer named Joe Bitterlin who took his celestial navigation duties very seriously. He took many observations of the sun and stars and posted our daily progress with our standing in the fleet each day. We had no reason to doubt his calculations but when Diamond Head appeared in view quite a few hours in advance of his prediction, he was very upset. As we swept down Molokai channel and across the finish line, Poor Joe was down at the chart table desperately trying to find where he had made an error.

We finished the race in 12 days, 6 hours and took 2nd place in class C. It was a better standing than Kialoa had ever made in the previous three attempts under the former owner so we were quite pleased. The festivities and the awards dinner were wonderful. I had promised my employer I would be back in no more than three weeks so I was soon on a plane back to San Francisco.

Jane seemed to be glad to see me back and we resumed our social life. She and her roommate, Ann, were well settled in their small apartment and I spent many evenings having dinner with them. This was a good thing because I was on a serious campaign to save money. My goal was to buy a boat of my own and in the fall I spotted an interesting little 23' sloop for sale at the yacht brokerage in Sausalito. She was a midget ocean racer, a type which had appeared in England recently and was popularized by one of the breed named *Sopranino* which had sailed across the Atlantic and was the subject of a recently published book. They were characterized by light but very strong construction of multiple layers of planking and typically had a reverse sheer which gave more room inside and provided more height above the waterline and were thus dryer and safer in rough seas.

The little boat had been designed and built in Japan for an American army officer who had shipped her back when he returned to the States. I <u>had</u> to have her. The asking price was $2800. I offered $2600 which was accepted, the only problem being that I didn't actually have that much money. I paid half down and promised to come up with the balance in 90 days. That's when the saving campaign really got serious. I even began to walk all the way to work and back to save the bus fare. As the 90 day deadline approached I sold the few old war bonds I had and put the proceeds together with my current paycheck (leaving me with zero funds for the coming month). Being still a couple of hundred short, I got a small loan from Household Finance Company and was suddenly the proud owner of my own yacht!

Jane and I didn't like the previous name, *Batara* (a combination of Bart and Barbara) so we changed it (a serious taboo) to *Ballerina*, which we thought appropriate for a lively little boat. We got a berth at the Sausalito Yacht Harbor for $15 a month and we were as happy as can be. As money became available I replaced her galvanized rigging with stainless steel wire, installed a pair of bronze sheet winches, which had been given to me and acquired a used outboard motor. Over the winter more improvements were made including re-finishing the varnished spars and painting the interior. She looked wonderful and was a joy to sail.

During this period I was still living in the small studio apartment in San Francisco. I was seeing a lot of Jane during the week in the evenings and on weekends sailing on *Ballerina*. I had come to the conclusion that I didn't want to continue on having sailing voyages with a bunch of guys that I seldom saw again after each trip. I was sure what I really wanted was a permanent partner to share my sailing adventures. My idols were cruising partners like Eric and Susan Hiscock or Peter and Anne Pye who planned and carried out their voyages and as a result had a lifetime of memories to share. The ocean races were wonderfully exciting and there was a sort of battle comradeship within the crew, but it only lasted the length of the trip. I wanted something more and I resolved to find the person who would fit my future sailing dreams. Perhaps Jane would be the right one. An opportunity soon arrived to test her sea legs.

Pete Fromhagen asked if Jane and I would like to come along with him and his lady friend, Mary, on a coastal delivery trip to sail *Kialoa* from San Francisco to Southern California in preparation for the next Acapulco Race which started in mid-January. Commodore Tompkins was invited to join the crew also. A mid-winter voyage of 500 miles on the California coast could be a pleasure or a nightmare depending on the weather. It would certainly be a good test of Jane's seagoing aptitude and attitude.

We started off from the marina near the St. Francis Yacht Club on Friday evening of the New Years weekend. It was inky dark as we left the harbor, hoisted sail and headed for the Golden Gate. It had been raining off and on all day and it looked like we might get more of the same during the night. Just as we were approaching the Golden Gate Bridge we were engulfed in a very heavy rain squall. There wasn't much wind but the rain came down in buckets. As we passed under the span of the Bridge, we were deluged with what seemed like a solid stream of water. We could hardly see and were frightened by the noise of the falling water which stopped as abruptly as it had started. Apparently we had run directly under one of the scuppers of the bridge roadway. No harm was done but it was a big surprise.

As we headed down the coast the sky cleared, the stars sparkled, and the temperature dropped. *Kialoa* was equipped with a handsome little soapstone fireplace which we attempted to fire up and make life more comfortable below decks. All our efforts produced was a choking cloud of smoke which forced everyone up on deck. Obviously the wind across the deck or the downdraft from the mainsail was not what the fireplace wanted. Eventually, after some experimentation, we rigged up a piece of canvass on the windward side of the chimney and achieved a cheery fire and some much-needed heat in the cabin. At dawn the next morning we saw that the coastal mountains near Point Sur were covered with snow.

Jane had been outfitted for the trip with a pair of 13-button Navy wool pants, jumper and watch sweater plus a set of green surplus foul weather gear. In lieu of boots she was wearing a pair of thin plastic fishing waders. Not very fancy stuff but she had no complaints, at least none that I heard. Actually none of us had very classy gear....it simply didn't exist in those days. At breakfast Pete handed her a glass of very acidic, canned grapefruit juice which made a quick return trip over the rail. It wasn't seasickness; it was just the wrong stuff after a stressful night. Actually, Jane was never seasick on the trip, a fact which I duly noted in the positive column. The remainder of the voyage was quite smooth and by the time we arrived in Newport I think both Jane and I were pleased with her ocean sailing trial.

I had been thinking for some time about a possible long cruise in my own boat but not before I had found my life/sailing partner. After our little winter voyage, I thought perhaps I could start getting serious about my plan. What I hoped to do was to buy a boat in England and spend a year sailing back to San Francisco. I loved to read *Yachting Monthly* and *Yachting World,* the leading British boating magazines, whenever I could get hold of them. From the ads I knew that there were cruising boats available at very reasonable prices in England and saw no reason why I couldn't save enough money in a few years to buy one and make my dream cruise. The trip would follow the Devon and Cornish coast of England, then across the stormy Bay of Biscay to Spain and into the Mediterranean. In the fall, after the hurricane season had passed, we could cross the Atlantic and spent the winter in the Caribbean then head up the coast from Panama in the spring. It could all be done in the best season in each area. It was a great plan; at least it seemed so in front of a blazing fireplace with a drink in my hand.

Jane and I talked about "the trip" at length during the winter and in spite of her limited experience, she was game to go. About this time I got my courage up and invested in an engagement ring which I presented to Jane after dinner one night. Without hesitation she said yes to my proposal and the die was cast. We decided on a wedding sometime in April.

I went up to Sacramento one weekend shortly thereafter to meet Jane's parents. This was all new stuff to me and I was more than a little nervous about the whole operation. I needn't have worried. Her father, Gary Lindley, was a wonderfully friendly man and being an engineer, I think he had an affinity toward me. He had graduated from the University of Arizona in 1913 with a degree in mining engineering and had lived an exciting life in Mexico in his early days. He told stories to Jane about how, being an educated American, he was presumed to know something about medicine. At one point he was ordered to remove a bullet from a bandito at the point of a gun and on another occasion he was put against the wall by some of Poncho Villa's men but talked his way out of the situation by speaking German, protesting that he wasn't a gringo and by bribing the bandits with a stash of silver. My visit was in the winter of 1955-56, a season of extraordinary storms and rainfall in California. Gary was working for the Bureau of Reclamation at the time, an agency which had just constructed Folsom Dam on the American River above Sacramento. The huge, earth-fill dam was still not quiet complete and had started the rainy season with a bone dry reservoir. When we drove up to see it, the water was in danger of overtopping the dam in spite of all the floodgates and penstocks being wide open. Knowing something about dams and hydroelectric projects, I was bug-eyed to see how the whole situation was near to disaster. Luckily the day we inspected it was the last day of a series of storms.

Jane's mother, Theresa was an elegant little lady who had left a comfortable, upper class, home life in Duluth, Minnesota in the early 1920's to come out West and take a job in a rough little mining community in Arizona as a school teacher. It was quite a bold move for a young woman in those days. While there, she met Gary who was assistant supervisor of the large Phelps-Dodge copper smelter. It was in

Arizona that Jane was born. In later years when the smelter closed because of the depression, they moved around the country as Gary worked at various jobs, mostly in Government service. During WWII he served as administrator of a Japanese relocation center in Colorado. He said he thoroughly disagreed with the idea of the camps but took the job as a patriotic war service in spite of his misgivings, believing that he could be a fair and sympathetic leader. Jane attended school with the Japanese children and was a schoolmate of Yutaka Kuwatani, our neighbor in Tiburon, who lives just down the street.

As our wedding day in April approached, we started to look around Sausalito for an apartment to rent. We hit pay dirt almost immediately when we were offered a flat in a big old three story, brown shingle building on Bridgeway Avenue, just across the street from the yacht harbor where *Ballerina* was berthed. It had been built in the early 1900's and was starting to look its age with slanty floors and an old fashioned interior including a big brown porcelain-enamel space heater, a claw-foot tub and a kitchen sink with wooden drain boards. The huge living/dining room had a redwood ceiling and wainscoting and an enormous brick fireplace. It also had a wonderful view of the Sausalito waterfront, Angel Island and the Bay. The rent was $65 a month. It was perfect in spite of the alpine walkway to get up to it from the street. We soon had it furnished in what a friend described as "young newly-wed" style. We lived there happily for 12 years.

Our wedding on April 14, 1956 in Sacramento was a modest affair with a ceremony at the Episcopal Church and a reception at the Lindley home afterwards. I think I was in a bit of a daze the whole time, but Jane looked lovely and everything went well. Jane has always insisted that her vow to me was to, "Love, honor and let go sailing." She said she was damned if she'd ever compete with my first love. We had planned to save our vacation time for a couple of cruising honeymoons on *Ballerina* so after the reception we drove back to the Bay and, though it seems ridiculous, we went to a party at the Corinthian Yacht Club to pick up a trophy before returning to our new home in Sausalito

On April 14, 1956, Jane and I were married in Sacramento

Life was grand. We both loved our unique apartment with its cozy interior and wonderful views. Our sailboat was right across the street and within a couple of weeks after our wedding we were into racing, having signed up to sail in the YRA (Yacht Racing Association) races in one of the performance handicap classes. The time allowances were based on past performance, presumed theoretical speed and pure guesswork so it wasn't the most scientific kind of racing but it was a lot of fun and quite exciting. We usually recruited an additional crew from among our friends. The normal drill was for me to sail the upwind legs and for Jane to steer downwind while the crew and I wrestled with the spinnaker. In those days a number of the regattas were two-day affairs with a big party at the host yacht club on Saturday night after which we enjoyed spending the night aboard *Ballerina*. We didn't always win but we always did quite well and over the course of the season we collected enough points that we were the class season's champion. To say we were pleased with our little boat (and ourselves) would be a big understatement.

In July, when the races stopped for a month, we slipped away aboard *Ballerina* for a 10 day "honeymoon" in the Delta. We had no dinghy and a rather dubious little outboard motor but were excited to be off on our first cruise on our own boat. Accompanied by our friend Jim Hurst on his boat, *Lady Carol,* we sailed up the Napa River to a charming little anchorage called Horseshoe Bend where we spent a couple of days. Sadly, this spot became completely silted up in later years. Then we continued alone up through the shallow waters of Suisun Bay and into the labyrinth of waterways in the San Joaquin River Delta. It was a different world then than it is today. There were only a few boats to be seen and the levees were mostly covered with willows and tall cottonwood trees making it a cruising delight. Having never been up the Delta before, we wandered up and

Cooking breakfast in Ballerina's cockpit in the Delta, July, 1956

down the waterways in *Ballerina,* chart in hand, exploring every day and finding a new, snug anchorage every night. All too soon, it was time to beat our way back down the Bay and return to our jobs and the world of reality.

     We planned the second half of our "honeymoon" to be a 10 day cruise in September to Tomales Bay, fifty miles up the coast. Now that I think back on it, it is a wonder it didn't end in disaster. At the very least it proves how lucky I am. I had never been up on that part of the coast and had certainly never been across the dangerous bar and into Tomales Bay. About all I had to go on was some advice from my friend Hugh Jacks, who had a piece of property up there and who had sailed into Tomales Bay numerous times, and, of course, the chart. Even today, most coastal cruising guides strongly advise that the place be avoided because of the treacherous shallows and breaking "sneaker waves" at the entrance.   And in addition, the exposed stretch of coast from the Golden Gate to Point Reyes and beyond can be very rough and windy even in the calmer days of the fall.   It was probably not the sort of trip to take one's new bride on in a little 23 footer.   During the later part of the summer I had built a nice little pram dinghy (named *Gimpy)* which was a big improvement in our equipment.   Our auxiliary engine consisted of a borrowed outboard motor of unknown reliability. Of course, we had no radio.

On September 1, 1956 we loaded the last of our stores aboard and shoved off at 6:30 A.M. to catch the ebb out the Gate.   According to our log book, it was a heavily overcast morning and we were accompanied by the fishing fleet as we passed Point Bonita with our little dinghy in tow.   As we progressed up the coast the clouds cleared, the breeze picked up from a favorable direction and we had a fine sail all day.   By late afternoon we had arrived in Drakes Bay and anchored amongst the fishing boats.   After dinner we rowed over to the fish dock where we watched salmon being unloaded.   Without a word a fisherman handed us a nice silver salmon which he indicated by a gesture, was too small to be landed from a commercial boat.   It was wonderful end to our first day.   We were exhausted and in bed by 8:30.

The next leg around Point Reyes and up the coast 15 miles to the Tomales Bay bar was the critical one.   To our dismay, the morning revealed nothing but pea soup fog and flat calm.   We got underway at 6:30 and ran a compass course to take us to Point Reyes then another course to take us up the coast, using the outboard motor.   The fog lifted a bit as we neared the entrance allowing us to find the sea buoy. Even better, right on schedule, the schooner *Altura* belonging to our friend Hugh Jacks came out of the bay for a day of fishing.   Their presence was very encouraging as we, with some trepidation, headed across the bar and into Tomales Bay.   The fog lifted. The breeze came up and with a song in our hearts we sailed down the length of the bay watching lovely little coves and beaches pass by until we anchored at Shallow Beach near the inner end of the bay.   Presently *Altura* returned and picked up her mooring then we all went ashore to Hugh's "base camp", a tent on the shore at the site of his future weekend home. That evening we had dinner around a campfire with our salmon as the *piece d' resistance.*

Sailing down Tomales Bay on or 2nd honeymoon cruise in September

During the ensuing week Jane and I had a delightful time roaming the ten mile length of Tomales Bay, anchoring off various pretty beaches and exploring by dinghy the tiny lagoons behind several of them. One day we anchored off the tiny settlement of Marshall on the northeast side of the bay. We had never seen it before and were enchanted with the little community centered on the old wooden Hotel Marshall. It was closed on the afternoon of our visit but by peering through the window of the lobby/bar we could see the proprietor asleep on the pool table. Nearby was the general store, which was jammed with essentials including buckets and suchlike hanging from the ceiling. In one corner of the store was a small enclosure containing the U S Post Office. We haven't seen it again in recent years but hope it hasn't changed.

We had been invited to visit an elderly couple named Les and Myrna Alexander who lived in a little cottage above the sand dunes of Dillon Beach, just to the north of the entrance to the bay. By studying the chart we saw that we could approach their house from a deep cove inside the bay. We carefully felt our way along a sparsely marked, narrow channel alongside Tom Point until we were at the edge of the shallows at the head of the cove Here we dropped the anchor and set it carefully then hung up the little kerosene anchor light. We rowed ashore, tucked the dinghy under the bushes then hiked along the shore and over the sand dunes to the little colony of Dillon Beach. Les and Myrna lived in a tiny cinder block weekend cabin which had become their home upon retirement. They seemed surprised and delighted to see us and learn of our unusual arrival route. We had a merry visit with drinks and supper then a quiet night on their fold-out sofa. Next morning we hiked back to find our dinghy undisturbed and *Ballerina* safely riding at anchor.

As the end of the week approached and our little honeymoon cruise on Tomales Bay about to end, we moved out to as close to the entrance as we dared and anchored for the night. Hugh Jacks had warned us that it was vital to cross the bar at slack tide or at least on a modest flood current. At all costs, we were advised to never enter or leave the bay on an ebb current which can cause the oncoming swells to trip and break on the shallow bar. We were underway at 6:30 in flat calm and were soon safely across the bar. Outside was an oily calm with the surface of the water coated with a red substance which we assumed was some sort of algae or "red tide". Beneath the surface were thousands of nasty looking, huge red jellyfish. We plowed along for hours using the outboard motor until right off Point Reyes it abruptly stopped. After much cleaning of spark plugs and pulling on the starter rope, we got it going again and limped into Drakes Bay on one cylinder.

To our great surprise, two other sailboats came into the anchorage, an event which ended in a great cocktail hour for the combined crews. The following morning the calm continued so we slowly crawled along using our barely-running outboard. As we poured the last of our gasoline into the motor off Duxbury Reef, it was obvious that we would not have nearly enough fuel to get home. However, our good luck continued and soon a little breeze came up and continued to freshen. By the time we sailed under the Golden Gate Bridge we were booming along, easily breasting a strong ebb tide. Evening found us back home in Sausalito at the end of our memorable little adventure. When we climbed the pathway to our apartment, we were greeted at the door by Mignon, our house-sitting friend who informed us that last night she had served as midwife to our cat, Topsy and her new litter of cute little kittens.

In November of this eventful year of 1956, I was asked to help fit out and sail a 42' schooner named *Reliance* from San Francisco to Southern California. It had been purchased by our friend, Dwight Long, together with a partner named Glen Johnston. Dwight had attained some renown when he sailed around the world in the 1930's as a young man and wrote a book about it called "Seven Seas on a Shoestring". I had gotten to know him when he was working temporarily in San Francisco a few years before. Unfortunately neither Dwight nor Glen were available to get the boat ready. I contacted the previous owner, Jim Denebeim, and arranged for the two of us to bring the schooner down from San Rafael to Sausalito. As we cleared the channel and entered the main part of the Bay, I started to hoist the mainsail but soon stopped when the wire halyard jumped off the sheave and jammed at the masthead. I got out the bosun's chair and with some help from Jim, got myself hoisted to the top of the mainmast. I led the free end of the wire up over a little cheek block above the sheave and called for it to be tightened on a winch. With a bang, the block broke loose and tore across my face cutting a nasty gash in my cheek which bled profusely. After our arrival in Sausalito, Jim drove me over to the Kaiser Hospital in San Francisco for a few stitches. It seemed like an ill omen at the time but it proved to be the only bad luck of the trip.

I spent a busy week in the evenings and during my spare time getting the schooner ready for the trip down the coast. On the day before Thanksgiving the crew arrived from Southern California. Together with Jane, it consisted of Glen Johnston and a pair of love birds named Jerry (a cement truck driver) and Marlyn (a cute blond) who were obviously smitten with each other and made billing and cooing sounds at all times. Glen had been in a motorcycle accident years ago and wore an artificial leg. He was a very capable guy and got around on the boat just fine with or without his peg leg. We had our Thanksgiving dinner at the little café under the old Sausalito Hotel, walked back to the boat and cast off.

It turned out to be a very easy trip mostly in calm or very light breezes. Off Point Sur we caught up with a Canadian ketch named *Flying Walrus* which had left Sausalito several days ahead of us and had been sitting off the Point for days drifting back and forth with the current. After seeing us motor by they gave up trying to make it under sail, started their engine and followed us down the coast. We stopped at the rickety pier in Port San Luis to buy gas then continued our leisurely way. The voyage ended in Santa Barbara on a calm, sunny morning (Is there any other kind in Santa Barbara?).

As a footnote to the trip, 48 years later I met Bob Vespa, a new member of our Cruising Club of America station, who told me that he was nearing completion of a total rebuilding of a 42', Schock-designed, staysail schooner built in 1927. I dug out some photos of our trip on *Reliance* and sure enough, it was the same boat. It is now reincarnated as *Scorpio* and is a beauty.

While on our cruise in Tomales Bay, Hugh Jacks announced that he planned to take his schooner, *Altura,* in the Transpac Race to Honolulu the next summer and asked if I would join the crew. He also asked if I would be interested in skippering the boat back home afterwards. Of course, I was ready to jump at the chance especially since it would be an opportunity for Jane to sail back too. It was a big step, however, because it would involve at least a couple of months away from work. After talking it over with Jane, who was game to go, we told Hugh OK. We were still focused on our idea to buy a boat in England and sail home so there were money issues involved too. In the end we decided to sell our beloved little *Ballerina* so that we could capture a sizable chunk of money toward our goal and be free to concentrate on the *Altura* project. It was a sad day in February 1957 when the new owner, a man from Stockton, sailed away with her. That night Jane shed bitter tears saying, "Without *Ballerina* now, we are nothing special, just ordinary people."

The 48' schooner, Altura, crossing the finish line at Diamond Head

CHAPTER 6

ALTURA

Hugh Jacks, the owner of *Altura,* although a generation older, had become my good friend and mentor when he had his schooner in the berth next to *Tai Fung.* He was a very friendly man with a keen sense of humor. I saw him as a grand person with a wealth of knowledge of boats and a quirky ability to always to come up with a funny quip. He was much more than this, of course, being a graduate of the London School of Business and an astute business man. Although he seldom talked about his affairs, I learned that he had acquired an old defunct company named the Pacific Coast Company which was still listed on the New York stock Exchange and turned it into a very successful holding company with many assets in shipping and other maritime enterprises.

One day I mentioned that I hadn't seen him for a while. He said he had been on a trip to England and then went on to say his company partly owned and managed a ship named the *Torrey Canyon,* which most people will recognize as the huge oil tanker which ran aground on the Scilly Isles and made a gigantic oil spill on the beaches of Cornwall. The recent newspapers had been full of the story. Hugh then mentioned that he had been in the awkward position of having to walk the beaches with the Prime Minister. When I asked Hugh if it was really as bad as portrayed in the press, typically, he said, "Oh, it was nothing that enough clean rags couldn't fix"

I had never sailed with Hugh on the *Altura* when he invited me to join the crew for the 1957 Transpac but I knew I wouldn't pass up a chance to be aboard. *Altura* was a 48' "knockabout" (having no bowsprit) schooner designed by Eldridge-McGuiness on the East Coast in about 1935. She wasn't built of very fancy stuff, but had apparently survived a hurricane in the West Indies at some point in her life. She had been sailed to the West Coast in the middle of WWII. I once met the man who did this trip and he showed me pictures of her with huge identifying numbers painted on her hull. When Hugh bought the boat in 1953, it had recently been cosmetically improved but was a bit shaky in terms of structural soundness. Still, he had taken it in the 1955 Transpac Race and a Mexican race and it had survived and proved to be quite a fast boat.

Measuring Altura's spars for a new suit of sails

Hugh went all-out for the upcoming Transpac Race, ordering a complete new suit of sails and a new engine in addition to lots of minor improvements. He also recruited a grand crew including Peter Sutter, a well known local skipper and sailmaker, Joe Miller, a talented sailor and mechanic, plus Burbeck Johnson and Dick Woodin, experienced racing sailors. Also aboard were a couple of Hugh's old pals, Red Laidlaw and Ned Boussange who had sailed all their lives and had lifetimes of stories about it. True to my expectations, they were all wonderful company.

Most skippers fitting their boat out for a Transpac Race spend a lot of time fretting about the food to be put aboard and the menus for each meal. Hugh, being a merchant shipping kind of guy, simply phoned one of the ship chandlers and ordered food for eight hands for three weeks and please deliver the stuff to *Altura* at Madden & Lewis Shipyard. We certainly learned what merchant marine sailors eat....lots of catsup, sauerkraut, strawberry jam and corned beef hash among other things. Still, Hugh was a great cook and we ate quite well on the trip.

We got off to a good start at noon on July 4, 1957 and by evening we had passed the west end of Catalina Island. About 5 AM the next morning, while sailing along smoothly, we suddenly saw the entire sky, from horizon to zenith, momentarily turn brilliantly white as though the sun had flashed like a gigantic light bulb quickly turned on then off. It happened in complete silence which made it all the more eerie. We were stunned. Then I remembered that I had read that an atmospheric test of the largest hydrogen bomb was to be done that day in Nevada. I knew that the Nevada Test Center was at least 400 miles from our location and it was difficult to grasp that the phenomenon we had seen had come from such a distance, but there was no other explanation. After a minute of shocked quiet, Joe Miller commented, "Well, there goes Los Angeles."

If the '53 Transpac was too calm and the '55 race was too windy, in '57 the winds were just right. We had nice breezes on the quarter almost from the start, allowing us to spread all of our canvas almost every day. On a schooner it can be a very big spread indeed especially with the huge gollywobbler flying. This sail fills in the entire area from the top of the foremast to the top of the mainmast and to end of the main boom. One memorable day when it was necessary for us to gybe the boat (change course to get the wind on the other side) we carefully assigned tasks for dropping the gollywobbler so that it could be re-hoisted on the other side. At the signal, both halyards and the sheet were cast off but instead of the sail coming down, it went *up* instead. In no time, the forward (throat) halyard took a couple of wraps around the light on the top of the foremast! At this point that sail wasn't going up or down so we were in a real fix until I was hauled aloft to the top of the mast and straightened things out.

Altura could really ramble when she had the wind she liked. One day in a nice fresh trade wind she was tearing along at full speed. Every time the Speedo hit 10 knots one of the crew would reach inside the porthole in the front of the cockpit and reward the helmsman with a peanut. The cardboard box on the inside full of unshelled peanuts, took a real hit that day. When *Altura* was sailing hard the poor old schooner tended to leak more than a little. Fortunately, a large pump was mounted right on the front of the engine so occasionally it was necessary to start the motor and pump out quite a few gallons. One time when someone commented on how much she leaked, Hugh quipped, "Considering how much water there is out here, I think she keeps out quite a lot".

The racing crew for the 1957 transpac Race
(rear L to R) Burbeck Johnson, Hugh Jacks, Dick Wooden, me
(front L toR) Peter Sutter, Joe Miller, Ned Boussange

We finished the race in 14 days, 21 hours which put us in first place in our class and 9th in the fleet of 34 boats. It was not a particularly fast race due to the moderate breezes but it had been extremely pleasant because of the nice sailing conditions and because of the wonderful shipmates I had. Jane joined us for the festivities, cruising in the Hawaiian Islands and the voyage home. Hugh and most of the crew, except Joe Miller, flew home and I was left to organize the boat for the voyage back to California.

Before he left, Hugh had suggested that we take the boat in the Kauai Race, a 102 mile, overnight race from Honolulu to the port of Nahwiliwili on Kauai. To fill out the crew and for local knowledge, we invited Louis Valier and his wife, Marge, who had spent many years sailing in these waters. Louis accepted with the proviso that we go on a little expedition he had in mind after the race. He said he had always wanted to visit an isolated valley named Nualolo on the west coast of Kauai but never had a big enough crew when he sailed his own boat near there with his family. Also along for the race were a group of local yachtsmen making for a total crew of nine.

We started the race in the evening off Waikiki and by morning were crossing the Kauai Channel between Oahu and Kauai. By early afternoon we were approaching the finish line and appeared to be well in the lead except for a 40' sloop named *Y Como* who rated exactly the same as us and who was just about even with us. We quickly figured the shortest distance to the finish was at the inshore end of the line. We put Louis on the bow because he was used to judging the depth of tropical water by its color, and began sailing as close to the reef as we dared. Of course *Y Como* did the same thing and as both boats got into shallow water we each began to surf on the face of the almost-breaking waves. First one boat would surf ahead then slow, and then the other boat would surf ahead. It was extremely exciting and risky. As we neared the finish line *Altura* surfed into the lead by a half a boat length then *Y Como* surfed past us right at the line. We couldn't tell exactly who was ahead when the flag went down because our view of the finish was blocked by *Y Como's* sails as she passed us on the crest of a wave. We were declared the winner by a half of a second.

But excitement wasn't yet over for the day. After the big luau at the Kauai Yacht Club that evening we returned to the boat and were getting some much-needed sleep when in the wee hours sirens began to wail and police loudspeakers began to warn of a coming tsunami. All boats were ordered to evacuate the harbor immediately and to head for deep water outside. As I recall, only one boat actually got underway and powered out into the darkness and rough seas. The rest were all too exhausted or too full of food and alcohol to make the effort in spite of the knowledge that tsunamis in Hawaii are serious business. Fortunately we had Louis aboard who immediately got on the radio and found out that the source of the tsunami was an earthquake in Chile a few hours earlier. Louis knew the time it takes for a tidal wave to travel from Chile to Hawaii and quickly determined that if it were coming it would arrive in a few minutes. Since there was no way we could get underway in that short time, we simply waited. It never arrived. With a great sigh of relief we all headed back to our bunks.

Later we were shocked to learn of the death of three crew members on a 36' yawl named *Typee,* owned by Dick Dole, a local yachtsman. They had left Kauai to return to Honolulu the day before we did and during the night while powering, the watch on deck went below to find the rest of the crew dead from carbon monoxide poisoning. In spite of the portholes and the companionway hatch being open, the deadly gas, which is heavier than air, had overcome them as they slept. In those days most sailboats (including *Altura*) had gasoline auxiliary motors which are much more prone to produce carbon monoxide than diesel engines.

The day after the tsunami alert, we left Nahwiliwili harbor and sailed along the south coast of Kauai to spend the night anchored off Polihali, the "barking sands" beach on the southwestern tip of the island. This spot marked the beginning of the spectacularly beautiful and precipitous Napali Coast and was our jumping off location for our attempt to reach the hidden and inaccessible Nualolo Valley. When we arrived off the valley Louis explained that since it would be impossible to land a dinghy on the shore, we were to divide into two groups. Jane, not being a strong swimmer elected to give it a miss. One group would remain with the schooner while the other would swim ashore from as close as the dinghy dared to go. He also cautioned us to be sure to keep our legs up on the surface because if we allowed them to get between the large rocks on the shore, they can easily be broken as the surf comes in. Under Louis's direction it all went well and the first group found themselves in a "Lost World". The valley was surrounded on both sides by impossibly steep and high cliffs. What a perfect place for an isolationist mini-kingdom. All that remained of an ancient tribe were the terraces for homes and communal structures but the whole valley simply echoed of a tragic end to a fascinating era.

Burbeck and I were in the second group to go ashore. Fortunately we were pretty much ready to come back about 30 minutes ahead of our allotted hour and a half because the weather was deteriorating rapidly. Louis rowed in to pick us up just as a heavy squall hit. From then on the weather just got worse. We got underway and proceeded along the incredible Napali Coast toward Hanalei Bay, about 25 miles away. The wind and sea built rapidly and *Altura* struggled to make headway. At one point we bucked into a big sea so hard that the heavy bronze manhole cover over the lazarette (the space under the afterdeck) jumped up and almost rolled overboard. Normally we needed a big prybar to get that hatch loose. Eventually we reached Hanalai Bay, undoubtedly the loveliest anchorage in the Hawaiian Islands.

After a couple of days we got under way for Honolulu and the start of our return trip to California. The Hawaiian Islands lie in a generally southeast to northwest direction which meant that we had gone as far downwind as we could go. We now would have to face the easterly trade winds and the rough seas they produce especially as they funnel between the islands. The passage between Kauai and Oahu across the Kauai Channel was no exception but luckily the trade winds were down a notch and we made steady, if wet and bouncy progress during the day and through the night. By dawn the next day we were in the lee of Oahu and enjoying blessedly smooth water as we approached Honolulu.

We returned to the Ala Wai yacht harbor and tied up in one of the wide berths between fixed concrete fingers (the berths were actually wide enough for three boats) with a small 26' folkboat type boat on the other side of the finger. Soon a little Japanese rigger appeared on his bicycle and proceeded to go to work on some project at the top of the slim wooden mast. He had pulled himself up to the top in a bosun's chair along with his little bag of tools. We weren't paying much attention to him until we heard a horrible "Yeoooow!" and saw him coming down along with the mast. It seems he had not realized the mast was stepped on deck and when he pulled a rigging pin the whole works let go. Lucky for him, the berth was wide enough that the mast didn't hit the adjacent concrete finger. We rushed over to fish the rigger and the mast out of the water. He was unhurt and didn't say much but soon he picked up his tools, got on his bicycle and disappeared, his day obviously not off to a good start.

I had arranged for a return crew including Jane, Joe Miller and Dick Simon, a sailing friend from Sausalito who owned a nice 33' cutter named *Kia Ora* plus Phil Price, my old shipmate from the *Tai Fung* trip. A few days later, after the arrival of Phil and Dick, we bashed our way across the rough Molokai Channel and made our way to the cozy

Altura moored in Lahaina harbor just before our voyage home

little harbor at Lahaina, Maui. There we renewed our acquaintance with the Troy and Collins families, our hosts on the *Tai Fung* and *Mistress* trips. It was an ideal place to get ourselves mentally and physically prepared for the upcoming long voyage back to San Francisco. I think it was especially good for Jane since this would be her first long ocean passage. On the 8th of August we said goodbye to our friends and set off on the 3000 mile journey home.

A hurricane had been rampaging around south of the Hawaiian Islands and had apparently disrupted the flow of the trade winds because instead of the strong headwinds we expected, we got moderate breezes and unexpectedly nice conditions for the first several days. In a few days we were out of the trade wind zone and began to enter the calms of the great Pacific high pressure area. Unlike the squally doldrums of the equatorial tropics, this area is characterized by clear sunny days and magnificent starlit nights. It seemed to me like ideal sailing, but Jane had a very difficult time getting used to the motion of the boat, the difficulty of sleeping at odd hours and the stress of the of the unfamiliar life aboard. Although she didn't get seasick, she felt very tired, flushed and feverish as well as nervous and had difficulty eating below decks. Her nerves also had her kidneys working overtime which added to her discomfort. In her notes of the trip in her diary she wrote quite a lot about her misgivings about going to sea and her doubts about our plans for a possible long voyage from England to California.

As we approached the Pacific High, Joe began work on a scoop net. He carefully fashioned the round hoop using split bamboo then attached it to a long bamboo pole. The net was woven with marlin twine using intricate fishnet knots. The purpose of this endeavor was to capture the prized Japanese green glass fish net floats which we anticipated finding in the calm waters ahead. Sure enough, we soon began to spot them on the smooth waters where they seem to accumulate. We found them in all sizes ranging from a few inches to over a foot in diameter. The best were the ones which still had their fishnet covering attached. Our progress slowed considerably as we zigzagged over the ocean when our prey was spotted.

After passing through the big high pressure area we picked up a brave westerly wind which allowed us to abandon our northerly course and turn the corner toward the east. We set the spinnaker and began to reel off the miles, running straight for San Francisco. Normally this is a risky strategy because if you are not truly over the top of the high, one can run right back into the calms, or even worse, run into the northeasterly trade winds. We were very lucky as we continued to sail for our destination without ever having gone north of the latitude of San Francisco. As we continued our voyage, Jane seemed to become better adjusted to life at sea. I gave her lessons in celestial navigation and soon she was taking sextant sights and working up our position with great accuracy and skill.

In 18 days, 21 hours we passed under the Golden Gate Bridge, having made an exceptionally fast trip (it took 26 days on *Tai Fung*). We tied up in our old slip in the Sausalito Yacht Harbor, tired but happy to be home. It had been a grand summer and an important experience for both Jane and me. She now had a taste of ocean sailing which left her with mixed emotions, and I had succeeded in carrying out the responsibility of bringing the schooner and her crew home safely from a long ocean crossing.

The return crew (L to R) Phil Price, me, Jane, Joe Miller, Dick Simon

As an epilogue to the *Altura* era, Hugh Jacks sold the boat shortly after our return. As much as he and all of us loved the old ship, he knew that she was clearly not seaworthy any longer. We were very fortunate to have avoided any serious weather on the trip back from Hawaii. She leaked a great deal in even moderate weather and heaven knows what would have happened in a serious blow. Before we left for the Transpac Race we had sailed her in a local ocean race around the Farallon Islands and up the coast to Bodega Bay Buoy (the Buckner Race). When we returned to Sausalito all the seams in the planking in the forward part of the hull were cracked open. It was a sobering sight.

About five years after she was sold, I got a call from Hugh asking if I knew who the owner of the boat was and where she was berthed. It seems he had just received a phone call from a distraught mother in Berkeley whose son had told her he was going on a weekend sailing trip on a boat named *Altura* to Half Moon Bay, about 30 miles down the coast, and had not returned. Apparently someone had remembered that Hugh had once owned the boat and put her in touch with him. I had an idea she was kept somewhere in the East Bay so I phoned Elly Dowd, a yacht broker friend in Alameda asking if she knew anything about the schooner. She groaned and said "I was afraid something like this would happen." It turned out *Altura* was kept in the harbor where she had her office and she knew the boat well because it was often seen coming back from sailing on the Bay looking like it was about to sink. She did some calling around and then filled me in on the story. It seems the owner and his wife and their two children plus the young man from Berkeley were seen leaving Half Moon Bay on a clear but very windy Sunday morning. They were never seen again and not a scrap of the boat or any bodies were ever found, not even a life jacket, a hatch or a lifebuoy. Apparently it had sunk very suddenly, probably from a loose or sprung plank. A tragic end to a fine old boat and an even worse tragedy for the two families involved.

Sali, a 26' Seabird yawl sailing off Sausalito, 1957

CHAPTER 7

SALI

In June 1957, prior to sailing in the Transpac Race, I had quit my job at International Engineering Company so now I needed to find a new one. I tore out the page in the Yellow Pages listing consulting engineering firms in San Francisco and hit the street. I soon landed work at John A. Blume & Associates, a rather small but well respected structural design firm on the corner of Howard and New Montgomery in the City. I was to remain with this firm for the remainder of my career. Meanwhile Jane returned to her job at the State Bar of California as secretary to the *Bar Journal* editor and public relations director. Thus both gainfully employed, we resumed our focus on the future.

We were still both aiming toward the idea of buying our own boat in England in a couple of years and sailing it back to California, however Jane's uncomfortable and difficult time aboard *Altura* on the way back from Hawaii posed a big problem. She was not at all sure she wanted to endure another long ocean crossing but without her to share the adventure with me, the trip didn't make much sense. I was not inclined to try to talk her into it if she would be miserable. On the other hand I was not going to easily abandon the plan which I had my heart set on. We discussed the situation endlessly then suddenly came to the conclusion that there was a simple solution. Since it was only the three-week ocean crossing that was causing the problem, why not have Jane cross the ocean from Gibraltar or the Canary Islands on a plane or passenger ship and meet the boat in the West Indies after the crossing. After all, the rest of the trip would be coastal sailing which Jane would surely enjoy.

With this obstacle out of the way, we resumed our enjoyable life on the Sausalito waterfront. Within a month I filled in a missing

piece of our life by finding and buying a rather bedraggled old 26'
yawl named *Sali* which was offered for sale at the yacht brokerage
across the street. She was a "Sea Bird" yawl, a design by C.A. Mower
which was published in Rudder Magazine in the early 1920's as an
example of a simple, small and easily constructed boat which could be
taken to sea in safety. To prove the point, Thomas Fleming Day, the
editor of Rudder Magazine sailed one across the Atlantic to the Mediterranean and on to Rome, a notable feat at the time.

Sail under full sail in San Pablo Bay

Sali was built sometime in the late 1920's in Alameda by a
young man named Jack Blinn while still in high school. He altered the
design slightly by giving it a raised deck forward, presumably to give
more interior space but also, I suppose, because that was a popular
style on San Francisco Bay at the time. She was built of pretty plain
stuff and had a canvas covered deck. Under the bridgedeck was an old
two cylinder "Blue Jacket Twin" Universal gas engine with a hand-
crank start. An old but functioning head (toilet) sat under a seat opposite the galley, right by the companionway. Her main claim to fame
was the fact that young Mr. Blinn had sailed her to Hawaii <u>and back</u>
with two of his friends sometime in the early 1930's. Whenever we

sailed on the Bay it was not unusual for someone to hail us and shout "I helped build that boat" or "I sailed to Hawaii on that boat". She was well known for sure. At one point she had been owned by Dick Simon, one of our shipmates on the *Altura.*

We had paid $1,800 for *Sali* and hoped to improve her enough to add to our cruising kitty for the trip to England. Finding things to upgrade her cosmetically was not difficult. As always, step one was to clean the bilge and paint it bright orange with red lead paint. Next we stripped off the old deck canvass and replaced it with new, a job which is not as easy as it sounds but which made a big improvement. Some new mahogany trim and a complete paint job on deck and below made her look quite smart. By spring we were ready to sail and looking forward to weekend cruising, racing and a trip up the Delta in the summer.

Our first race was the annual Richmond to Vallejo Race, near the end of April. This was (and still is) an enormously popular event attracting a fleet of over 150 boats. We were pretty excited and had prepared to give it our best. I had even sewn up a spinnaker and a mizzen staysail for the event. As we sailed up windy San Pablo Bay under a full press of sail, we were shocked to see that the bow was being forced down level with the surface of the sea and waves were washing over the foredeck. Obviously we were driving the poor old thing a bit too hard! After enjoying the big party that night at the Vallejo Yacht Club, we had yet another big surprise. The next morning, as we were maneuvering in light airs near the starting line, we noticed smoke coming out of the hatch. The engine was on fire. Fortunately it was just the wires on the motor that were burning and we soon had it under control. Getting our nerves under control was not so simple.

We entered all of the races in our class that season and did quite well considering we had such an old fashioned boat. Moe Witzel, a friend and racing competitor, told me after one race that he was amazed that we could get so much out of such an old boat. At the end of the racing season we were second place in our class.

Sali was quite an amazing boat. One day we were sailing near San Quentin when suddenly the helm went dead. The rudder stock (shaft) had broken off just below the hull. We couldn't run the engine because it had an offset propeller which would simply make the boat run in circles and we had about six miles to go to get back to the harbor. With a little experimentation we quickly found that the boat was quite controllable under sail alone. We could make her go in any direction by simply adjusting the trim of the sails, and to come about all we had to do was slack the jib and haul in the mizzen slightly to weather. In the end we sailed all the way back to Sausalito, into the marina and <u>right into the slip,</u> entirely under sail with no rudder.

She was a very old boat however, and she could leak plenty when sailed a bit too hard. One weekend we were encouraged by my boss at work, who was a sailor too, to sail down the South Bay to Coyote Point, spend the night and meet him and his wife for lunch. All went well on the run down and we enjoyed a leisurely lunch at his country club the next day. By the time we got back to the harbor, however, it was getting rather late in the afternoon and the wind was blowing strong. The South Bay can get mighty rough and soon *Sali* was making heavy weather of it as we pounded to windward. Before long the floor boards were floating, a bag of charcoal had broken open allowing a mass of briquettes to float around the cabin, and various cushions were in the mess too. We pumped long and hard on the bilge pump before we reached smooth water a few hours later.

In June, 1958 a pretty 30' canoe-stern sloop named *Calypso* from Portland, Oregon sailed into the Sausalito Yacht Harbor. As was our custom, we ran down and invited the crew to come up for a drink and a shower, an offer we made to every boat visiting our shore, and one which was never refused. The owner of the boat was Bob Petersen, a fellow about my age or a little older, who worked for a shipping company and had been transferred to San Francisco. He had built the boat himself on the Columbia River and wasn't about to leave it in Oregon, so he sailed it down the coast with a couple of pals. We soon became good friends and went on numerous weekend cruises together either on his boat or ours or, more often, with both boats. Just about this time the flat above ours in the old shingled building on Bridgeway Avenue became vacant so Bob Petersen and a couple of other yachties, including Derek Baylis, moved in. Derek had arrived a few months earlier from Australia on a schooner named *Carla Manus* and became another of our collection of friends who arrived in Sausalito on cruising boats.

A humorous incident in the shallows of the Napa River while on a weekend cruise
in company with Jim Palmer and his date Mignon

I had loaned the beautiful little dinghy I had made the previous year to a friend who lost it when it blew over at the end of a long tow line and in a panic was cast loose. I needed a replacement, and Bob Petersen, who had no dinghy at all, needed one too. We set to work on the porch of our flat to build a pair of 6'6" "Pootzy" dinghies, a design by A. Mason which was published in Rudder Magazine. It was a remarkable little dinghy for such a small size. It fit on the foredeck of just about any boat, carried a huge load and towed nicely. The fact that the earlier one had capsized was not the fault of the dinghy but was caused by not keeping the dinghy close to the stern of the yacht when towing in a rough sea. Bob and I planked the little boats with 1/8" plywood which made them very light, then covered the skin with fiberglass cloth. Appropriately, *Calypso's* dinghy was named *Bongo* and *Sali's* dinghy was named *Sili*. Building small boats became a favorite hobby for me and over the years I can count over 22 boats I have built ranging in size from the little "Pootzy" dinghies to a 17' motor launch.

In midsummer we decided to take *Sali* on a two week cruise up the Delta in company with Bob Petersen on *Calypso*. Jane had given me an old 16mm movie camera for Christmas which she bought for $50 from a TV photographer at KPIX where she had worked when we married. The idea was that we would try to make a film of our planned cruise from England the following year. Our little cruise up the Delta would be a good chance to make a short test film. We took along our cute little calico kitten, Becky, who turned out to be the star of the show.

At the end of the first day's run we ended up in Mayberry Slough, a narrow cut in the marsh opposite Antioch, California. As might be expected, a strong chilly wind was blowing up the Bay and sweeping the treeless banks of the waterway. I now know that it is useless to even think of anchoring under these conditions up there. One must find a lee behind some tall bushes or trees. We didn't know that then and moved around in the gathering darkness trying to find a suitable spot. After we finally got the hook down we rafted up and attempted to make supper on one of those early, round cast iron Hibachis in our windy cockpit. Of course neither boat had anything resembling a spray dodger for shelter. Bob Petersen, who had read stories of the wonders of cruising in the fabulous Delta, was not impressed.

After that, things improved. We had been told about a seldom visited place at the junction of Cache Slough and Miner Slough on the Sacramento River side of the Delta. It was idyllic. A lovely little cove was formed by the banks of the slough and the enclosing islands at its mouth. There were little beaches, blackberry bushes abounded and there was enough open water in our little lake to try the sailing rig I had made for the dinghy. I am sorry to say that the place no longer exists. A few years later a huge ship channel was dredged right through it to form a way for large cargo ships to reach the new inland Port of Sacramento.

Our itinerary then took us to Steamboat Slough, a very popular hangout for yachts in those days. The slough is a shortcut of six miles for water coming down the Sacramento River to reach Suisun Bay. A sizable portion of the river water is diverted into the slough and as a result of its steeper gradient, a very strong current flows through it. This makes anchoring in Steamboat Slough something of an art form. The only successful way to do it is to: (1) drop a bow anchor, (2) row a bow line ashore, tie to a tree and haul the bow close to the levee, (3) carry a stern anchor out in the dinghy, (4) row a stern line to a tree and make fast, (5) spread an awning and make a gin and tonic before you expire of the heat and exertion. In midsummer boats would be moored under the big cottonwood trees, bow-to-stern on both sides of the slough for half a mile. It was a wonderful social scene too with lots of kids playing on the beach and cocktail parties aboard the boats in the evening.

Next we sailed down Georgiana Slough, a sinuous waterway connecting the Sacramento River with the San Joaquin River. I have been told that in earlier times the trees on both banks were so large that they almost touched overhead. A few years before our cruise, however, the Army Corps of Engineers cut down all the trees on the slough, apparently because they believed that they were weakening the levees. It was a sad sight to see, but I am happy to say that a new crop has largely grown up in the intervening years.

Once on the San Joaquin River we roamed around the levee-enclosed islands and spent time at Fig Island on Potato Slough (we were the only boat there). Before we knew it, it was time to sail home. The trip back was an arduous but not uncomfortable beat to windward which took two days with a stop overnight in Vallejo.

Back in Sausalito our attention turned to our upcoming adventure in England. In the fall we sold *Sali* for $3,000 to a group of three young men. She had been a lovable old boat and she had served us well. We added the dollars to our fund which we were desperately trying to make large enough to carry out our plan. Certainly we were going to need every cent we could find. In the end we scraped together $14,000, an amount which, in the best of circumstances, we knew would be barely enough. Still, our hopes were high as we plunged ahead in the winter of 1958-59 toward our goal.

Jane and I decided that a crew of four would be ideal. This, of course, was before the days of windvane gears or affordable autopilots, so we had to think in terms of steering the boat every inch of the way back to California. We invited our old shipmate Phil Price to join us. He was just finishing up a two-year hitch in the Navy and jumped at the chance. We knew him to be a quiet, competent sailor with lots of handy skills and 100% reliable. He was 20 years old at the time. We also asked Bob Petersen to come along. He readily agreed, in spite of the fact that he was just settling into his new job with States Lines on the San Francisco waterfront. We had not sailed with Bob at sea but had been with him around boats a lot. He had served in the Naval Reserve aboard ships, had lots of sailing experience and was very pleasant. We were sure we had an ideal crew.

In thinking ahead, we tried to make use of all the materials we had on hand that might be useful in terms of time and money in getting a boat fitted out in England. We found five large "foot locker" trunks and filled them with tools, clothing, foul weather gear, books and navigation instruments. I even packed up an assortment of bolts and screws. I bought a chronometer and a used shortwave receiver for getting WWV time signals. I had been given a beautiful British sextant by Walter Johnson, the owner of *Nordlys*, and a set of navigation tables by Cap Ferdinandsen, the old sailmaker in Mill Valley. We had a friend who sold pharmaceuticals who put together a medical kit for us. I even had a dentist friend make up a small dental repair kit. The stuff all went into the trunks. If we had it and it might be useful, we packed it up. I even boxed up all the leftover canned goods from the *Altura* trip and built a folding dinghy, but in the end decided to it wasn't worth the expense to ship them over.

It was an exciting time. We poured over the ads in every British yachting magazine we could get our hands on, looking at boats for sale and checking the prices. I didn't bother to contact any yacht brokers over there because I knew it would be useless to receive a lot of specifications on available boats if I was not in a position to look at them. I also knew that a good boat offered at a low price would not still be there by the time we arrived. I was sure we would find something to buy that we could afford. We would soon find out.

Meanwhile the fall and winter seasons were enlivened by the arrival of a rather large ketch named *Romayne* which sailed in from Vancouver, Canada, with a lively group of six young Canadians aboard. She had a gaff rigged mainmast with a topmast, high bulwarks and a very old fashioned look about her. It seems she was built of riveted steel in Germany by Krupp not too long after World War I. They had broken their topmast on the way down the coast when a running backstay failed and would be in port until it was repaired.

Our future Canadian friends arrive aboard Romayne.
Sterling Hayden's schooner, Wanderer, is in the background

We soon got to know her crew by means of the usual drink-and-shower offer at our flat. The owner, Stuart Riddell, was a sort of jack-of-all-trades who was rather short on sailing experience but had been a pilot, lumberjack, sheep rancher and gas station operator among other things. Among the crew were his cousins Anne Cowan and Mickey Kinloch, along with a young yachtsman named John Yuell from the Vancouver Yacht Club. Also aboard were Mike Gunning, a young former British merchant marine officer, and his wife Valerie. Their plan was to sail around the world.

We had much in common to talk about and had a big farewell party for them before they sailed away with a newly spliced topmast. Two days later as Jane and I sat down to breakfast we noticed a large boat with no mainmast tied up to the breakwater across the street. I said to Jane, "That looks an awful lot like *Romayne*, but if it's her, she must have lost her stick." We soon got the story: On the first night at sea the helmsman saw the jib and headstay swinging far out to lee-ward. Although the rig was not in any imminent danger since they were running before the wind, they instinctively headed up into the wind which they now realize, was exactly the wrong thing to do. As the boat came up into the wind, the mast broke and went over the side. It seems the crew, while waiting in Sausalito, had carefully taken apart the rigging turnbuckles and greased the threads but had failed to secure them before going to sea. Inevitably, the turnbuckle on the headstay unscrewed and the mast lost its support. Stuart told us they cut away the wire rigging with a huge pair of wire cutters and left the mast in the water with the US courtesy flag fluttering from the starboard spreader. "You would have been proud," he added.

Well, that certainly changed their plans. After much discussion and an offer from Ronnie Wise, a Sausalito spar builder, it was de-cided to get rid of the old gaff rig and build a new modern Bermuda-type mast. Meanwhile there were crew changes too. John decided to return to Vancouver on his Vespa motor scooter (a disastrous idea). Mike and Valerie also left, which was a good thing because they were always fighting. On the plus side they invited our old shipmate from *Altura*, Joe Miller, to join them, bringing his vast experience, skills and good humor to the ship. Two more members of Stuart's extended family, Hans and Pidge, also joined the crew.

The boat stayed in Sausalito for the winter while the re-rigging project took place. The mast building culminated in a big "glue-up" session one afternoon when a large crew assembled to spread the Weldwood glue, assemble the planks and tighten the clamps on the huge new spar which Ronnie had prepared. Stuart often said the dis-masting was the best thing that could have happened because it gave them a far better and safer rig and a much better crew.

We had grand times with the *Romayne* gang that winter, a regular feature of which was to get together every Friday evening aboard an old wooden 110' subchaser named *Telesis* for a "finish up the beer keg party". The owners of the vessel had a standing order for delivery every Saturday morning of a keg of beer which lived in its own little refrigerator aboard the boat. We always did our best to make way for the new one. One Friday evening Jane brought along Emily, her co-worker at the State Bar, an event which had important consequences. She was a pretty gal with a vivacious way about her and she soon was a regular. It turned out that Stuart wrote to her later from Tahiti and invited her to join the ship as they cruised the South Pacific. Inviting a girlfriend to come to Tahiti had to be a historic first. Later, Stuart and Emily were married in New Zealand. They are still happily married 46 years later and are among our best friends.

As the spring arrived Jane and I and the *Romayne* crew made preparations for our separate adventures.

Armorel, our 40' cutter sailing off Cowes under a previous owner

CHAPTER 8

ARMOREL

March 13, 1959 arrived almost before we knew it. I remember it like yesterday, when we took the Greyhound commuter bus from Sausalito to San Francisco, transferred to the airport bus and boarded a Lockheed "Constellation " plane to New York and were on our way.

We stuffed our belongings at home into a little glassed-in portion of the front porch, which had earlier served as a small workshop, and sublet our flat to a couple of sailing guys from the harbor. My old '35 Ford sedan had worn out a year or so before and was replaced by the current family car, a cute green '34 Chevrolet coupe (with a rumble seat) which was driven to the weekend cabin of some friends in the East Bay town of Sunol and left under an oak tree. Our calico cat, Becky, was given a new home, and I took a leave of absence from my job. I had planned to just quit, but my boss suggested a leave would preserve my vacation status and my miniscule profit sharing vesting. Jane simply quit her job. It was all pretty simple considering we had no children, no big careers, no house with a mortgage, and no ageing parents.

Bob Petersen (who we had begun calling Pete since one Bob on a boat would be enough), had a theory that Denmark might be a likely place to find a cruising boat. He had subscribed to a Danish yachting magazine and learned enough of the language to decipher the ads. He decided to go on his own to Copenhagen shortly after we left to check out some of the ads he had seen and would contact us when we arrived in England. Phil Price would fly to England after we had found a boat.

We stayed in an old flea-bag hotel near New York's Times Square for a couple of days, watching the St. Patrick's Day parade and taking a tour boat ride around Manhattan Island, then took a train to Boston to catch our ship. We had purchased tickets on the *RMS* (royal mail ship) *Newfoundland*, a fancy title for the cheapest passenger ship crossing the Atlantic. It took 13 days and cost $154 each. Actually, it was a combination cargo and passenger ship and was a showing its age, but was not at all bad, especially considering the price. Jane and I had a comfortable little stateroom with a porthole and two bunks. The heads and showers (with rusty water) were down the passageway. It even had two classes of passengers, although there were only two couples in the 1st class section. Mostly the ship carried young people like us, with their guitars, on their way to a tour of Europe.

We stopped in Halifax, Nova Scotia for three days while the ship worked cargo, and then went on to St. Johns, Newfoundland for another day in port. It seems the ship's rules decreed that passengers were allowed in the crew's quarters on days in port, and since beer was freely available on those days, there was no reason not to have a party in the evenings. The crew was mostly young lads from Liverpool who spoke in an outrageous "liverpudlian" dialect, loved to sing and sounded like the Kingston Trio (accent and all) as well as the Beatles. We had some jolly times. On other days at sea we mostly huddled in the heater-less deck saloon, playing cards and waiting for the next meal or for the "pub" to open on the traditional English time schedule: i.e. 11:00AM to 1:00PM and 4:30PM to 6:00PM. On deck, with the ship's course on the great circle route taking us north across the Grand Banks, it was bitterly cold and rough. Along with half the passengers, I had a short bout of flu, but neither Jane nor I got seasick. It was comforting to know that our sailing route back across the Atlantic would be far to the south.

We disembarked in Liverpool and caught a train to Bristol where we had an introduction to the parents of one of our friends who had turned up in Sausalito on a cruising boat. We spent a night at their modest home and, mercifully, they allowed us to unload some of our backbreaking luggage at their home when we set off for the south coast to begin our search for a boat to buy. We really had no clear plan in mind so we decided to start our hunt in the westernmost part of Cornwall and work our way east along the coast.

With an introduction to Captain Mitchell, the harbormaster of Fowey in hand, we started there. It was a wonderfully quaint little port with a scattering of yachts lying on moorings in various corners of the harbor and adjoining creeks. We rented a rowboat and spent a pleasant day rowing around looking at the boats, but without a yacht broker in town it was impossible to know what might be for sale or even who owned them. We quickly realized that this approach wasn't going to work, so we said our goodbyes to Captain Mitchell and his wife and took a train to the bigger harbor of Brixham. Even here it was difficult to get an idea of what might be for sale so we pushed on again by train to Southampton, the biggest yachting center in England.

Once checked into a suitable bed & breakfast, we contacted Pete in Copenhagen. He hadn't had any luck in finding a boat there, so we agreed to join forces and get properly organized. When he arrived, we rented a car and visited the office of Laurent Giles, a famous yacht designer who ran a yacht brokerage on the side. It was the start of a frustrating period in which we would get information on one or two boats, then get in the car, drive to some obscure anchorage or boatyard and have a look. Inevitably, the boat would either be in deplorable condition or be designed with some impossible features. There were some very weird boats in England. Also it appeared that the supply of cruising boats had been pretty much picked over, and with economic conditions what they were in England, few new yachts were being built. Our budget for a boat was only $7,500 which didn't help. It was a slow process, but eventually we did find one which came close. It was a 35 footer named *Blackjack* owned by Mr. Thorneycroft . Naturally, it had a huge Thornycroft diesel engine which took up a lot of space. Unfortunately it wasn't really big enough for four people. It was a discouraging business.

Another boat which we looked at was a sort of motorsailer named *Lady Amanda* with an honest-to-gosh bronze plaque on her bulkhead commending her role in the Dunkirk evacuation at the outset of WWII. It seemed almost worth buying her just for the historic medal.

After several days we shifted our search to the Hamble River and a broker named Mr. Pittfield who had the biggest nose I had ever seen. After listening to our needs he suggested we take the ferry over to Cowes on the Isle of Wight and look at a nice boat which exactly fitted our desires, but was listed for far more than our budget. When we mentioned this fact Mr. Pittfield said, "Take a look and make an offer. You never know."

We followed his suggestion, took a ferry across the Solent and found *Armorel*, a 40' cutter at Lallow's boatyard on the Medina River. She was a beautiful, roomy cruising boat in fine condition and perfect for our voyage in every way. The only problem was the asking price was $14,000. We came back to Mr. Pittfield and offered $11,200 (4000 pounds) which was still way over our budget but, fortunately, I had an ace in the hole.

Before we left, Hugh Jacks took me aside one day and told me if we couldn't find a boat within our budget or if we found a good boat that was above our budget, to let him know and he would be glad to arrange a loan. It was a very generous offer. Above all, he cautioned, don't try to sail back on an unsuitable boat just because you are short on funds. I didn't expect our low offer on *Armorel* to be accepted but if it was, I knew we had a way to come up with the purchase price.

Without waiting around, we got in the car and headed up the east coast to Burnham-On-Crouch to check out a couple of boats. The first one, named *Lylie,* was within our budget and about the right size. She had been built at a barge building yard and was kind of rough. She had a plumb stem with a deep draft forward (with the head right behind the stem) and about a 16' bowsprit to balance her up. With this awkward rig she would likely be difficult to handle and probably would not have much resale value back in California. Scratch that one off.

The next boat, *Liza*, was our back-up boat. We had seen her for months in the ads (which should have been our tip-off). She was advertised as a 40' ketch with much new renovation with an asking price of $7,500. We figured if all else failed we could always buy this one, but when we saw her our hopes sunk. It seems she had been sailed from Norway to England at the start of WWII as an escape boat and was left to rot on a mud bank. After the war, she was dragged out of the mud and used as a project to keep the boatyard workers occupied. Not much thought had gone into the rebuilding work. For instance, Jane noticed that the hole for the mainmast was centered right over the doorway to the head! She was a hopeless old thing, so scratch that one too.

We were a discouraged trio as we checked into the "Ye Olde White Hart Hotel" that night. But the next morning when we phoned Mr. Pittfield, he told us our offer on *Armorel* had been accepted. He said, "The owner didn't think much of your offer, but he liked what you intended to do with her and didn't want to watch her ever being neglected." When I said "Well I guess we better get right back to see you." He replied, "Sir, I think you would be very foolish if you didn't." We could hardly believe our good fortune as we jumped into the car and sped for the Hamble River.

Armorel as we found her in Cowes, Isle of Wight, April 1959

The next few days were a blur of activity. We signed a contract to purchase the boat (subject to survey), wired Hugh Jacks who generously loaned us $4,000, engaged a surveyor, moved ourselves into the "Anchor Inn" at Cowes and dispatched Jane back to Bristol to retrieve our luggage. The surveyor spent all day poking and tapping.

He even had us lift up two and a half tons of lead inside ballast so he could check the bilges and keelson underneath. In the end he pronounced her a perfectly sound boat.

Armorel was designed by a Mr. Anderson, the owner of a small boatyard in Penarth, Wales and was patterned after a Falmouth Quay Punt, a smaller type of gaff rigged cutter which worked as shore boats for the big windjammers anchored in Falmouth Bay. She was built in 1935, but had been used only a few seasons before the war and had been laid up ashore for a number of years after the war, so she looked quite new. Her hull had a transom stern with a huge outboard rudder, was quite deep drafted (7.5') with a long keel which started at the bow and sloped back to the rudder. Her beam was only 11' which was rather narrow for a boat of her size by American standards. She was rigged as a Bermuda cutter with the mast stepped right in the middle of the boat. The size of the rig appeared to be rather modest, which meant she would probably be easy to handle.

Below decks she had a nice layout with a grand aft cabin behind the companionway ladder, a galley to port, and a head to starboard at the foot of the ladder, then a lovely saloon with two comfortable settees. Forward was a roomy fo'csle set up for a paid hand with a little folding table, toilet and a folding pipe cot. All of the trim was of teak. There were two big teak skylights, one over the aft cabin and one over the table in the saloon. It was one of the best layouts I had ever seen except that the galley was a bit small. She even had such amenities as a large folding chrome plated ring alongside one of the bunks in the aft cabin which the broker explained was for the "sick bowl". A previous owner had installed a very large fan in the head which provided distracting noise for his modest wife.

She was powered by a 25 HP Britt gas engine, a sort of workboat motor. It had electric start but also a convenient hand start arrangement. The ignition was by magneto (with a spare in a sealed tin). In addition to the generator on the motor, there was an auxiliary generator from a Sherman tank mounted in a locker in the cockpit. The best piece of equipment, however, was a hydraulic windlass which was powered by a pump belted to the main engine. It was a beauty and so powerful we raised a heavy mooring to the surface one time without realizing we were hooked on to it. She also had a marine radio and an electronic depth sounder, the first one I had ever used. In all, she was a very well equipped boat.

The boat was maintained by a full time, year-round boat keeper who had recently painted the entire boat on deck and below. All the spars and blocks were stored ashore and were glistening with fresh varnish. She came equipped with a nice ten foot sailing dinghy of cold molded plywood, built by the makers of the famed British Mosquito bombers. About all we needed to do below decks was to install some kind of gimbaled cooking stove. On deck we needed to build a boom-kin so we could have a permanent backstay, install a pair of sheet winches and fashion a spinnaker pole. We also needed to order a large genoa jib. It was really a trivial amount of work compared to what all the other boats we had seen would have required.

In less than a week the boat was launched and rigged. The launching was an amazing process where the boat was jacked up and skidded into position, then slid onto a launching cradle all with the aid of wedges, blocks, greasy planks, tackles and infinite skill. After she rolled down the launching ways, the mast was lifted into position and lowered onto the mast step. A mechanic came aboard and started the engine and we were on our own. We moved out to a mooring between a pair of pilings and heaved a huge sigh of relief. It had been a very exciting day.

As much as we enjoyed The Anchor Inn and the owners, Peg and Sam Hawke, we were glad to move aboard. It happened on April 28th. The weather was still very chilly and wet and there were as yet few tourists or yachtsmen to be seen in Cowes. One weekend the previous owners of *Armorel*, Barry Heath and his wife, came down to Cowes and looked us up. They were a very polished and extremely pleasant couple. They introduced us at the Island Sailing Club, where we were welcomed and invited to use the facilities during our stay. They also took us to see the Royal Yacht Squadron, but tactfully suggested we would probably be more comfortable using the ISC. They also showed us their flat which they shared with their friend Max. It took us a while to figure out that Max was Max Aitkin, better known as Lord Beaverbrook. We learned years later, when a subsequent owner of the boat researched her history, that Barry Heath was the elder brother of Sir Edward Heath, prime minister of Britain between 1970 and 1974. No wonder it was such a nice boat.

Jane had been working on a list of our stores which amounted to about 600 cans of food plus other things. She placed the order with the local grocer and in a few days the whole load appeared at the boatyard. It looked like an impossibly large pile of groceries, but we set to work stripping off the paper labels, varnishing and labeling each tin, then carrying them out to the boat in the dinghy. Our five big trunks which we had shipped to England also appeared about this time. I had sent them to the American Express office in London and when I called to tell them to forward them to Cowes, they informed me that they had been very annoyed to have them underfoot for the past several weeks and were only too glad to get rid of them. Another American was in Cowes, like us, outfitting a boat to sail home to California. When he saw us unpacking the trunks he groaned and said, "I had all that kind of stuff at home! Why didn't I think of shipping it like you did?"

Fitting out: shaping a new spinnaker pole

We had written to Phil about *Armorel* and suggested he meet us in London. We played tourist for a couple of days, met Phil, did a bit of shopping to round out our stores, and returned to Cowes to continue our preparations. We had become very fond of Cowes and were on friendly terms with the shop keepers and tradesmen. Procuring fresh food meant visiting the baker, the butcher and the greengrocer. Jane had her favorites. One evening Jane and I were invited by our butcher and his wife to come up to their flat for cocktails. When I asked about what things were like there in WWII he became very animated and was full of stories. Their apartment, which was over their shop, overlooked the waters edge. "Oh. One night a bomb landed at low tide right behind the building. It blew mud everywhere. When the tide gets a bit lower you can still see where it hit." On another night a German pilot parachuted into the town and was grabbed by the locals. It turned out that he was a former yachtsman and had been to Cowes for regattas. He asked where he was and when he was informed that he was in Cowes he said "Vunderful. Take me to the Hare & Hounds Pub."

During the month of May the weather improved, yachting activity around the harbor began and our fitting-out jobs progressed nicely. The weather was fine and we were anxious to get underway. We went ashore on the morning of June 1 to say good bye to our old inn keepers, Peg & Sam, who we have exchanged Christmas cards with until their recent deaths, and to settle our account at the ship chandlers. I asked for the amount we owed and was told, "The bill hasn't been made up, but it will quite alright if you just give us your forwarding address sir" Only in friendly, trusting England! I insisted in paying off the bill and they set to work to add it up. At three o'clock in the afternoon we slipped our moorings, hoisted sail for the first time and set forth down the Solent. To cap off our departure, a beautiful big Royal Navy cruiser passed us heading east. We had quite a tall flagstaff on our stern and, on an impulse, I uncleated the little halyard and dipped Old Glory. To our astonishment we saw a sailor racing toward the cruiser's stern and then saw a return dip of the huge St. George's Cross ensign. It was a perfect start to our voyage.

*   *   *   *

We were on our way, with a little over 11,200 miles to go before we sailed under the Golden Gate Bridge. The trip was most definitely not about finding and bringing back an inexpensive boat. It was about seeing and doing the things I had read about in cruising books and magazines for years. If any one book was the inspiration for our venture, it was probably *A White Boat from England* by George Millar.

Next best was *Red Mainsail* by Peter Pye. I was simply in love with the idea of seeing the shores of the places I had read about and making an Atlantic crossing in my own boat. We were off to a good start, with a good crew and a better boat than I would have dreamed possible.

One small problem was that Jane had to deal with her BIG LIE. Her mother was a lovely lady, but was deathly afraid of boats, especially sailboats that tipped when the wind blew. I tried to take her for a short sail on *Ballerina* once but had to return to the dock when she became hysterical with fear when the first puff of breeze caused the boat to heel just a little. Jane knew that she would worry herself sick if she had months to think about us sailing across the ocean. Thus was invented the big lie. She was told that we had chartered *Armorel* for some coastal sailing in Europe and in the Mediterranean. Jane's father was in on the real story; in fact it was he who advised Jane to keep our plans a secret. Still, it was a strain for Jane to keep up the fiction, and she had to be careful about what she wrote in her letters home. In the end her mother found out about our intentions shortly before we set off across the Atlantic. She was mildly annoyed at being kept in the dark, but nonetheless acknowledged that she was relieved she didn't know any sooner.

As we neared the western end of the Solent, the broad expanse of water between the south coast and the Isle of Wight, we stopped for the night at the pretty little port of Yarmouth. It was Eric and Susan Hiscock's home port and we had hoped to see them there, but they were off cruising on their famed little cutter *Wanderer III*. The next day we passed the craggy chalk columns known as The Needles at the western tip of the Isle of Wight, and then sailed on to Poole on the Devon coast. It was lovely harbor with a nice wooded park named Brownsea Island next to the anchorage. It was a bird refuge and the air rang with birdsong every hour of the day.

Our next challenge was to get around Portland Bill, a prominent headland which sticks out into the English Channel and is famed for the vicious tide rips and overfalls which have terrified yachtsmen. We were expecting the worst, in spite of carefully studying the tide book to pick the time of slack water. Our departure from Poole was timed to take us around the notorious headland in the middle of the night at the best time. It was a quiet night and a bit of an anticlimax when we saw nothing more menacing than a few swirls in the water.

The anchor went down in the very early hours in Brixham. In what I like to remember about England, we awoke at a rather late hour to find a little brochure from the Brixham Yacht Club lying on our bridgedeck with a card from the secretary inviting us to come ashore and use their facilities. Simultaneously, the customs officer came by in a boat to politely inquire where we had come from. He had waited until he was sure we were awake before making his call. I don't know how things are now, but in 1959 it was a very civilized place.

The coast of Devon is a surpassingly beautiful scene, but nothing, we thought, could compare with the sight of Dartmouth which greeted us as we entered the River Dart. Jane described it in a letter to her parents. "The River Dart is absolutely the most beautiful place I've ever seen. The river entrance is rather narrow with cliffs covered with the greenest of forest. The colors were spectacular; it's the closest thing to the Emerald City of Oz that I shall ever see." We anchored in the basin with the charming, compact little city on one side and a pair of rakish, side-wheel river steamers on the other side. At the Christopher Robin Milne's Bookstore (Christopher Robin was out of town) we met a nice lady who, with her husband, were boating enthusiasts, and who invited us to the local yacht club for drinks and a shower. Later in the day Phil returned to the boat with a little black kitty. Naturally, we named her Dart.

When Jane and I were traveling east along the coast earlier on our search for a boat, we met a couple in Plymouth named Roy and Ailsa Lanouette who owned a cruising boat. They suggested on our return we visit the Yealm River where they moored their yacht. They gave us instructions on how to enter the river (line up the church steeple with the left side of the bluff, etc). It was a tricky approach and we were pretty nervous as we crossed the shallow bar at the entrance, but found our way up the narrow river to a wide spot where several boats were lying on moorings. We got our anchor down between the tiny hamlets of Newton Ferrers and Nos Mayo, and soon spotted our friends waving to us from ashore. The next day the Lanouettes took us on a drive over the moors and a distant view of notorious Dartmoor Prison, then to lunch at their flat. Best of all, Roy, who ran a scrap yard, presented us with a collection of items he thought might be useful, such as a roll of sheet lead, various hoses, pieces of brass and such. It was a very thoughtful gift.

Roy agreed to sail with us on the next leg to Fowey. Just beyond Plymouth is the famed Eddystone Lighthouse. As we sailed past, the crew sang the verses of the well-known tune "The Keeper of the Eddystone Light." To our astonishment, Roy was delighted and said he had never heard the song before. By late afternoon we entered Fowey Harbor, said goodbye to Roy, and looked up our friend Captain Mitchell at the Harbormaster's Office. To our embarrassment he insisted on giving us a large, framed, hand-drawn chart of the harbor dated 1678. When we protested that we shouldn't take away such a historic local artifact, he waved our objections aside and said, "There is a roomful of old stuff like that around here." We stowed it under a mattress and now it hangs in our den in Tiburon.

The next leg of our cruise along the South Coast took us to Falmouth, the westernmost port in England and our proposed jumping off point for the crossing of the Bay of Biscay. Initially we anchored in a quiet cove named St. Maws in a corner of the harbor. In no time we were invited ashore by the residents of the house opposite the boat. They insisted we have drinks with them and invited us to have a shower. It reminded us of our routine with cruising boats in Sausalito.

For the first time we had an opportunity to try out the sailing rig in our 10' dinghy in the sheltered waters of the cove. Also in the cove was an antique Falmouth Quay Punt, the ancestor of *Armorel's* design. It was an idyllic spot, but soon we moved into the main harbor and anchored off the Falmouth Yacht Club. I was puzzled by the Irish flag flying from the club flagpole, but soon an American flag was hoisted as well. It then dawned on me that the yacht near us was Irish and the flags were in recognition of the club's foreign visitors. The hospitality and adherence to tradition of the English yachting fraternity was a marvel to us. The Irish crew (a man and his daughter) invited us over for drinks. They were from Bantry Bay on the west coast and were returning to their home waters with their new Dutch-built steel yacht. They told us that the appearance of a yacht (Irish or foreign) in their area would be remarkable and most unusual.

It was now June 16th, and we had arrived at the end of our coastal cruising and had to now face the loathed and feared Bay of Biscay on our 550 mile passage to Spain. The weather so far in England had been nearly perfect. We kept telling ourselves that we ought to get the heck out of here before the weather turned bad, but in fact, it remained nice all that summer until the end of September. In later years the British yachting magazines referred to 1959 as "The Summer."

I had read so many stories in books and magazines of yachts coming to grief in storms in the Bay of Biscay that it had taken on a mythic role in my imagination. I was fully expecting to receive a real hammering from one of the famous southwesterly storms that made its reputation so fearful. We were happily disappointed. The weather on our day of departure was perfect with only a light breeze from the north. During the passage we got some moderate wind at times but always from a favorable direction and not a drop of water ever came on deck. We couldn't believe our luck. On the fifth day we raised Cape Finisterre (end of land), the northwesterly point of Spain.

The little piece of Spain above Portugal on the Atlantic coast is the province of Galacia and it is a cruising paradise. At the time I knew nothing about it and was prepared to sail right on by. Then I read an account by Eric Hiscock, in one of the books we had aboard of a cruise he made in the area. It convinced us to have a look. There are five big bays here, called *rias,* each one about the size of San Francisco Bay. They are set in picturesque, wooded terrain and with one exception, are the site of only very small villages. Our little cruise here was a total surprise and one of the high points of the voyage. During our time here we saw only one other yacht.

We put into Ria Corcubion, the most northerly of the bays, late on a Sunday afternoon. We put up the "Q" flag and anchored off a small but attractive, sandy beach just above the little town, expecting to go ashore and check in the following day. At the time Spain was under the rigid dictatorship of Generalissimo Franco and we were rather leery of what the officialdom would be like. We spent the rest of the day aboard, and except for some small boys who came by in a rowboat and a couple of uniformed guys armed with their rifles watching from the shore (who it turned out were just relaxing), we were totally ignored. Late that evening several officials came out to see us and came aboard. They were very cordial and seemed to have almost no paperwork or formalities for us. We decided we were going to like Spain!

The next day we went ashore and wandered around town. It was like we had stepped back a couple of hundred years in time. Here is Jane's description from a letter home: "The village is very tiny and has no outskirts to speak of. Lots of buildings, all crowded into a small area, and then just countryside. We found ourselves out of Corcubion almost before we realized we were in it! We continued beyond Corcubion and found ourselves in the slightly larger village of Cee. There was much more activity in Cee. Tiny, narrow winding streets, most buildings three stories high, with dirty dark doorways, although the windows up above had spotless curtains in them, and most of the people seemed clean and neat. The place was littered with kids and animals. Pigs and chickens wandered about the streets. Cats and dogs all over the place. Chickens seemed to have as much run of the houses as the cats and dogs. They strutted in and out of doorways followed by their brood of wee chicks. An oxcart came squeaking through a narrow street…its wheels were solid wood…a primitive mode of transportation indeed. And what was the cart carrying? Electrical equipment. As we passed the church the padre stopped us and invited us in to see it. The outside was plain; the inside elaborate with intricate religious statuary, shrines and altars."

We saw women carrying water in wooden casks on their heads, and a life style I didn't know still existed in western Europe. Jane saw some women scrubbing clothes along a wall near the beach, so she took our laundry ashore and joined them. She knelt on a stone by a tiny pool under a running stream of water and set about soaping and rubbing the clothes on a big flat stone, then spread them on some bushes to dry. Hard on the knees, back and arms, I'm sure, but the clothes got clean.

We sailed the next day for the next bay, Ria Muros, just a few hours to the south, and anchored off the village. As soon as the anchor was down a rough fishing skiff loaded with officials came alongside. It contained the Harbormaster, a talkative and likable middle-aged man, the Port Doctor, a slight, gentle man, and the Police Captain, a sullen, brutish guy who brightened immediately when the booze came out. Also along were a couple of others who probably tagged along for a drink. It was all very friendly and informal.

This was a slightly larger town and rather more attractive than Corcubion or Cee. At the wharf was a sailing cargo vessel carrying a load of bricks which were being brought ashore by hardworking local women who carried them in baskets on their heads, up a ramp, across the street and into a building. They were laughing and appeared to be happy as they did it which amazed us as it seemed like darned hard work. We soon learned that a feature of Spain is hordes of boys. Nice kids, but something of a nuisance because they mostly didn't go to school and had too much time on their hands. They would follow us around like we were the Pied Piper and were especially attracted to our dinghy when we came ashore. They seemed to have no concept of the meaning of the word "no", especially as it pertains to playing in the dinghy and visiting aboard *Armorel*.

Jane tries the local laundromat in Corcubion, Spain

One evening while at Muros we walked to a tiny village nearby to attend the Fiesta de San Juan (lots of fiestas in Spain). It was after dark, of course, and the festivities occupied the length of the little main street. There was a large bon fire, a miniature Ferris Wheel big enough for four and a tiny merry-go-round (both hand-pushed), plus ice cream, beer and firecrackers sold on the street. At 10 P.M. an orchestra set up on one side of the street and began to play. Soon dancing commenced on the dusty, stony street, which we joined with enthusiasm. It was quite a lively scene.

Before leaving Muros the next day, we bought a case of excellent Spanish brandy ($1.00 a bottle) We were learning to adapt our taste in liquor to match the local stuff. The *Terry Brandy* was fine and came in an attractive bottle with a gold mesh covering it. Later, in the West Indies we found the best Barbados rum for 75 cents a bottle and even better, in Mexico we enjoyed *Oso Negro* gin for 65 cents a bottle (including a little black bear on a key chain). We also acquired a couple of wicker-covered demi-johns and kept them filled with red and white wines we selected at the local *bodega* while we were in Spain. With booze at these prices, I can see that it would be easy to become alcoholic but in truth, we were quite moderate drinkers. We even found that having a glass of wine for lunch was too much of a soporific so took up the Spanish custom of adding fruit juice to make a nice *sangria*. We also astonished many Spaniards who came aboard and discovered that none of us smoked.

The last of the five rias is Ria de Vigo, the site of the small city of Vigo, a sort of miniature version of San Francisco, situated on hills rising from the Bay with cute little tram cars running up the streets. We anchored in front of the impressive Real Club De Yates (Royal Yacht Club) and rowed ashore. As soon as we stepped onto the quay, the club secretary stepped out of the very impressive building and greeted us warmly, grandly waving his arm toward the Club and saying "This is your home." He had the club register in his arms and wished us to sign in immediately. We were impressed.

He invited us to join the members that evening for a dinner dance, an invitation we readily accepted. We assumed the dance would be following dinner, and since Spaniards eat quite late, we were sure we would have plenty of time to take showers and get dressed. By the time we leisurely returned to the clubhouse in our best clothes it was about 8 o'clock and we learned the dinner dance was long since over. There was no mention of a dinner at the club. Obviously something had gotten lost in translation.

When we arrived at the yacht club, we noticed that there lines of cork floats laid out to form lanes for a swimming race which took place in the early evening. About this time we also became aware of a foul smell around the boat where we were anchored and realized that we (and the swimming area) were awfully close to a large sewage outfall. We moved the boat a respectable distance away from the sewer pipe to get away from the smell, but we certainly had to admire the hardy constitution of the local swimmers.

A small American ketch named *Gitano* was anchored off the club, the first yacht we had seen since leaving England. It was owned by Jim Scott of Fresno who had the hull built in Britain and finished up the rig and interior himself. He was sailing with Rex Wright, a friend from San Francisco. Like us, they planned to sail for the Mediterranean and eventually cross the Atlantic. We were to more or less sail in company with them for the remainder of the summer.

The hospitality of the yacht club and the little city of Vigo were nice, but we soon moved over to the other side of the bay to a cleaner and more peaceful anchorage at the tiny village of Con. The whole setting was made interesting by a book we had aboard named "The Treasure Divers of Vigo Bay." It describes a famous battle between a Spanish treasure fleet and a Dutch squadron in 1699 in which gold-laden Spanish ships, which had just returned from America, were trapped in the bay by the Dutch. While the Spaniards worked desperately to unload the ship's treasure and take it inland by mule train, the Dutch broke the chain boom protecting the Spanish ships and engaged in a furious battle, sinking and burning the entire Spanish fleet. Some believe that much treasure remains on the bottom. We met the author of the book in nearby Bayona where he had been diving on a Spanish ship which was believed to have been sunk at the entrance to the bay while trying to escape. To my knowledge, they were unsuccessful in recovering any gold.

Our final anchorage in the Rias was at Bayona, just outside Vigo Bay. It was a perfectly protected spot, a sort of bay-within-a-bay. There was a picturesque stone castle with crenellated walls overlooking the cove and a quaint little town ashore, all set within wooded hills. We celebrated July 4th in delightful sunny weather here with our American friends on *Gitano* and the American author/diver, John Potter. It was a splendid little anchorage and a good departure point from Spain for our sail down the Portuguese coast toward Gibraltar.

We stopped overnight at the fishing port of Leixoes (pronounced approximately like lay-so-engeh) and entered Portugal with much paperwork and formalities at the police station. At the time Portugal was under the iron rule of strongman, Antonio Salazar. We were enchanted with the colorful fishing boats and the lively activity of the fishermen but were a little intimidated by the officialdom. Soon were on our way down the coast in a fine wind bound for the Tagus River and the resort town of Cascais at its entrance.

Cascais had an imposing yacht club, a spacious anchorage and a spic-and-span town of pretty buildings and beautiful houses. We anchored among the many fishing boats and were welcomed at the yacht club. There were, however, no other yachts to be seen until our friends on *Gitano* arrived the next day. We took the spotless little electric train to see the capital, Lisbon, some miles up the Tagus River and generally were enjoying ourselves a lot until tragedy struck one night. After dark, when we were in bed, we heard our little black kitty, Dart, scampering around on deck as she often did. Next morning she was nowhere to be found. We think she just got going too fast and ran off the end of the boat. We searched the beaches and inquired amongst the fish boats for a sign of her but without luck. It was a dark event and Jane spent the day in tears. Little Dart had become the fifth member of the crew and was the source of endless entertainment and fun and now she was gone.

The steady northwesterly winds which blow down the coast of Portugal are often called the "Portuguese Trades" and they lived up to their reputation on our way to Gibraltar. We sailed in company with *Gitano* who struggled to keep up with us in spite of using her impressive squaresail. We both bowled along in brilliant sunshine for three days with a strong following wind and steep seas until we rounded Cape Trafalgar and closed with the Straits. It was a thrill to make out the unmistakable shape of the famed Rock of Gibraltar. This was exactly the kind of experience we hoped to have when we planned the trip.

On the advice of yachtsmen in England, we had written to the Queen's Harbormaster in "Gib" for permission to tie up in the Naval Dockyard as there were no civilian marinas or wharfs for yachts there at the time. We had received a reply in a tan official envelope, marked "On Her Majesty's Service", informing us that we were welcome. When we arrived we were assigned a berth at the Commercial Quay inside the massive walls of the dockyard and settled in to enjoy this unique maritime community which was a blend of Britain, Spain, Africa and most especially, Malta. It reeked with history and it was fascinating to explore the narrow streets of the town and the tunnels and fortifications of all ages on "The Rock". Gibraltar was also a crossroads for yachts entering and leaving the Mediterranean and those on voyages in the Atlantic. Our nearest neighbor was a large Norwegian salvage tug with a friendly crew patiently waiting for the inevitable call from a ship in distress. On July 23rd, our day of departure, I visited the harbormaster to pay our very modest port dues. When he asked when we might be coming out in the fall, I made a guess by saying about October 6th. He welcomed us to come back.

Sailing down the coast of Portugal in company with our friends, Jim Scott and Rex Wright on Gitano

It was our plan to spend the summer in the Mediterranean, going as far east as time permitted, then return to Gibraltar to begin our Atlantic crossing after the threat of hurricanes had passed in the fall. Originally we had dreamed of going as far as the French or Italian Riviera but now realized that a more logical destination would be the Balearic Islands, about 550 miles away, a goal which would give us time for the leisurely cruising we craved. As we started along the south coast of Spain a dramatic change in the weather and sea took place. Gone were the chilly, windy days of the Atlantic, replaced by sunny, warm, mostly calm days and the deep blue of the Mediterranean Sea.

We left the massive bulk of Gibraltar astern and sailed smoothly along the south coast of Spain. We exchanged our woolen sailing clothes for shorts and swimming suits and at times towed behind the boat hanging onto the end of the main sheet. We stopped each night at an interesting Spanish town, a nice change from our day-and-night passages in the Atlantic.

At the end of eight days (including four days in Cartagena), we entered the harbor at Alicante, a good-sized city on the east coast. We moored with our stern to the quay ("med style"), set the large awning and sat back to observe the life around us. Most noticeable was the heat. It was really hot. Luckily, we shipped over a big white awning I had sewn up in Sausalito. It seemed to create its own breeze underneath and made a huge difference in our comfort level. Our next surprise were the Gypsies. We had first encountered them in northern Spain one day while walking in the countryside when we came upon a picture-perfect Gypsy encampment complete with colorful clothing and little, gaily painted covered wagons. I had no idea they still lived in Europe in such a seemingly storybook lifestyle. On the Alicante waterfront, however, they were of the pestiferous urban variety, apparently harmless, but relentless in their begging for money and their offers of dubious services. We were not moored in the best part of town and eventually moved the boat well out from the quaywall for privacy and security.   Otherwise we found Alicante to be a busy, interesting and friendly city.

Phil and Pete took advantage of our proximity to Madrid to make a side trip by train to the capitol for few days. This was a nice break for Jane and me to have some time aboard to ourselves. Upon their return, we headed east for the Balearic Islands, about 100 miles away, where we were to spent the rest of the summer.

We made our landfall at Puerto Antonio, on the island of Ibiza, the southernmost of the three main Balearic Islands. It was a bit of a tourist trap, so we left as soon as possible and found a cozy little cove named Puerto San Miguel. It was big enough for only one or two boats, had an ancient watchtower overlooking the anchorage and had a narrow path leading to the tiny village about a half-mile inland. It was so charming we stayed for a week and never saw another boat or visitor ashore. We varnished the brightwork (we had lots of it), tried our hand at fishing (without success), hiked ashore and generally enjoyed the relaxed solitude. After a brief visit in the village of Portinaitx, where we took in a local festival and had a wonderful dinner ashore, it was on to Palma de Majorca, the yachting capitol of the Balearic Islands.

We tied up at the Club De Yates, an impressive facility with a large, beautiful clubhouse, marina and boatyard. We understood that it was one of the largest yacht clubs anywhere with about 9000 members, mostly non-resident, on its books. They were very hospitable and assigned us a spot to moor, (Med-style). We also got a date to haul out the boat on the club slipway. The bottom was getting a bit foul and needed a coat of anti-fouling paint, but more importantly, the propeller shaft bearing needed attention because of the excessive leakage which was taking place. The club shipyard crew hauled us and took care of our needs with great efficiency and at minimal cost. I think it was the first time I had actually enjoyed having my boat hauled out.

The leakage problem was caused by loose packing around the shaft which could only be adjusted from outside, in the water. On our way from Gibraltar the bilge water got so high one night when we were under power, that water got up to the flywheel and threw salt water all over the starter and generator, putting them out of action permanently.. This would have been serious indeed on most boats but *Armorel's* motor could easily be started by hand, and with magneto ignition, needed no electricity to run. Power for lighting could be generated by our little ex-Sherman tank auxiliary generator. We sailed the remainder of the trip with this arrangement.

Palma de Majorca was a lovely city with a magnificent cathedral nearby, pretty wooded hills, and a large central boulevard shaded by huge trees. The waterfront adjacent to the yacht club was home to a fleet of large, picturesque cargo schooners which were a delight to look at and were undoubtedly the last of a dying breed. Another fixture was the net menders who repaired fishing nets on the quay. In the background were several ancient windmills which had long since ceased to function, but were nice to see. But best of all, was the low cost of everything, including very nice quality leather and woolen goods. Food and restaurant meals were ridiculously cheap. A complete steak dinner with wine was only $1.25 and the price of fresh produce in the huge market was virtually nothing. We attended a bullfight which we mostly enjoyed for the drama of the thing. Our friends on *Gitano* arrived, which gave us opportunity to discuss our adventures over cocktails and meals ashore.

After two delightful weeks in Palma we departed for a circular voyage around Majorca with stops at several interesting and snug anchorages. At Cala Gran we encountered a movie set where a sea drama was being filmed using a sistership to the *Romayne*, the old Canadian yacht which had wintered in Sausalito. We anchored nearby and became friends with some of the film crew including the cameraman, Lenny South. He was a very experienced cinematographer and had filmed most of Alfred Hitchcock's pictures. Lenny was quite disgusted with the current project and over cocktails on *Armorel* would regale us with stories about how screwed up everything was. The film was being made in 3-D and, from the tales we heard, seemed doomed to be a dud. It opened in San Francisco shortly after our return under the name *September Storm* and closed after only a few days.

Our last stop on our little circumnavigation of Majorca was at Puerto Soller, which I still consider the perfect harbor. It was a small circular bay with ideal protection, set in a ring of mountains. We moored to a small concrete quay in water so clear we could see our anchor easily in 50' of water. The town of Soller was located several miles inland (for protection from pirates in the old days) and was connected to the port by a tiny "Toonerville Trolley." We entertained a couple of young Belgium girls, one of whom was delighted for a chance to practice her English. We corresponded with Greta, who later became a high court judge, for many years until her untimely death in 2004. In spite of the beauty of the place, we knew we should move on. It was now September 5th and the summer was coming to an end.

We returned to Palma for a few days to get organized for our passage to Gibraltar and took a berth alongside the big, 118' schooner, *Zaca*, which had been built in Sausalito in 1930 and was then owned by Errol Flynn. It looked to be in fair shape but was definitely showing her age. A pleasant young American couple was aboard who explained that Flynn had loaned them the yacht for a short cruise in the Mediterranean. They were working hard to prepare the boat and to receive friends who would be their crew. The next morning, with long faces, they informed us that they had received word that Flynn had died the night before (in bed with a young lady) and the trip was off.

On the way back to Gibraltar we stopped again in Cartagena to renew our acquaintance with an American military couple stationed at the USAF base there and to take advantage of their offer to take us to the PX (a source of rarely-found peanut butter). While there, they presented us with a black and white replacement kitty who we named "Scupper". She was a tough little Spanish cat with a zest for life who survived the entire voyage back to Sausalito.

As we neared Gibraltar in the middle of a black night, we found ourselves in the midst of a horrendous electrical storm with lightning bolts striking the sea all around us. To me, there is nothing more worrisome than lightning at sea, knowing that our mast is the only thing sticking up and by far the best target for a stray bolt. After getting past the storm, we approached the Naval Dockyard in the dark and were hailed by a navy launch who called, "Ahoy. What boat?" When we answered, "American yacht *Armorel*," they replied, "Right O, follow us. We've been expecting you." I was flabbergasted then realized it was October 6th, the day I had told the harbormaster we might be back.

We took up our old berth at the Commercial Quay along with *Gitano* and a small British ketch named *Raider*. She was a little double ender about 30' long with a gaff rig and an open (non self-draining) cockpit. We had seen her earlier in the summer and had met her owner, a quiet, competent chap named Colin Gallon who intended to sail to the West Indies. When we asked him if the boat's open cockpit worried him, he replied, "Well, the boat has sailed for forty years in the English Channel, and I'm sure the trade wind passage across the Atlantic will not have conditions nearly as severe." Unfortunately it was a misjudgment which was to have tragic consequences. Colin was in Gibraltar with an American girl named Harriet Benton who had been traveling around Europe with a girlfriend on their Vespa scooters. Harriet had decided to sell her scooter and join Colin for the trip across the Atlantic.

Jane had become so accustomed to our life aboard *Armorel* that she had completely forgotten her misgivings about another ocean crossing and the plan for her to take a ship or plane across to meet the boat in the West Indies. The subject just never came up so we sailed across the Strait of Gibraltar to Tangier and entered the harbor to be surrounded by boatmen waving soiled letters of recommendation and shouting for us to avail ourselves of their services as our watchman. We moored, stern to the rocky mole, and asked the owner of an old subchaser, which was obviously a smuggling boat, if it was wise to hire one of those characters to be a watchman. His reply spoke volumes about the place. "If you don't hire one of them, they will steal the nails right out of your hull." We took his advice and engaged a piratical-looking fellow who actually was well worth the $4 a day we paid him. He not only slept *on top of* the companionway hatch at night, he watched the boat by day and ferried us between the boat and the shore. Tangier was a fascinating place, particularly the Casbah, but I must admit I was a bit uneasy there. When an east wind (a *levanter*) came up the next afternoon we decided to cut our visit short and bailed out.

A six-day passage in moderate northerly winds took us to Las Palmas on the island of Gran Canaria in the Canary Islands. We anchored off the yacht club in the midst of several sailboats planning to make a transatlantic crossing. There was an American schooner named *Mystic*, which had been waiting for months; a small folkboat-style sloop named *Jellicle*, whose owner, Mike Bayles, had a gimbaled bunk (it didn't work); an old ketch named *Si Ye Pambili* crewed by five Rhodesian bobbies; an English schooner, *Penella,* with a retired couple on their way to Australia; and about four more of various nationalities. They were an interesting group and we got to know all of them as we compared notes and stories.

A couple of days after our arrival in Las Palmas, Peter Tangvald, a well known single-handed sailor, arrived on *Dorothea* from Casablanca. He immediately asked us if we had seen anything of Colin Gallon on *Raider*. He was concerned because *Raider* had left Casablanca a day ahead of him and he feared for her safety, because on his second day at sea, in a severe wind, he had been pooped (flooded from astern) by a big breaking wave. Peter said he was not sure *Raider*, with her open cockpit, would have survived a similar incident. During the remainder of our stay at Las Palmas we watched anxiously for the little gaffer to show up but without luck. Later on the other side of the Atlantic we saw Peter again and heard more details. It seems Peter had been sent a newspaper clipping about a missing American girl on a British boat. The story was very garbled with the British yachtsman named as a retired Army officer, who was obviously Colin's father. The article did, however, give the name and address of Harriet Benton in upstate New York. In order to at least straighten out the story, we wrote to Harriet's parents and told them of our meeting them in Gibraltar, Colin's identity, and even a photo of Colin and *Raider* plus other details we thought might help. Later we received a very sad letter from the Bentons thanking us and asking if Harriet was happy when we last saw her.

*   *   *   *

We enjoyed our eight-day stay in the Canary Islands, but were anxious to begin our Atlantic crossing. So on October 25, 1959 we weighed our anchor, waved goodbye to our friends, stopped briefly at a small beach to get a supply of sand for Scupper's sandbox then set sail towards the west with Barbados 2,700 nautical miles ahead.

Our strategy was to drop south to pass fairly close to the Cape Verde Islands, then when we had picked up the trade winds, head directly west for the West Indies. It was the usual route taken by sailing ships since the days of Columbus. We had nice breezes from aft almost from the start and beautiful weather all the way across. In fact, it was a dream crossing. It seemed like the wind would blow nicely for several days, then lighten up for a few days before picking up again. We spread every stitch of canvass we could, with our usual rig being the full mainsail, a genoa jib poled out to windward, a jib and staysail set to leeward and a watersail under the long main boom.

The transatlantic sailors: me with Scupper, Jane, Bob Petersen, Phil Price

We did not have an autopilot or windvane steering gear, but we soon learned that *Armorel*, with her long raking keel, needed very little help from us to hold a straight course. It was not unusual for us to lash the wheel and all go below for a leisurely meal with the boat sailing as if she were on rails. One small problem became apparent immediately, however. Cotton sails and galvanized rigging wire do not get along well together with the sails pressed against the rigging and the boat rolling heavily. We set to work and soon had the shrouds covered with the traditional "baggywrinkle" from top to bottom. This was easily made from short strands of manila rope and marlin, which were then wrapped around the rigging wire. It stopped the chafe and gave the boat a fine seagoing appearance. Nowadays smooth stainless wire and tough dacron sailcloth have made the technique extinct.

Another problem soon became known as well. Phil had sported a magnificent set of red whiskers ever since the cruise started. When he shaved them off one day we were shocked. After a day or so he admitted that the reason he had taken such drastic action was because his body hair was infested with crabs, which he presumed he had picked up in the showers at the Las Palmas Yacht Club. We got out our copy of *The Ship's Medicine Chest and First Aid At Sea*, the green book found on all merchant ships, with lurid color photos of ghastly venereal diseases, and looked up crabs. The recommended cure was to dust the victim liberally with DDT and roll him up in blanket for several hours while the critters died. It just happened that we had a supply of DDT for Scupper's fleas, so poor Phil was stripped, doused and rolled. We thought it was hilarious. Phil thought otherwise, but it worked.

Armorel under full sail in mid-Atlantic as seen by the crew of Penella on our 10 th day.
Note the watersail under the boom and the baggyywrinkle on the rigging.

On our 10th day at sea we spotted a sail on the horizon ahead of
us. As we got closer, we recognized it as *Penella,* a 40' English
schooner owned by Leigh and Dorie Rankin, a middle-aged couple
bound for Australia to visit their son. Leigh was a retired Royal Air
Force officer who had taken up sailing only recently. Their introduction to ocean sailing had nearly ended in disaster when they encountered a series of severe gales off the North African coast and had to be
towed into Casablanca with severe damage to the rig and steering gear.
They had left Las Palmas a whole week ahead of us, which meant that
we were going almost twice as fast as they were. The difference in
speed had mostly to do with the fact that they were sailing with only a
pair of twin staysails and were more short-handed than we were. Certainly *Armorel* was no racing boat, but we were carrying a lot more
sail and we were sailing with a full crew. It was a big surprise to come
upon another sailboat in the middle of the ocean and we were quite
excited to see them. We shortened sail to match their speed and sailed
alongside for awhile, then made full sail again and left them in our
wake. They eventually arrived in Barbados about seven days after us.
She was the only vessel of any kind we saw on the entire crossing.

We tried fishing all the way across by towing a line astern with
various lures. Our only catch was a snake mackerel, an unappealing
eel-like fish with long sharp teeth. We didn't try eating it, but Scupper
eagerly gobbled her share. The cat was always on the lookout for fish,
especially at night. She would prowl the decks for flying fish which
often hit the cabin or sails and landed on deck. This was fine except,
for some reason, she would try to sneak them below and devour them
in Jane's bunk. Jane quickly learned to do a "fish check" when she got
off night watch and retired to bed.

As we neared Barbados, I checked and rechecked my celestial
navigation. Finally I announced that we should raise land the next
morning, on our 21st day at sea. That afternoon a tropic bird with brilliant white plumage and a marlinspike tail appeared and circled our
masthead, a sure sign of the proximity of land. At 1000 the next morning we sighted land ahead. What a thrill. To have GPS these days is
nice, but it has taken all the excitement away. For real satisfaction,
give me a good old fashioned landfall, made with celestial navigation
and dead reckoning. Our taffrail log showed 2,760 miles as we sailed

into Carlisle Bay at Bridgetown on November 15, 1959 and dropped the anchor off the Aquatic Club, a funky little bar on the end of a pier.

Jane has success on her second attempt to bake bread

Our arrival in Barbados marked the beginning of an extremely pleasant two and a half month cruise in the West Indies. We had chosen our landfall because it was at the eastern end of the islands, making our route mostly downwind with easy sailing. After a week in Barbados we sailed overnight to the island of Bequia in the Grenadine Group. Then we continued up the chain of Windward and Leeward Islands, stopping at nearly every one. By Christmas we had arrived at English Harbor on Antigua. We moored to the quay in Lord Nelson's old dockyard along with three or four other boats which had sailed across the Atlantic. We were in high spirits with a major portion of the voyage behind us, and it was wonderful to compare stories and celebrate the holidays with friends.

Our cruise in the West Indies in 1959-60 was at an ideal time. Almost all of the former British colonies in the West Indies from

Trinidad to Jamaica had organized themselves into the West Indies Federation the previous year. It was a time of great optimism amongst the islanders and there was a uniformity of formalities which made it easy to travel from island to island with little fuss. Unfortunately, the federation fell apart only a couple of years later, in 1962. Maybe we were just naïve, but we enjoyed all the natives we met and sensed no hostility or unpleasantness anywhere we went.

Unlike the Mediterranean, we found the islands to be an underwater wonderland. The water was warm and clear and full of fish and colorful coral. We acquired snorkels, fins, facemasks and spear guns and spent a lot of time in the water. Of course, Scupper grew sleek on her share of the fish and langouste we brought aboard. Jane even found a recipe for Moray Eel poached in beer. The sailing was wonderful too. Except of the occasional light airs in the lee of the islands, there were none of the calms we encountered in the Med. Mostly we had rollicking sails between the islands in the kind of wind that *Armorel* loved.

When we were in Martinique, Jane treated herself to a pair of gold earrings. This called for having her ears pierced, something she had always been tempted to do. The jeweler sent her to the dusty little workshop of a goldsmith, an imposing and handsome black man, who readily agreed to carry out the operation with what appeared to be a sharpened bicycle spoke. (Jane said it looked more like a #3 knitting needle.) He simply passed the spoke through a Bunsen burner flame, held a freshly cut potato behind her ear lobe and pushed it through. A little alcohol was swabbed on, a pair of "trainer rings" was inserted and the process was complete.

Although there were no outward sign of infection, there was apparently some from the ear piercing because by the time we got to the Virgin Islands, she noticed a hard lump under one arm. The doctor at the St. Thomas Hospital said it was a swollen lymph node and said it should be removed. Jane spent a couple of days in the hospital in a room with two very pleasant native women and recovered nicely. Jane later told how, when the lights were turned off and the room became dark, Christianita, a cheerful black woman with breast cancer, said softly, "Now we are all the same."

On February 26, 1960 we departed from St. Croix, Virgin Islands for Panama after a wonderful cruise through the West Indies.

Our non-stop sail to the Panama Canal took us seven days for the 1,117 mile passage (shortened considerably by the west-going current in our favor). The first night we had the hell scared out of us when a patrol plane appeared out of nowhere and centered us in an incredibly powerful spotlight. The Cuban Missile Crisis was a year and a half in the future, but obviously tensions were building as we sailed toward Cuba. The rest of the way to Panama was entirely uneventful with fresh trade winds on the stern and warm sunny skies by day and balmy nights.

In the West Indies, anchored off The Baths, Virgin Gorda

When we arrived off the breakwater at Christobal in the Canal Zone, we were greeted by a Canal Company launch with a customs man, a quarantine man who handed us a big bug bomb and an admeasurer who quickly calculated our net tonnage which determined our canal dues at $1 per net ton ($10 total.)   All of this was done while we were motoring into the harbor. It was a demonstration of efficiency. We took a berth at the Panama Canal Yacht Club and settled in for a two week stay at the friendly little club while we completed our canal passage formalities, purchased stores for the trip up the coast and hauled *Armorel* on the club slipway. This latter task almost turned into a disaster when Jane took off her engagement and wedding ring and put them in her shirt pocket to keep them clean on the day the boat was launched. As the cradle rolled down the ways she saw something sparkling in the water and yelled for the winch to stop. There were her rings on one of the timbers of the hauling cradle!

While at Panama, Pete received a message to call his employer, States Lines, offering him a job in Japan as assistant manager of the Tokyo office at an excellent salary with an apartment, car and maid thrown into the bargain. It was much too good an offer to turn down and besides we were all feeling that the trip was winding down with only one lap left to go. A couple of days later we saw Pete off as he boarded an airplane to his new career. He had been a wonderful crew and friend but on the other hand we really only needed one person in addition to Jane and me and there would be more room and less friction with only three of us aboard.

The day we transited the Canal was packed with interest and excitement. A canal pilot came aboard at 0830 and gave us the order to get underway. Fortunately we had managed to schedule our passage in company with a Canal Company tugboat which allowed us to lash alongside and let her take the bumps against the rough lock walls. This was important on the three upward locks when the tremendous volume of water entering the lock chamber from big orifices in the bottom causes immense turbulence with scary looking boils and swirls on the surface. Upon reaching the top of one lock, the tug, with *Armorel* clinging to her side, would simply move to the next lock. When we reached the level of Gatun Lake the pilot suggested we hoist sail and take the "Banana Cut", a shortcut behind several lush islands. By late afternoon we had been lowered via three locks to the level of the Pacific Ocean. We moved a couple of miles to the west and picked up a mooring off the Balboa Yacht Club at Panama City. It had been quite a day!

Unfortunately a few days later when approaching a dock I misjudged the fast-moving current and hit the dock heavily with the bobstay, pulling the bottom eyebolt, at the stem, out of position. This was potentially a serious weakness so we scheduled a brief haulout on the club slipway to examine the damage and make a repair. While up on the slipway, Scupper (who seemed to be in heat) decided to take unauthorized shore leave and disappeared. We relaunched the boat the next day and spent an anxious time searching for the cat. That night we found her on the bow of the next boat hauled out, meowing loudly.

Entering Galliard Cut in the Panama Canal

We sailed out of Panama Bay on February 24th with San Francisco 3650 miles ahead. I had been dreading the trip up the Pacific Coast ever since the voyage started. It had hung over the whole enterprise like a dark cloud with the expectation of endless headwinds and difficulty. As it turned out, I need not have worried. What I hadn't realized was that for the first third of the trip, the wind mostly blew up the coast, and to help us along there was a north-going current. There were a couple of places in this stretch we had to be concerned about including the Gulf of Papagayo and the Gulf of Tehuantepec where very strong offshore winds can kick up, but mostly it was easy going for a long way.

On our first night out of the Canal we very nearly lost the boat while we were crossing the Gulf of Panama toward Cape Mala. Phil was on watch in the wee hours when he woke me up to tell me that he could see the loom of the Cape Mala lighthouse on the port (left) side of the boat. Obviously a current had set us to the north so I told him to just alter course to put the light on the starboard (right) side. What I should have done was to plot the reciprocal of the new course from Cape Mala on the chart. If I had done so, I would have seen that it took us right over an island. About an hour later I heard Phil rushing about on deck, starting the engine and gybing the boat. Phil was always a very alert watch keeper so I knew something was badly amiss as I jumped out of my bunk and scrambled up on deck. He told me breathlessly that he had seen the dim outline of the island and white breakers right in front of the boat, leaving him barely enough time to maneuver out of danger. I learned a vital lesson: Always. Always. Draw a new course on the chart to be sure it runs clear of danger.

We stopped for a couple of days in Costa Rica at the little banana port of Golfito, where we became acquainted with two American expatriates living on the beautiful little beach opposite the anchorage (they weren't speaking to each other), and then carried on non-stop for Mexico. One day as we were sailing slowly along the coast of Nicaragua, Phil spotted a dugout canoe drifting ahead of us. It was a rather large one and appeared to be quite new. It was about 18' long and was obviously very heavy. We surmised that it had probably blown off a beach in an offshore wind. Phil insisted in getting a line on it and taking it in tow, heaven knows to where. We weren't sailing very fast and there was a swell coming up from the south so naturally the canoe kept running up and bumping *Armorel's* stern. This was clearly unacceptable (to me anyway) so after several hours Phil regretfully cast it loose.

The scenery along the coast of Nicaragua was quite spectacular with many active volcanoes in view, some of them puffing smoke out of their pointed summits. We were making slow but steady progress, almost entirely under sail. During the day an onshore sea breeze would usually build to a decent sailing wind by afternoon and then abruptly die after sundown. In an hour or two a soft offshore breeze would usually begin and carry us smoothly along until sunup, when it would die and the cycle would start again. All the while, a north-going current added to our daily mileage. We were a bit apprehensive about the Gulf of Tehuantepec and had planned, or at least hoped, that we would have a bright moon during our crossing of the Gulf so that we could safely hug the beach at night. As it happened, we had a full moon and happily we did not encounter any strong offshore wind as we had feared.

Off the coast of Nicaragua we encounter a drifting dugout canoe

That night when Jane was on watch, she excitedly awakened both Phil and me and told us to quickly come topside. She had been sailing along under the brilliant moon when she suddenly realized the lights had gone out and that she was witnessing a full eclipse of the moon which now looked like a piece of dull orange construction paper pasted into the black sky. I must confess that Phil and I weren't too excited about it, but to this day Jane considers it one of the more memorable experiences of the whole trip.

On our 14th day out of Panama, we entered Mexico at the tiny fishing village of Puerto Angel. We were now at the top of the Gulf of Tehuantepec and the entire system of winds and currents changed abruptly. The halcyon days of drifting along with the flow now became one of bucking the prevailing wind and wind-driven current.

Not that we necessarily had a lot of wind on our nose, it was mostly a case of seeing a marked drop in our daily progress especially on days when we had only light breezes. *Armorel* was a heavy cruising boat with a modest rig and thus was no flyer to windward especially in light airs and the Britt engine began to get some heavy use. We had put aboard a large deck load of 200 gallons of gasoline in cans and a couple of small barrels in Panama and now began to use it up. At the same time we found that the motor would gradually begin to lose power. We correctly diagnosed the problem to be a build-up of carbon which would cause the cylinders to pre-ignite from the glowing carbon and subsequent burning of the valve surfaces. Phil and I became expert at removing the heads (there were two of them with 2 cylinders each), scraping off the carbon, touching up the valve seats with grinding compound and reassembling the works, all in an hour or so. On a couple of occasions we even did this operation at sea. It seems the basic problem was that the engine had no thermostat and was running too cold. We were quite proud of ourselves that we managed to keep this problem under control without professional help.

At last we entered Acapulco, a major milestone, being roughly the half way point between Panama and San Francisco. We were given a berth at the Club de Yates which had recently moved to the west side of the bay and had built a striking new clubhouse and modern marina. In 1960 Acapulco was still a spectacularly lovely city and we were thrilled to be there. Ultra modern hotels lined the shore and crowned the hills along with homes of striking design. The downtown waterfront was clean and had only modest traffic on the bayside boulevard. At night the bay and surrounding slopes sparkled with light.

Our old shipmate and friend, Dick Simon, who we had invited to join us for a few weeks, soon appeared with, predictably, a pretty stewardess named Ann he had met on the plane. After purchasing fresh things from the open air market, filling our tanks with bottled water and hauling cans of gas from the filling station across the street, we headed out of Acapulco Bay in the evening, heading north in a flat calm.

One of the jobs I had undertaken while in Acapulco was to try to have the generator on the motor restored to life after its drenching in salt water early in the trip. The Mexicans are famous for being able to fix anything and I had no trouble in finding a little repair shop who agreed to undertake the rebuilding job. I picked up the repaired generator and installed it just before we left. Once we got underway I was pleased to note that it was putting out lots of juice but was puzzled by the fact that it showed discharge. After about two hours I noted that the generator was awfully hot, so I disconnected it. A couple of days later, Phil was swimming around the boat and said I better take a look at the propeller. What I saw was a prop resembling the fluted edges of a pie crust. On further inspection I noted that all the bronze thru-hull fittings had large indentations. Yikes! The generator, instead of pumping juice into the batteries, had been pumping it into the water. Apparently the polarity of the thing had been reversed in the repair process. What a good thing I had disconnected it.

In spite of the minor problem with the generator, we were in a frame of mind to slow down and enjoy our cruising in Mexico. We felt we were definitely on the last lap before home and additionally were pleased to have fresh faces aboard, especially Dick with his zest for new experiences and delightful sense of humor. An overnight passage from Acapulco brought us to the picturesque little village of Zihuatenejo and the adjacent island of Isla Grande, both of which we explored at leisure. While wandering around the dusty streets of village, Dick stubbed his toe and knocked off a toenail, an incident which was to have a near-disastrous ending a couple of weeks later. We said goodbye to Ann, Dick's pick-up friend, and continued our pleasant cruise up the coast.

Within a few days we arrived at Banderas Bay and anchored off the tiny Mexican Indian settlement of Yelapa. Although the anchorage was far from perfect (a deep, rocky bottom) the place was a delight. We had been told there was a waterfall and pool above the village and as soon as we landed on the beach a small boy named Rafael insisted on showing us the path and leading us there. It was a little paradise with a clear cool stream tumbling over a small cliff into a lovely basin surrounded by boulders. After nearly a year craving for unlimited fresh water, we felt in heaven and spent a portion of each day there.

On the beach was a ramshackle little bar/restaurant where Dick soon met a trio of off-beat American gals, art students from San Miguel de Allende, plus a raffish British expatriate named John Langley.

He claimed to be a concert violinist who was down on his luck and who now lived in a tiny thatched house he had built on the hillside. With this cast of characters, Dick devised a dinner party ashore after which the entire group stumbled in the dark up the rutted road to John's rustic abode for more drinks of the local moonshine served in jelly jars. The next night the whole troupe assembled again aboard *Armorel* for a spaghetti dinner and a sing-song under the stars.

After a brief stop at Puerto Vallarta we proceeded to Mazatlan where Dick planned to fly home. By this time his toe with the missing toenail was obviously infected. We had a reasonably good medical chest aboard which had been assembled by Clint Hanger, a sailing friend who worked for a drug company. It included a supply of penicillin and syringes. Moreover, I had been instructed by Ann, the Canadian nurse on *Romayne,* on the art of giving shots in the bum and was eager to try my skill. Dick readily agreed, even insisting we take a photo of the procedure. When he arrived back in San Francisco he was feeling very sick and upon consulting a doctor learned that he was allergic to penicillin and easily could have died from the shot. When I found out about it, my brief career as amateur doctor came to an abrupt and final stop.

We sailed across the Gulf for Cabo San Lucas which in 1960 was just a small dusty village and a fishboat pier extending out from the shore. We took on fuel and headed up the coast of Baja. To our surprise, we found that we were freezing in the suddenly lowered temperatures. Of course, we had just come from almost a year in the tropics and had few warm clothes aboard. Phil reckoned that our blood had all turned to beet juice in the tropics. On night watches, a favorite tactic was to open the engine room hatch under the cockpit floor and stand on the engine for warmth as we motored along.

After a brief stop in Turtle Bay for gas, we continued on, finally coming to a stop at the north end of Cedros Island to take shelter before crossing the notoriously windy patch between Cedros and San Carlos. We noticed a Mexican fishing camp ashore opposite the boat and soon a couple of fishermen in a skiff came alongside to ask if we would trade rum for lobsters. When we said "S*eguro!*" they zoomed off and returned with a huge lobster trap full of langouste and several gunny sacks of the Mexican equivalent of abalone. Our offer of a bottle of rum was met with dismay and the question *"Una botella solo-*

mente?" In our fractured Spanish we tried to explain that there were only three of us and we had no refrigeration. We could tell that they were going to endure some tough questioning from their pals ashore but in the end they understood and selected three nice little lobsters and a suitable pile of abalone for us and departed with a smile.

Three days later we entered the USA at the San Diego Customs dock, then moved to a berth at the hospitable San Diego Yacht Club. On the assumption that we would probably be too distracted to get the boat looking good when we got back to Sausalito, we decided to give her a paint and varnish job while at San Diego and in less than a week we had her shining from stem to stern. Then it was on to Newport Beach where we met our old friend, Dwight Long, the circumnavigator and author who now owned a jewelry store on "Main Street" in the newly-opened Disneyland theme park. At his insistence, we spent a delightful day in nearby Anaheim visiting the place. For sure, we were now back in California.

We offered to take Dwight along with us for a few days, an offer he readily accepted. We stopped at Catalina Island and Santa Cruz Island and on the third day dropped him off at Santa Barbara. He was good company, but in spite of his circumnavigation 25 years earlier, we sometimes wondered if he had ever actually learned to sail. It was a phenomenon I have seen frequently, wherein a person who has only sailed on his own boat and never benefited from the experience of others, especially while ocean racing with a crew of skilled sailors, never really becomes much of a sailor in spite of traveling long distances at sea.

At Santa Barbara Phil's father, Bill Price, joined us for the trip up the coast to San Francisco. He was a fine, soft spoken man who was eagerly anticipating his first ocean passage under sail. He had some limited sailing experience on San Francisco Bay and was under no illusions about the potential for a rough trip. We got underway in the morning and had a smooth sail under the lee of the land until we neared Point Conception in the late afternoon. It was obvious that it was blowing a gale beyond the Point so we retreated to Coxo Anchorage, just under the Point, set the anchor and waited until midnight for the wind to die down before starting again. There was still a gale of wind and a very rough sea the next day but we were able to struggle up to the open but reasonable shelter of Port San Luis Bay. After a day at anchor we tried again to head north in the middle of the night but were forced to retreat in the face of howling winds and breaking seas. In the end we spent four days waiting at Port San Luis for the winds to die down. Unfortunately, Bill had to return to work so he took the Greyhound Bus home. It was sad to see that he had been deprived of his sea voyage, but at least he had a memorable experience rounding the loathed and feared Point Conception. It was by far the most trying segment of the entire trip. In fact, it was the *only* rough part of the trip. Which was as it should be, since we had carefully planned to be in the best season for each part of the voyage, i.e. Summer in Europe, Fall after the hurricanes for the Atlantic crossing, Winter in the West Indies and Spring for the trip up from Panama. We were also very lucky.

On May 22, 1960, just a week short of a full year since our start, we sailed under the beautiful Golden Gate Bridge with the flags of the 17 countries we had visited flying from the rigging and 11,371 miles recorded in the log. We pulled into an empty slip at the Sausalito Yacht Harbor and had a joyous reunion with our family and friends. It was hard to believe we were back after such a wonderful and fulfilling experience. To this day we still sometimes refer to the *Armorel* voyage as "the trip". Until we had kids, it was the milestone in our life. And how fortunate we had been. We not only accomplished everything we set out to do but had done it in a lovely, comfortable boat with our best friends as crew.

We suddenly found that we were minor celebrities with articles about us in all the Bay Area newspapers and many visitors eager to talk with us asking a hundred questions about how to do it. I had made a 16mm film of the trip and we were much in demand to give a showing at just about all the yacht clubs in the area. It was even shown on TV on a show called "Golden Voyage" featuring amateur adventures, hosted by Bill Burred. Dwight Long, who dabbled in travel lectures, had made the connection for me so I boarded a Greyhound Bus with the film under my arm and traveled to Hollywood. I arrived at the studio in the morning and by noon it had been edited and spliced together. After lunch the music was picked out and at 7:00 PM I returned to the studio, met Mr. Burred, got a bit of make-up on and, bingo, I was on the air live! It was quite an experience and the check for $500 was nice too. About a year later we got a check in the mail for $150 as payment for a rerun. Thus ended my short career in Show Biz.

Scupper anticipating our return through the Golden Gate, May 22, 1960

Jane and I decided to continue the sub-rental of our flat and live aboard *Armorel* for the time being partly to save money to pay off our debt to Hugh Jacks. We installed a nice little wood burning cabin heater and changed our cooking stove to use propane. Our cat, Scupper, took to wandering away from the boat and was soon pregnant on a regular basis. In spite of the comfortable living quarters on the boat, the inexpensive lifestyle and the camaraderie of the other boat dwellers in the harbor, it was not a perfect life for me. I found that we almost never went sailing and suspected that we were getting just too much "boat". On the weekends our days were usually taken up with visitors who wanted to talk endlessly and I missed the anticipation of getting away from home and down to the harbor for a project, a race or a short cruise.

We knew we would have to sell *Armorel* at some point since it was obviously a much more elaborate and expensive yacht than a couple of young people of our means could reasonably afford to maintain. After a year of living aboard, a yacht broker friend came to us with an offer which would double what we paid for her so we reluctantly faced reality and agreed to sell. The first buyer needed only a year to find out that he didn't have the skill or time to maintain her. The next owner was Glen Yarborough, the tenor in *The Limelighters* group, a nice guy who owned the boat for 14 years. Next was a retired Navy man who sailed her on a two year cruise to South America. Presently she is owned by Bob Diecks an ex-Navy SEAL who has had her for over 25 years and has poured all of his time, love, and money into her. He wanted to know everything about her. He copied our movie and our log books and traveled to England to meet the widow of Sir Barry Heath who had sold *Armorel* to us. He even tracked down her origins by finding the son of the original owner, a gentleman who kept the small boatyard in Penarth, Wales in business all through the Depression by ordering a new yacht nearly every year. *Armorel* was the biggest, best and last of the line. The yard was bombed and burned early in the war. In 1999 Jane and I saw her at her homeport in Monganui, New Zealand and she looked beautiful. In my mind, she will always be beautiful.

The 26' yawl, Woodwind, reefed in breeze off Sausalito

CHAPTER 9

WOODWIND

While still living onboard *Armorel* in the summer of 1961, I was invited to sail in the Transpac Race aboard a new 45' yawl being built by the legendary sailor, boatbuilder and designer, Myron Spaulding, at his boatyard in Sausalito. She was named *Chrysopyle* and was owned by Dean Morrison of the St. Francis Yacht Club. There was some doubt as to whether the boat would be finished in time for the start of the race on July 4th so I and other members of the race crew pitched in whenever we had time to work along with Myron and his crew to try to finish the construction and get her launched. It was a real race against the calendar, but by late June she hit the water, the compass adjuster came aboard to swing the compass, food and fuel were hastily put aboard and we were off down the coast. We arrived in San Pedro only a day or two before the start.

I scarcely knew the owner, Dean Morrison, but had heard that he could be a difficult person because of his temper. Among the eight crew were three good friends, including Myron Spaulding, Dink Crawford, and Bill Clum, who I had crewed for on *Kialoa* in the '55 Transpac. Also aboard were Dean's son, Bruce, and another pair of young sailors with limited experience.

We got off to a decent start, but within a couple of days we started to have diminishing winds. Myron was the designated navigator, but he was obviously exhausted from the effort of getting the boat finished and had done nothing for the past three days to pinpoint our position. When questioned about it, his reply was, "Don't worry there will be plenty of time to navigate, right now just sail the course." By the fourth day, with still no effort to navigate by Myron, I got out my own sextant which I had brought along as a spare, and took a morning sun sight. I tried to get a "Sumner Line of Position", a calculation which would yield a line on the chart along which the yacht would be located. I could not make it work out based on our dead reckoning position as a starting point. Finally, by moving our assumed position further and further south, I was able to get a reasonable result. At noon I was able to cross the earlier line of position (advanced for our distance run) with a "Meridian Latitude" and knew we were about 200 miles south of where we thought we were. We had literally sailed ourselves out of the race!

Of course, there was endless discussion of how this could have happened. We were all capable helmsmen and had carefully sailed the compass headings Myron had given us. The problem turned out to be a 20 degree error in the compass in spite of the compass having been adjusted by Mr. Stevens, an expert, old time adjuster. It remained a mystery, but later I heard knowledgeable people say that a newly launched vessel must be turned around a few times before the compass is adjusted in order for the ship to acquire its natural magnetic signature. In our case the compass was "swung" right after launching with the boat being turned around just once. Maybe this was the problem.

About this same time we tried to start the engine to charge the batteries and found that there wasn't enough juice to make the starter work. This was a serious problem with no apparent solution until someone suggested we try to start it with a rope like an outboard motor. It turned out that there was a spare pulley on the front of the motor so we wound a rope around it, then led it up through a snatch block under the boom. The whole crew took hold of the rope, and at the signal of "One, two, three," we gave a great pull. *Viola!* It started.

As we neared the mid-point of the passage I was hoisted aloft in a bosun's chair to the top of the mainmast to change the spare wire spinnaker halyard (they seldom lasted the whole distance). We were sailing in a fresh trade wind with Dink at the wheel and with the boat rolling heavily. As I got to the top of the mast, Dink neglected to keep his eyes on the road (the compass) and instead started to look up at me. Inevitably, the boat went into a series of spectacular rolls with equally spectacular results.

The spinnaker pole dipped deeply into the sea causing a huge rush of water to burst the spinnaker like a water balloon. Then the boat took a giant roll the other way causing the main boom to dip deeply into the water and shatter with an explosive crash where it was held by the vang. Meanwhile I was going through at least 5G's at the top of the mast while hanging on for dear life. The owner went nuts!

We managed to strap some spare wood to the broken boom for an emergency repair in a few hours and set another spinnaker, but all of this didn't help our speed or our morale. During the entire race we were walking on eggs whenever the owner was on deck or whenever things weren't going just right, because of his unpredictable temper. It was an unhappy crew. We were probably going to finish at the back of the pack because of our navigational error early in the race and there was little enthusiasm aboard. Finally we crossed the finish line in the only ocean race I did not enjoy. As I recall, the boat was shipped home.

Later in the summer of 1961 we moved back into our old flat across from the waterfront at Sausalito. It felt nice to be back in our comfy old digs with its interesting view and shady surroundings on the hillside. Apparently Scupper thought otherwise because within a week she disappeared. We reckoned she took the first cruising sailboat out of town. No matter. We soon found a replacement in the form of a large yellow tomcat named Sam. He was a nice cat, but a bit wild in his approach to the opposite sex. When we wearied of the spraying around the apartment, the midnight yowling, the abscessed puncture wounds and the complaints of the cat-owning neighbors, we arranged for his name to be changed to Sam Spade, after which he lived a long contented life with us.

With the proceeds of the sale of *Armorel*, we paid Hugh Jacks back the remainder of our debt with grateful thanks, replaced our antique Chevy coupe with a nifty little '59 VW bug, and made a down payment on a tiny rental duplex in Mill Valley as a modest investment in real estate. Meanwhile, I had resumed my job with John A. Blume & Assoc. Engineers in San Francisco and Jane got a job working as a secretary in the City.

Just before we moved off the boat, a little yawl from New Zealand named *White Squall* sailed into the harbor with a crew of three who were to become great friends. Ross and Dorrie Norgrove, the owners, and their crew, Doug Duane, were the quintessential Kiwis, full of energy, fun loving, and endlessly amusing with their zany slang and funny expressions. In addition, Ross had a grand tenor singing voice and played a wicked guitar. Ross was also one of the most unforgettable characters I have ever met. His career included vaudeville as a small boy in his parent's act, a prize fighter, a sailor on one of the last sailing cargo vessels in New Zealand, a tug boat skipper and commercial fisherman. When in Sausalito he tried his hand at carpentry and soon was foreman on impressive apartment building projects. Later he took up writing and authored several books on chartering, rigging and even fiction. He and his crew were always the center of the parties we often hosted at our flat.

Jane and our cat, Sam, at Sausalito

Another couple who entered our life at this time was Sidney and Laila Messer who appeared in a gaff-rigged schooner named *Sadie* which they had built in Washington and sailed down the coast in a semi-finished state. They lived aboard, and after completion of the interior, shipped her to Nova Scotia and spent a year sailing back to Sausalito via the West Indies and Panama. We liked to think that they were at least partly inspired by our voyage on *Armorel*. They added Tuuli, a baby daughter, to the crew shortly after arriving back in Sausalito and later exchanged the schooner for a lovely old English-built ketch named *Margaretta*. This vessel carried them on cruises to Hawaii, Alaska and Mexico and remained their home for many years.

Also about this time we heard through the sailor's grapevine that the well-traveled cutter *Stornoway* was on its way to Sausalito from New York, and in due course the little gaffer with tan sails appeared in our view. Al and Marjorie Petersen were a delight and became our fast friends. Their little 33' double-ender had been built in 1928 and had already been sailed around the world by Al shortly after WWII. Marjorie, a keen dinghy sailor, had her eye on Al before he left on his circumnavigation and after his return marched him to the altar. They had completed a cruise to the West Indies and a lengthy cruise to Mediterranean before sailing to California. We spent many evenings together over cocktails and dinner aboard their boat or at our flat. From Sausalito they sailed on a 24,000 mile circuit around the Pacific and later on a five-year cruise to Europe and back to Sausalito.

I mention these three examples of the many cruising sailors in our circle of friends we met, partly as a result of our voyage from England. We were still very much interested in ocean voyaging, but were ready to settle down for at least a little while as we looked ahead to a having a family and a home of our own. At the top of the list, however, was a boat we could afford and enjoy.

Bob Petersen, now working in Tokyo, kept in touch with us and told us of the little 25' sloop he had purchased and the sailing he did along the coast of Japan (almost all yachts in Japan were under 26' because of a heavy tax on bigger boats). He sent us a drawing of a 26' yawl being built at the Okamoto Boatyard in Yokohama. It was designed by a Mr. Oda and was similar in style to *Ballerina* but larger and with a more modern underbody and rig. It looked good so we ordered one to be built for us. Bob was on hand to keep an eye on her construction and offered to ship it to San Francisco on one of his company's ships. We decided to name her *Woodwind* and eagerly awaited her arrival in time for the 1962 sailing and racing season.

Naturally, something was bound to go wrong with this perfectly organized operation. Just as the new boat arrived in port, the waterfront was paralyzed with a bitter longshoreman's strike which seemed destined to last for quite a while. For weeks on my way to work and home again in the evening I could see poor little *Woodwind* sitting in her cradle on the deck of the ship at Pier 17 as I rode the commuter bus along the Embarcadero. Meanwhile, the first race of the season was approaching. Finally in frustration, Jane and I decided to take a trip to Eugene, Oregon where my folks had moved the previous year. As might be expected, the strike ended within a day of our arrival so we turned around and hustled back to see to the unloading and claim our new yacht.

She was a little beauty and nicely built too. She had a double layer of planking riveted to oak frames and had that unique smell of Japanese cypress and keyaki oak I remembered from *Ballerina.* Inside she had a clever little galley and four bunks plus a place for a proper marine toilet, all on a rather small (Japanese-size) scale. The cockpit had pretty varnished gratings to sit on and a hatch at the stern to stow an outboard motor. Aft of the cockpit was the miniature mizzen mast for her yawl rig. The boat had arrived only a week before the Vallejo Race, the first of the season, so we had a lot to do, especially as we had requested that she be sent without rigging as stainless steel wire was not available in Japan. We worked like fools to get organized for the overnight race and barely made it to the starting line across the Bay at Richmond. We had literally not sailed the boat before and got a surprise as we crossed the line, sheeted in our sails and felt the full force of the wind. She lay over on her side and tried to round up into the wind even as I pulled desperately on the tiller. She was one hard-mouthed, cranky boat and way under-ballasted too. By reefing the mainsail and dropping the mizzen, I was able to keep her moving until we were able to slack sheets and run up San Pablo Bay toward Vallejo where we finished near the bottom of our class. It was a very disappointing day! The return leg the next day wasn't much better.

I knew we would have to put more weight on the bottom of the keel, so as soon as we got back I went to work to make a pattern of the keel in order to build a mold for a lead shoe to be bolted on the keel. Having seen many boats "legged up" at low tide in some of the shallow ports in England, I decided to try the same thing. Using a pair of 4

x 4's, with a plywood pad on the bottom, as legs, we ran her aground
on a beach at high tide, adjusted the legs, waited for low tide then
made our pattern when she was high and dry.   Next I made a mold for
the lead and took it the boatyard to cast the lead shoe and have it
bolted on.   It made a huge difference in our stability, and together with
learning to keep the boat "on her feet" by shortening sail when necessary, we gradually learned how to make *Woodwind* sail quite well.

The boat is "legged up" on the hard to make a pattern for more ballast

We went in the Bay handicap class races during the 1962 season and did quite well.   We even went in a couple of the newly-
organized Midget Ocean Racing Class events along the coast.   On the
race from San Francisco to Half Moon Bay I took along the Kiwi crew
of *White Squall*.   It happened that *Woodwind's* sails came from the
Ohara sail loft in Japan.   Naturally, the New Zealanders couldn't resist
having fun mimicking an Irish brogue each time a sail was set with
such comments as "Tis a pleasure to set a sail made by the hand of
O'Hara is it not?."

*Finishing a short ocean race to Half Moon bay
with Doug Duane and Alex Crichton*

The next year, in midsummer, Jane and I made a vacation cruise in our little yawl, beginning with a cruise in company with our friends' boats to Horseshoe Bend in the Napa River, then continuing on our own up the Delta. We roamed around the Sacramento and San Joaquin Rivers, visiting familiar anchorages and new locations, enjoying every day. Just before we set off on our cruise, I read in the newspapers that a huge project to dredge a ship channel to the new Port of Sacramento was complete and would be officially opened in a week or so. The newspaper stories also mentioned that the project included a navigation lock which would connect the Port with the Sacramento River to allow barges of agricultural products and other stuff to be loaded on ships at the Port. Since Jane's parents had recently moved back to Sacramento from Carmel, we decided to pay them a visit by boat.

We sailed under the Rio Vista drawbridge and on up Cache Slough, intending to stop at our favorite spot at the mouth of Miner Slough, only to discover that the new ship channel had gobbled up our little paradise. Bummer! We sailed on up the channel for hour after hour with no chart and no way to judge our progress since it was absolutely straight except for one almost imperceptible bend in alignment. Adding to the strange environment was the fact that it was all very new with absolutely no vegetation on the banks anywhere along the way. Eventually we reached the huge ship basin and spotted the navigation lock at the far end. I had no assurance that the lock was completed and ready for business, but as we neared it, a drawbridge lifted and the huge lock gates swung open. We entered the cavernous lock, the gates behind us closed, a small adjustment in water level took place and the gates on the far end opened to reveal the Sacramento River. All of this took place in total silence. I was convinced that we were surely the very first boat to pass through the lock. When we moved a short distance up the river and moored at the friendly Sacramento Yacht Club we saw our friend Martin Kenoyer on his little Bear Boat, *Cinnamon*, who informed us he had gone through the lock the day before and claimed the title of being first. Ironically, the lock was obsolete before it was even finished because barge traffic had already been displaced by trucks. After a decade or so the expensive and beautifully built lock was permanently closed to traffic.

We sailed down the Sacramento River with the help of the considerable current, spent time at Steamboat Slough, and then moved over to the San Joaquin River via Georgiana Slough. At the end of two satisfying weeks, we beat our way down the Suisun and San Pablo Bays and home to Sausalito.

We had learned to love our unique little yawl, but there were other things going on which made us consider selling her after only a little over two years. In the end a fellow offered to buy her and made and acceptable offer. He said he <u>had</u> to have a wooden boat and boasted of his $50 badger-hair varnish brushes. Regrettably, we let her go and then watched poor *Woodwind* deteriorate in full view of our living room. After a couple of years the varnish peeled off, the masts turned black, a thick mat of seaweed grew on her bottom and eventually the worms ate through her hull and she sank in her slip. I felt like I had betrayed a beloved child.

Hugh Jacks had bought a replacement for the old schooner *Altura* in the form of a sleek 45' fiberglass yawl, also named *Altura* (his wife Ellen used to refer to the old schooner as the "real *Altura*"). It was the first large fiberglass design by Sparkman & Stephens and she sailed wonderfully. Interestingly, a sistership arrived on the Bay at the same time. In the process of learning to sail the boats, we would often have little match races in the evening. Sometimes one or the other of the two boats would pull out the mizzen mast and sail as a sloop. It turned out that whichever of the boats had the mizzen <u>out</u> would invariably win. It seemed the sail area of the mizzen would not compensate for the extra weight and windage of the mizzen mast. No matter, the yawl rig was much prettier and that's the way we kept her. Hugh raced her regularly in the Bay and local ocean races, and I usually crewed for him after *Woodwind* was sold.

Sailing toward the Delta on one of several cruises

These were fun days. Hugh always attracted a lively, likable crew who, I think were more interested in enjoying the race than in winning it. Regulars were Joe Miller, my shipmate on the schooner trip to Hawaii and back, and Red Laidlaw, Hugh's oldest sailing friend, plus an assortment of other jovial characters of varying experience. *Alltura* was a sizable, powerful vessel which sailed beautifully, but needed more than a little skill to keep up to speed and under control, especially when running with her huge spinnaker and mizzen staysail. There were times when we had some scary moments. One day when we were running down the Bay in an especially strong wind with all the big "kites" set and pulling like crazy, we were set by the current a little closer to Point Blunt than we realized. Suddenly we bounced off a rock with a terrific shock. The whole boat jumped and shuddered then kept on going. Typically, Hugh, who was suffering from a chronic stomach ulcer at this time, simply said, "I think I need a drink of milk."

Jane and I were hoping to start a family but nothing was happening. At the same time we were still thinking about the possibility of making another long ocean cruise. I had not forgotten the excitement and romance of Tahiti and the Tuamotu Islands I experienced on the *Mistress* trip and longed to sail to the South Seas again. Just about this time our friends George and Pat Renfro bought a superb 55' schooner named *Samarang* and began planning a year-long cruise to Tahiti and return via Hawaii and invited Jane and me to join them. They were a very fine couple with lots of sailing experience, including an earlier cruise to Tahiti on a smaller boat. It was a great opportunity, but foolishly we turned it down because I really wanted to do the trip on my own boat. I think the great success of our *Armorel* trip had made me overconfident that we could repeat our wonderful luck. Thinking back on it, we let slip a chance to have a worry-free voyage with good company on an excellent boat. One bad decision can often lead to more bad decisions and that is exactly what happened.

Whistler, a 42' Murray Peterson "coaster" schooner

CHAPTER 10

WHISTLER

Our friend, Clint Hanger, the man who put our medical chest together for the *Armorel* trip, bought a 30' Tahiti Ketch named *Taihoa*, which had appeared in Sausalito after a long trip up from New Zealand. It was powered by an ancient, rusty *Hupmobile* car engine (which gives some idea of her condition). Clint, who is inclined to be the over-enthusiastic type, especially when he gets hold of a new idea, happily moved his wife, Sara, and little daughter, Linda, aboard to try the liveaboard lifestyle. After a couple of years it became apparent that the boat just wasn't right for a family of three so they moved ashore and Clint began to dream of his perfect boat.

The dream boat began to take the shape of a gaff-rigged schooner of a type known as a "coaster schooner" so named because the designer, Murray Petersen, always named his own boats by that name. They were modeled after the two-masted, working schooners of the 19th century and were exceptionally handsome. They were usually between 40'and 50' in length with a clipper bow, a topmast on the mainmast, a graceful sheer and invariably painted dark green with white trim. They were popular in Southern California where they were perfect for sailing to Catalina Island under a cloud of sail while looking very classy indeed. A number of them had been built by a Swiss boat builder known as "Squeaky," who used a set of pirated of plans and produced a good looking boat but of dubious quality. Clint was determined to have one.

By chance, Clint made the acquaintance of a US Army psychiatrist who was stationed in Japan and had built a sailboat at a nearby boatyard. When Clint asked him if he could arrange for a coaster schooner to be built at the yard, he agreed. In due course a contract was produced offering to build a 42' Coaster III schooner based on a set of the pirated plans for the bargain price of $11,000. Additionally, the psychiatrist agreed to oversee the construction. Clint was ecstatic and soon was showing us photos of the boat as it was being framed up and planked. The letters from the psychiatrist also gave glowing reports of the progress. The only problem was that Clint was so wrapped up in the project that he was driving his wife crazy. It finally got to the stage where Sara told him it was either the boat or her. Something had to go.

He wisely decided that he simply had to give up the project and asked if we would be interested in taking over. He had about $7,500 invested so far and the boat seemed to be well along in construction. Just at this time we needed to make a decision on whether of not we were going on the *Samarang* trip to Tahiti. Suddenly it seemed like the stars were aligned. Here was an opportunity to acquire a nice new yacht for a bargain price which would allow us to make a cruise to the South Seas on our own boat. The success of our *Armorel* trip had lulled me into thinking I could do it again because, without investigating further, I agreed to take over the project for the amount he had in it. I could easily have found out more about the boatyard and the schooner because Bob Petersen was right there in Japan and as a matter of fact, knew all about it. But we didn't consult him. It was a big mistake.

What neither Clint or I knew was that the boatyard had apparently decided that they could not possibly complete the schooner for the contract amount so they simply stopped work on it and shoved it out of the shed and onto the beach. Why the psychiatrist/inspector hadn't told Clint about this situation was a mystery. I only became aware of it when there was no answer to my communications with the yard. In desperation, I finally asked Bob Petersen to look into the situation. He came to the rescue by arranging for the hull to be launched and towed to the Okamoto Boatyard in Yokohama who agreed to finish the boat on a time-and-material basis. This was the boatyard where both *Ballerina* and *Woodwind* had been built, so we knew they could do a good job. Bob also arranged for a competent marine surveyor to oversee the completion of the boat. It was a huge relief to get the project back on the track, but I was quite sure that the final cost would be a lot more than we had originally planned.

*The partially finished hull our schooner was simply shoved
out on the beach by the boat yard*

One of the first things our new inspector found out was that the
planking had been attached using brass screws rather than bronze. In a
few years brass in salt water sort of melts away in a process called de-
zincification (brass is an alloy of copper and zinc). There was no
choice but to have the yard remove and replace every one of the many
hundreds (or thousands) of screws in the hull and replace them with
bronze, an alloy of copper and tin. It was not a happy start. Later I
found that much of the interior work done by the original yard had
been done with <u>brass plated</u> steel screws. Still, the Okamoto Boatyard
did the best they could to finish the schooner in a creditable fashion,
but there was not much they could do to correct some of the flaws in
the basic structure. The one thing the original yard did right was to get
the shape of the boat done correctly. In spite of many structural short-
comings, it had a lovely sheer and a perfectly fair and smooth hull.

At the time we agreed to take over the schooner project, one of
the first things I did was to redraw the sail and deck plan to bring the

pirated drawings into correct scale. I also located Murray Petersen's original *Coaster III* in Long Beach. Having obtained permission to go aboard, I drove to Southern California and took lots of photos of the details of her rig, deck fittings and accommodation. I then made new drawings of the layout below decks the way we wanted it. It was a good thing I did all this because the Japanese craftsmen in the Oka-moto Boatyard slavishly copied every detail, and on the surface at least, produced quite a good looking vessel.

It was a busy time in the winter of '63 and spring of '64 order-ing equipment and shipping it to the yard in Yokohama. We sent over a Grey Marine engine, a windlass from Scotland, cabin lamps, and all kinds of stuff. A suit of sails was ordered from a sailmaker in Japan, and I even found time to build a little dory to hang in the stern davits. The bills kept coming too and soon the cost of the schooner had almost tripled. We had a tiger by the tail and had no choice but to keep on going. In September 1964 Bob Petersen notified us that the schooner had been loaded on the SS Chester Arthur and would soon arrive in San Francisco.

I went to the US Customs building on Sansome Street, paid a modest duty, then paid the shipping and obtained the papers for her release. The next day my friend, John O'Brien, and I took his little Monterey fishboat alongside the ship and waited while they offloaded the schooner. The mate was in a foul mood because he could not get to the cargo under two of the hatches until he got rid of the blasted yacht and her masts. He needed to lift the boat using the shipping cra-dle, which would not have been a problem if the boat was to be set on the wharf. What we needed, however, was to have her set in the water. Eventually he piled a huge weight of chain on the schooner's timber cradle so that it would sink and let the boat float free. He then lowered the masts and a big pile of booms, gaffs, topmast, etc. which we lashed to the deck of the schooner. Mercifully it was a very calm day as we towed the boat to the Madden & Lewis shipyard in Sausalito where she would be rigged. We decided to name her *Whistler* after a pictur-esque West Indies cargo/ferry schooner we had seen plying the waters between the islands of Bequia and St. Vincent when we were on *Ar-morel*.

An exhausting week followed in which I sorted out the maze of rigging wire, fitted the topmast and readied the deadeyes and lanyards for adjusting the standing rigging. While this was going on I had a sickening feeling that a huge mistake had been made in the size of the masts. They looked much too big and heavy. Worse, they were built exactly to the dimensions I had shown on the rigging and sail plan I had redrawn. When the masts were stepped however, to my immense relief, they looked perfect. The following weekend, with the help of a group of friends, the entire spider web of running rigging was completed and the sails all bent on. Not a small job with a schooner, gaff-rigged on both masts.

At this point she was looking pretty good, but I already knew that there were serious problems. The large fuel tanks (for gasoline) were of stainless steel, but were made using soft solder, an impossibly dangerous condition. I could see that narrow brass straps had been used instead of the heavy forged iron frame-keel connections as specified, creating a serious weakness in the forward part of the hull. After only a couple of weeks in Sausalito, the hull planking had shrunk alarmingly which indicated that she was not very tightly caulked, and she leaked a lot even as she sat in her berth. She also had a rotting mass of sawdust and shavings in the bilge which added a worrisome aroma. On deck it was obvious that the seam compound had failed to stick to the planks and would have to be redone immediately. It was a good thing that we had long since dropped any idea of a south sea voyage in this boat. Anyway, we were plumb out of money so we weren't going anywhere.

By November we took *Whistler* for her first sail on a windy, almost stormy day. She actually sailed quite well in spite of being a bit tender (tippy). I thought a lot better of the boat seeing her under sail and away from the problems I had been dealing with. She seemed a very interesting and fun boat when romping along under her big gaff sails and double headsails. When we turned on the power and tried to get to the harbor, however, we found that the propeller was so undersized that we could scarcely move against the wind. One more problem to fix.

By spring 1965, the schooner was in about as good shape as we were likely to get her. We had a "For Sale" sign on her, but since people weren't lined up to make an offer, we sailed her often on weekends with a group of loyal friends who had helped us get her in commission. At this time a couple of Sausalito Yacht Club friends, Jim Enzensperger and Robin Hobart conceived the idea of reviving a race on the Bay for working vessels called the Master Mariners Race which had been immensely poplar almost 100 years earlier. It had been started in 1867 by the Master Mariners Benevolent Association, a charity to benefit orphans and widows of lost sailors. For several years it pitted the local brigs, schooners and sailing barges in a spectacular regatta on the waters off the San Francisco waterfront then died away.

Our first sail on Whistler in December 1964

The revival of the race was designed to attract interesting, old fashioned-looking boats with plenty of gaffs, bowsprits and yardarms for maximum spectacle effect. One had to submit a photo of the boat as part of the application to enter. It didn't really matter when the boat was built or what it was made of provided it looked like another era. *Whistler* was perfect for the part. Each boat was to be sponsored by a shipping or tugboat company or other maritime enterprise. The revival generated a lot of publicity in the newspapers and a big pre-regatta lunch was scheduled for participants and sponsors at the St. Francis Hotel. We were quite excited.

I invited Hugh Jacks to be our guest skipper, sewed up a main gaff topsail (set above the mainsail), and accepted an offer of the loan of a large genoa jib and a fisherman staysail (set between the masts above the gaff foresail). We would have plenty of canvass. The race was arranged so that each boat started at a different time such that, theoretically, they would all be together at the finish and the first one over the line would be the winner. This plan had the advantage of mostly eliminating close maneuvering at the start, a very good thing considering there were at least three square-riggers in the fleet.

The day of the race was a typical windy day on the Bay. When the gun went off for our start, we immediately hoisted every sail in a fine show of bravado. Immediately *Whistler* lay over on her beam ends with the lee rail way underwater, the rigging combing the water and the sea rushing past the cabin sides. What a photo opportunity! Pictures of poor *Whistler* staggering under her press of sail appeared in newspapers, magazines and even on a German calendar. Needless to say, we immediately shortened sail. We didn't win the race, but it was a great day.

A few weeks later we took the boat on out first little cruise on the Memorial Day weekend to Black Point at the mouth of the Petaluma River. We took along Clint Hanger and his family, Sara and Linda, age 10. Clint was ecstatic to sail on what was to have been his dream ship. All went well the first day as we sailed up the shallow channel across the mud flats leading to the river entrance and anchored below the railroad drawbridge. We had a lively cocktail hour and a BBQ dinner on deck then about sunset decided to proceed further up the Petaluma River to visit a yacht we knew was anchored in a narrow waterway named San Antonio Creek. By the time the last glass of wine was drained it was quite late and the tide was high but starting to ebb, so we said our goodbyes and motored smoothly back to our anchorage below the highway and railroad bridges. It was difficult to see just where we were in the darkness because the extremely high tide made the river look very broad. We anchored in what we thought was a good location, hung up the anchor light and went to bed. A few hours later we felt a bump as the boat went aground on the falling tide then a swirling sound as the current forced the keel into the mud and swung the boat broadside to the current. There was nothing we could do to get into deeper water and worse, the pilings of a derelict pier appeared to be close along side. What would happen when we lay over at low tide?

Dawn finally came after a sleepless night to reveal the schooner high and dry on a sea of mud. She lay on her side with the deck at a steep angle. The pilings we had feared during the night were nothing more than rotted 2x4's. We were in no danger, but very embarrassed, which became acute when everyone we ever knew seemed to be driving by that morning and stopped to walk out along the bank and comment on our predicament. The height of the ridiculous came when a fisherman in a small skiff hailed us and asked if he could perhaps help by towing us off the mud into deep water.

Whistler well aground at the Petaluma River

We were determined to get off on the midday high tide (which was not as high as the one the night before), so as soon as the dory would float we began the process of laying out three anchors to kedge ourselves off the mud. As the tide rose the schooner gradually began to straighten up and we winched in the anchor lines until they were bar taught. Finally as a last resort, I ran the engine at top speed in reverse. Suddenly the anchor lines all went slack and she began to move swiftly toward the center of the River. There was frantic action to stop the motor before a line got in the propeller, tie life jackets on a couple of the lines and throw them clear to avoid a snarl and move one of the lines to the bow as the boat snubbed to a stop in the strong current. What a mess! It took at least a couple of hours to retrieve the anchors and stow all the gear. Otherwise it was a fine weekend.

The summer of 1965 passed with still no buyer for the schooner. We took part in a newly-organized Schooner Association race/cruise to Vallejo and a Sausalito Yacht Club event or two but otherwise *Whistler* got little use. In August we were invited to join Jim and Betty Wilhite's lovely 67' yawl, *Athene*, on a two week cruise in British Columbia and suddenly the summer was gone.

And there was much more going on in our lives besides the schooner. Jane and I had been unsuccessful in getting a family started and this was an unhappy note for both of us. It had been common knowledge that adoptions were difficult to arrange because of a shortage of adoptable babies. At least that was what we believed. To our surprise, however, we saw a notice in the local newspaper to the effect that the County of Marin had started up an adoption unit and invited interested couples to attend an informational meeting at the Civic Center. Naturally we attended and signed up for a possible adoption.

About nine months later, a proper gestation period, we got a call from the County that they had a healthy three week old baby girl available. Were we interested? Wow! Were we ever! Previous to the call we had been "vetted" by a social worker who came to our flat to verify our living conditions and to be assured that we had suitable accommodations for a child. She even wanted to take a look at our marriage license. Obviously we had passed muster. We were almost holding our breath as we arrived at the adoption office to have a look at the little girl. It was love at first sight. She was a beautiful baby, a chubby, smiling little angel, and we were able to take her home with us that very afternoon. January 6, 1966. We named her Anne Lindley and installed her crib at the end of the hall, a space which had formerly been my closet. What a difference in our lives took place! The photos in our albums changed from boats to babies.

In April we drove up to Oregon to show Anne to her grandparents and in May we again sailed in the Master Mariners Race which had now become firmly established as a San Francisco Bay institution. I had been elected commodore of the Sausalito Yacht Club at this time so I suggested that we host the Master Mariners fleet at the club following the race. It was grand sight to have all the picturesque vessels anchored off the clubhouse in the evening sunlight and spirits were high when the skippers and crews came ashore for drinks and BBQ steaks on the deck. The bar did a roaring business and everyone was happy right up until the steaks ran out before everyone was fed. It wasn't quite a full scale riot, but almost.

Anne, our new crew, out for a sail with friends,
Stephen Parker and Marion Smith

In midsummer we took baby Anne along on *Whistler,* at age 7 months, and sailed "up the river" on a cruise to our favorite anchorages in the Sacramento and San Joaquin River delta. With her broad decks and large cockpit, she was actually quite a nice boat for this sort of thing. She was very good-looking too. As we were sailing up the narrow reaches of the Sacramento River cars and trucks on the levee road would honk their approval of our romantic vessel. As we neared Steamboat Slough where we intended to stay for about a week, we noticed that an outboard-powered skiff was following us with a man aboard who appeared to be perhaps one of the local farmers. After the drawbridge opened to let us into the Slough, the skiff continued to follow us and came up alongside and asked if the boat was for sale. We said yes but asked him to wait while we got moored. We probably appeared to be finished when he politely called, "Permission to come aboard." Unfortunately, I was busy up forward when our crew snapped at him, "Can't you see we are trying to get moored!" Obviously insulted, he zoomed off. Considering how much we wanted to sell the boat and how rich most of the farmers in the Delta are, it was a major *faux pas*.

Contrary to my expectations, having little Anne aboard was no problem at all. We hung up one of those "bouncy seats" under the main boom which worked well and her daily baths took place in a big plastic dish pan on deck. Below decks, with a lee cloth pulled up at one of the settee berths, she had a snug sleeping place. We had a huge awning over the main boom which made the cockpit and after deck a shady cool place. After a week at Steamboat slough, we wandered down to the San Joaquin River via scenic Georgiana Slough and anchored for a few more days at Fig Island in Potato Slough. In good "delta style", it was all very leisurely.

There were about 30 boats in the anchorage at Fig Island including a handsome 72' schooner named *Constellation* with a group of about six young people aboard who were working on the boat in preparation for a world cruise. The owner was not aboard and the tempo of the work being done by the crew, which seemed to be mostly sanding the varnish, was definitely not being rushed. One of the crew, a very affable young man who we dubbed "the ambassador," came by one day in the schooner's outboard speedboat and said they were organizing a little dinghy regatta after lunch amongst the boats at anchor with El Toro sailing dinghies, and since we had a similar sailing pram dinghy, invited us to join the regatta and have lemonade and cookies afterwards. He was sitting casually on the side deck of the speedboat with his hand on the wheel. When we said "sure," he shoved off, spun the wheel, opened the throttle and promptly fell overboard as the speedboat accelerated in a fast turn.

At first it headed at full speed for the open slough, then turned and terrified us by zooming through the boats at anchor, missing all of them by a miracle. Next it shot out of the anchorage and around the corner of the island which horrified us because we had just seen a boatload of kids going that way to pick blackberries. A moment later we heard a crash as it hit the island and plowed its way up into the bushes with the motor screaming at full throttle. A half minute later all became quiet as the engine fried and seized. All was quiet on the schooner too, but they soon regained their composure and took a second outboard boat to retrieve the speedboat. They gamely ran the little dinghy race and entertained the participants afterwards. Later that evening the owner came to the schooner and joined a very, very subdued crew. After that excitement, the trip home seemed an anticlimax.

In the fall we received two offers on the boat subject, as usual, to inspection by a marine surveyor. The first buyer said he would use the services of Frank Olivera, who we knew quite well and who was reputed to be the most thorough in the business. Before we even had the boat hauled out, Frank got started with his survey. That night he phoned me and said he was sorry to tell me that there was a lot of rot in the stern timbers of the schooner and what should he do. I told him to stop and send his bill to me, then I phoned the buyer and told him I had accepted a second, higher offer. He was outraged but couldn't do anything since no money had been exchanged. I then phoned the second buyer and told him the boat was available, hoping that he would skip the survey or at least use a less meticulous one. He simply got one of the boatyard workers to take a look at the boat and was informed that it looked fine. We had a deal! Jane and I danced for joy. The buyer, whose name I can't even remember, and I sat down in a little café in Sausalito and agreed on the details of the purchase. I was to get $10,000 cash, a small 2nd mortgage on a house in Carmel, a pair of practically unbuildable upslope lots in Fairfax, five acres of desert between Las Vegas and Henderson and three small lots in the ghost town of Goldfield, Nevada. I called it my schooner empire. It took awhile, but we disposed of all of it. The 2nd mortgage was paid off while mailing a little account book back and forth for a few years and the Fairfax lots were sold by simply nailing a "for sale" sign on an oak tree. The neighbor saw me doing it and asked what was going on, then bought them for $2500 to keep them from being built on. A Las Vegas realtor sold the desert land to a man who planned to put a dog kennel on it and I sold the ghost town lots for $150 each at a cocktail party to a man who wanted a bona fide Nevada address to avoid state income tax when he retired. In all we got about $18,000. We had lost about $10,000 on the schooner which seemed like a lot at the time and missed a chance to make a south sea voyage, but we quickly moved on.

Whistler was sailed to Southern California then resold to a couple, one of whom was a stunt woman for the movies. She had supposedly received a big sum of money as compensation for an injury while doing a stunt, so they bought the schooner and sailed for the South Pacific. We heard a report that the boat had been damaged but survived a typhoon in Suva harbor then went on to New Zealand. Several years later I was in American Samoa working on a hydrographic survey of Pago Pago harbor and saw a schooner which looked a lot like *Whistler* but different somehow. When I had the boat driver swing by the boat, sure enough, there was her name on the transom. I had failed to recognize her from a distance because she was now painted white, her trailboards (carved decorations) on the bow were missing and she had a windvane steering gear on the stern. I hailed the man on board and suggested we meet after work at the hotel.

Over drinks he explained that he and his lady friend had indeed sailed the schooner to New Zealand and tried to sell her there but had little success because of the high duty on imported yachts. Finally a buyer was found and it was agreed that they would make a deal in American Samoa. That sale fell through, but he had found another buyer who was coming tomorrow to take over the boat. The new owners were a family from Alaska with two children. I made a subsequent trip to Samoa a couple of months later and learned that they had made it to Fiji. After that I never heard of the boat again which worried me because I was pretty much in touch with the cruising scene in the Pacific. Knowing the structural weakness of the boat, I have always had an uneasy feeling about what might have happened to her.

Vim, a fine little 26' "Sea Islander" sloop

CHAPTER 11

VIM

The sale of *Whistler* in the late fall of 1966 was a great relief. Although she was a pretty thing to look at, her defects and general unsound structure haunted me. With her big gaff rig she needed a large crew and wasn't a very suitable boat for Bay sailing. Also I think our difficulties and expense in getting her built had prejudiced us against her. Anyway, she certainly was a much larger boat than we needed once we made the decision to forget about a south sea voyage in her. There were no regrets in seeing her go.

Jane and I had been living in the nice old flat in Sausalito for over ten years and although we loved the location and low rent, we were now free to look for a house of our own with more space for our family of three. House prices and interest rates were low and with some cash in hand from the sale of the schooner, we had no trouble in finding plenty of places to look at. There was talk of a passenger ferry starting service between Tiburon and San Francisco, so moving there had a special appeal. Jane found a fairly plain but pleasant three bedroom house with a good view of Richardson Bay and the Golden Gate Bridge on a modest street in Tiburon for $27,000. We moved in on January 1, 1967. 40 years later the view has mostly disappeared behind all the trees but we are still here.

The rumors of ferry service to the City proved to be true. A group of commuters in Tiburon headed by a jovial fellow named Ned Towne bought a 50' antique motor yacht which they kept at the Corinthian Yacht Club and began to use her as a ferryboat. It was a great idea, but sometimes the weather was bad or the motor wouldn't start resulting in frequent canceled trips. Also there was really no suitable place to tie the boat up on the San Francisco waterfront which was both secure and safe. Finally, there was the problem of maintaining the boat. In the end, they approached Russ Lewis who owned a charter fishing boat named *Blue Horizon* in Sausalito and suggested he take over the ferry run. He agreed, but within a month Tom Crowley, the tugboat and excursion boat king of San Francisco Bay, announced that he would use one of his tour boats to run a cheaper, faster ferry on the route. That was the end of the competition and the beginning of real passenger ferry service across the Bay for the first time since they had quit running when the Golden Gate and Bay Bridges opened in the late 1930's. We moved to Tiburon just as the new service started, and I rode the boat to work for the rest of my career.

We enjoyed our new home and made various improvements. I especially liked having a big garage for a workshop and almost immediately started building a 14' chamberlain dory skiff, a slender pulling boat suitable for either one or two rowers. Eventually over the years I was to build a total of 14 of these boats. But most importantly, after a year we decided to put our name in at the County for another adoption. In quite a short time we were invited to come up and meet a little three week old baby boy who was available. He was a cute little fellow with snow white hair and we took him home immediately. We named him Robert Gary, after his dad and his maternal grandfather, but to avoid confusion called him Robby. We were now a happy family of four.

My job at John A. Blume & Assoc. Engineers was interesting and enjoyable. The first years were spent mostly working on structural design of buildings, but gradually I became more involved in the marine aspect of our work. The firm had always done a lot of work for the US Navy designing wharfs and shore facilities and now in the 1960's there was a lot of interest in building marinas sparked by a large California bond issue to construct harbors of refuge and marinas plus the explosive growth of boating in general (probably spurred by the invention of fiberglass boats). Naturally I gravitated toward this field at every opportunity. I was project engineer for the design of the South San Francisco Marina, the Berkeley Marina and I carried out feasibility studies for many others. It was like being paid to have fun. A little later I found myself in charge of a project to build a navigation lock for yachts at Bel Marin Keys in Marin County and subsequently designed four more similar locks around the country. There was a certain amount of travel to foreign projects, enough to make it interesting but not an excessive amount. I was able to travel to jobs in Hawaii,

Samoa, Guam, Malaysia, Brazil and Alaska. All of which I enjoyed. Gradually I was given more responsibility, and eventually I was promoted to vice president in charge of the civil/structural division.

We were without a boat of our own for five years, but that didn't mean we were divorced from the boating scene. We belonged to the Sausalito Yacht Club and I had been invited to join the Cruising Club of America (CCA), a national yachting organization and we had a wide circle of friends with yachts, so there was no shortage of boats to sail on. Hugh Jacks generously loaned us his elegant yawl, *Altura*, three summers for two week cruises in the Delta. Early in the spring of 1970 a friend who was a trustee of the San Francisco Maritime Museum phoned to tell me that a nice 35' ketch named *Pocahontas* had been donated to the museum for a tax deduction, but it could not be sold right away. Were we interested in taking care of it for a year? Of course I said yes. The arrangement was that the museum would insure the boat (I doubt if they ever did) and I would pay for the slip rental and maintenance. We enlisted our friend John O'Brien to be a partner to help with the maintenance and the cost.

Before buying Vim I had a free charter for a year of Pocohontas,
a pretty, 35' Italian-built ketch

Pocahontas was a William Garden "Seal" design, a pretty, traditional double-ended wooden ketch with double headsails. She had been built in Italy using beautiful hardwoods and had lots of varnish work including bulwarks, wide rail caps, cabin sides and masts. Below decks she was nicely finished but with an unusual European layout, with the galley forward. She had a big powerful diesel engine. Unfortunately her sails were horrible, so my first job was to try to make them set better by re-cutting where necessary and re-sewing the bolt ropes. I was able to do this at home and was more or less successful. After hauling her out to paint the bottom and topsides, we gave her a coat of varnish and we were all set to enjoy her for the season.

We signed up for the Master Mariners Race in May and got off to a good start, but as we neared the first buoy we heard a nasty thump and saw the bowsprit bend upward and the headstay go slack. We instantly slacked all the sails and discovered that the bobstay had broken loose from the hull. We could have easily lost the whole rig! We put new fastenings into the stem at the bobstay connection and for good measure we fashioned a pair of stainless steel plates to screw to the hull to reinforce the connection. Not wanting to haul out again, we simply drove the bow of the boat up onto a beach near the harbor on a rising tide to do the job.

In July we sailed *Pocahontas* up the Delta with our kids and our sailing friend, Jim Algert. We had a smooth sail almost all the way to Steamboat Slough but had the motor running for the last few miles. Suddenly the transmission went out and oil spewed all over the engine compartment. We dropped the anchor and tried to diagnose the problem. It seemed an oil fitting on the hydraulic gearbox had burst. We were near the tiny historic town of Locke so I rowed ashore looking for a mechanic but the best I could do was to find some transmission fluid. Jim and I set to work to solve the problem with the meager resources we had on board. In the end we were able to make a repair by cutting up a toothpaste tube to make some discs which we used to close the blown out fitting on the gearbox. Underway once more, we arrived at the Steamboat Slough drawbridge just in time for one last opening before the tender went off duty for the day.

In September we once again took our friend Jim Algert with us for a trip on *Pocahontas* to Tomales Bay, about 50 miles up the coast, to participate in a CCA cruise. We got off to a good start on perfectly clear, sunny morning but by the time we were no more than ten miles up the coast, we were bucking into a very strong headwind. This was no surprise as it tends to do this on sunny days out there, but this time it was blowing especially hard. Knowing that even if we did manage to get to the entrance to Tomales Bay before dark (which looked unlikely) the waves would undoubtedly be too big to allow a safe crossing of the shallow bar. It was an easy decision to forgo the CCA cruise and go for a short cruise inside the Bay instead, so we turned around and raced back for the Golden Gate Bridge. Our first idea was to sail up to Montezuma Slough in Suisun Bay, but when we arrived at Point San Pablo we found that San Pablo Bay was a froth of muddy waves with a full gale blowing. Once more we turned around and spent the night in a snug cove at Angel Island. The next day we tried again to go up the coast and sailed up to Tomales Bay without incident.

It was a good thing we had turned back to Angel Island because the weather was raging in the Delta. Late that afternoon an outbound ship from Stockton was being buffeted by gale force winds and as it approached the old drawbridge between Antioch and Sherman Island, a black squall roared down on it and wiped out all visibility. It couldn't have happened at a worse moment. The bridge was a tower-lift type where the draw span is lifted vertically by cables on the tall towers on each side. Usually the bridge tender's control room is on the side; however, on this bridge it was located *on top of* the draw span. One can imagine the terrifying ride he got way up there when the ship plowed into one of the supporting towers. When he was eventually rescued from the jammed drawbridge span, he quit his job on the spot and vowed to seek safer employment. The bridge was later demolished and replaced with a handsome high-level structure.

The "charter" of *Pocahontas* worked out very nicely. Anne and Rob were old enough to sail with us on all our little cruises, except the one to Tomales Bay, and enjoyed the boat on day sails around the Bay. As winter approached, we gave the boat back to the Maritime Museum and she was sold. Years later I was boarding an airplane for a flight back to San Francisco from Honolulu when I noticed a man in line ahead of me with the distinctive sort of varnished box that is used to hold a sextant. When I asked if he had sailed over to the Islands, he told me he had just finished a wonderful trip on a dandy little ketch named *Pocahontas.*

By the spring of 1971 I was getting eager to have my own boat and began to look around. I noticed a Sea Islander sloop named *Vim* for sail in San Rafael and stopped by to have a look. I knew the yacht broker, Scott Baxter, well and had crewed for him many times. He suggested I take her out for a sail, which was a bit unusual since normally brokers insist that an accepted offer accompanied by a deposit be negotiated prior to any sea trials. I got the sails bent on and shoved off for a spin on the Bay. There was a stiff breeze blowing, so I had a good chance to try her on all points of sail and found that she sailed very nicely, especially for a cruising boat. When I got back in I got a jolt when I noticed that the stainless end fitting (swage) of the headstay was not just cracked, but split wide open. It was amazing that I had not dismasted, but then I have always been lucky. I don't remember the asking price, but I made a low offer of $5,500 which was accepted partly, I think, because the boat was owned by Howie Allen, a wealthy man from Belvedere who, I suspect, wanted me to have her.

Vim was a 26' sloop with a transom (square) stern and an outboard rudder. She had a 25 HP gas engine and had bunks for four. The head was in the forepeak under the end of one of the bunks. She wasn't fancy but was very pretty (I thought) with her classic, pure cruising boat style. She had been designed by a southern California naval architect named Merle Davis. The design had been featured in *Sea Magazine* as a build-it-yourself project, which was a little ridiculous because she was of quite sophisticated construction. Apparently only a couple of them had been built, one of which was built by Sid Hall of Sausalito and ended up in the hands of Dick Miller, a popular local yacht broker. One day a stranger named Bob Moore wandered into Dick Miller's office saying her had found a very competent German boatbuilder in Japan and wondered what would be a good design for him to use to construct a few "spec" boats. Naturally, Dick told him the only thing to build was a Sea Islander, like his own boat. In due course, a pair of the trim little sloops appeared for sale. They took a long time to sell because their price of $11,000 was way too much for boats of that size at the time (1957). Eventually they were sold and one of them, *Avanti,* ended up right across the dock from our yawl,

Sali. At the time I envied the owner and never lost my desire to own one of them. And now I did!

Buying a boat is easy. Finding a place to keep her, especially in those days, was not so simple. After a several days of panic, I was able, by pestering the manager, to get a slip at Paradise Cay Marina in Tiburon. It was quite handy to our home, but it was no paradise. The mornings were fine, but at precisely noon the wind would start to blow and within minutes all the halyards in the harbor would be knocking and clanging against the masts. It was the only harbor I have ever heard of where the monthly rental of a downwind slip was cheaper than for an upwind slip, and for good reason. Naturally, we had a downwind slip which added lots of spice to getting into and out of our berth on windy afternoons.

When we bought *Vim*, Anne and Rob were about six and four years old, a good age for getting used to being on a boat. Jane and I have albums full of photos of the four of us on little sailing trips around the Bay. We quickly learned that kids don't especially like to just "go sailing." They like to have a destination, preferably one with a beach. One of the favorites was to simply sail a couple of miles to Red Rock Island where we could land on the shore and explore the island including the abandoned mine shaft. Angel Island, Yerba Buena Cove and China camp were favorites too. Although I never raced the boat, I was surprised at how fast she was. This was largely due to her tall mast and large sail plan for a boat of her size. She was very comfortable too with a large cockpit and sizable cabin. In all, considering the age of our children and the sort of sailing we doing at the time, *Vim* soon proved to be an ideal boat.

Within a few months of buying the boat I got a call from my friend Peter Passano asking if I would be interested in having him as a partner in the boat. He had recently sold his ocean-going sloop, *Aka,* and according to his wife, was going crazy being without a boat. Peter and I had sailed together as crew on Hugh Jacks' *Altura,* and he had been one of the group of young men who had bought *Sali* from us. He and his wife, Brooke, had sailed their own boat from England to San Francisco in a trip similar to our voyage in *Armorel.* I had never considered a partnership before, but after thinking it over I decided it would be OK, especially considering our interests and skills were so similar. It was the start of a 20 year partnership in three different boats. We simply shook hands then took a calendar and marked every other weekend for our respective use. Of course we did lots of trading of weekends and sailed together many times. Peter and Brooke had a young family also, so there were many times when all of us would sail together and go for pizza afterwards. Peter had a good workshop and was handy with tools with the result that I would frequently return to the boat and find some nice improvement completed. I used to tell my friends that having him as a partner was like having a fairy godmother.

Vim on a quiet morning in Paradise Cove. Peter Passano asked to be a partner, a relationship which lasted for 20 years and three boats

At the time I bought *Vim*, she was getting on to being 20 years old and was showing her age a bit. She leaked a lot if she was sailed hard and some of the woodwork was getting a bit loose. On one occasion as we were headed up to a CCA cruise in Montezuma Slough we encountered a real blast of wind as we were getting just beyond the "mothball fleet" in Suisun Bay. We didn't have time to shorten sail so we just carried on running very hard before the wind. I could feel the mast bending fore and aft (pumping), but there was absolutely nothing we could do about it at the time. Naturally, we forgot all about it when we got into smooth water. A week later up in Steamboat Slough I was horrified to see that the side planks of the wooden box-shaped mast had become almost completely unglued. It was amazing that we had sailed all the way up there from Montezuma Slough without having the mast collapse. Peter was due to come up in a few days to help me sail back home so I told him to bring up some Weldwood glue and all the C-clamps he could find. Working from a bosun's chair, we worked as much glue into the joints as we could, clamped the mast planks together and held our breath all the way home whenever the wind got strong. Later we pulled the mast out and completely rebuilt it.

Peter was elected to membership in the Cruising Club of America so we regularly sailed together on all the CCA cruises including the annual fall cruise up the coast to Tomales Bay. These trips were sometimes a bit strenuous for a little 26 footer, but I can think of only one time when we were defeated by strong winds and rough seas and had to return home. In addition to being a lovely bay with lots of anchorages, Tomales Bay was always fun because Peter's wife Brooke had the use of the family weekend cottage at Shallow Beach, a private enclave in the State Park. Since there were several CCA members who had homes at Shallow Beach, it was always the focus of the CCA cruise. It was our habit to leave *Vim* at anchor for a week or two off Shallow Beach so that we could return on weekends to enjoy Tomales Bay with our families before sailing the boat home.

On one occasion however, for some reason, it was necessary for me to sail the boat home alone along with the other CCA boats at the end of the 3-day cruise. I left the anchorage early and got to the entrance while the flood was still running strongly over the bar and into the bay. It was dead calm and the little gas engine running at full speed had barely enough power to overcome the current. When *Vim* was only a quarter of a mile or so outside the bar, the motor stopped cold. I quickly hoisted the sails but with no breeze I could see that we were being set by the flood tide back toward the rocks around the entrance. It was too deep to anchor so I hopped into the dinghy and tried desperately to tow the boat to safety but soon realized that any progress I made was more than offset by the current. I was in real trouble. I had seen the other boats in the CCA fleet pass me on the way out of the Bay, but I knew there was one more boat still to come. Desperate to have that one see me, I abandoned *Vim* temporarily and rowed closer to the entrance channel. When I saw her cross the bar I raised an oar and waved it wildly to attract her attention. It worked. Aldo Allesio, the owner, at some peril because of *Vim's* position near the rocks, came over and passed a line to tow us clear. It was a close call and in the end I got towed nearly all the way to Point Reyes before a breeze came up and allowed me to sail home.

My partnership with Pete Passano worked fine for five years, but then he was transferred by Bechtel to work on management of a job in Algeria where a large liquefied natural gas (LNG) facility was under construction. We broke up the partnership by sailing up to San Rafael and having Scott Baxter give us his best estimate of her value. After some thought he felt she would fetch $11,000. I had the dubious pleasure of buying Pete's half for the same price I had paid for the whole boat, but it had been worth it to have such a good partner. Not long afterward another friend, Bill Hickman, came by saying he had sold his boat and offered to become a new partner. He was a member of the San Francisco Yacht Club in Belvedere which was by far the most desirable location for keeping a boat on the Bay. He explained that if he got another boat within three months he could keep his berth in the club marina. I would have to join the club, of course, but since it was near our home and had a wonderful junior sailing program which would be good for Anne and Rob, it made sense for us to belong anyway. With real regret, I resigned from the Sausalito Yacht Club and joined up. It was a good decision and 30 years later I still belong. Having *Vim* in the snug, sunny, calm harbor only minutes away from our home was nice too.

After my perilous experience at the mouth of Tomales Bay, it was obvious that the engine badly needed an overhaul. Bill, being a mechanical engineer, had lots of contacts and suggested an expert mechanic to do the work. First however, we thought it would be a good idea if we cleaned all the rust off the old engine by having it sandblasted. Anyway, it <u>seemed</u> like a good idea. We pulled the motor out of the boat, stripped it down, plugged up all the holes and hauled it off to the sandblaster. After giving it a coat of primer, we took it to the mechanic who thoroughly overhauled it. When we got it back we painted it a lovely green color and re-installed it. After five hours of running, it made ghastly noises and died. Bill and I decided a second opinion was in order so we pulled it out again and took it to an engine shop in San Rafael. A couple of days later they called and suggested we come by to get the diagnosis. It seems grit in the engine had completely eaten up the bearings, cylinders and just about everything else. The shop mechanic said he had never seen anything quite like it. Apparently in spite of the motor being rinsed in a barrel of solvent it had retained a deadly trace of the sandblasting grit. Moral: Never sandblast a motor. We replaced it with an old, used "Atomic 4" which is probably still in the boat.

Rob, Anne and Chipper rowing one of my 14' dory-skiffs

One Sunday Anne, who was about 8 years old, and I sailed up to Gallinas Creek, a winding, shallow tidal estuary east of San Rafael. The tide was rising so we sailed all the way up to a pleasant little spot by Margarita Island and anchored for lunch and a swim. When the tide changed and began to ebb we raised the anchor and got underway to sail home. As we neared the entrance where the creek opened onto the wide expanse of San Pablo Bay, we approached the line of stakes which marked the unseen channel across the shallows. Anne, who was steering, asked, "Daddy, which side of the boat should I leave the markers on." Without thinking clearly (I had consumed a couple of beers), I said, "Leave them to starboard". This was obviously the wrong answer since we had left them to starboard on our way in. Needless to say, we quickly ran on the mud.

I tried to back off with the motor and when that didn't work I jumped into the dinghy and rowed an anchor out into deeper water in an effort to kedge (winch) the boat off. With the tide dropping rapidly all these efforts were of no use and within 15 minutes we were solidly aground and starting to heel over. There would be no getting off until the next high tide well after midnight. It was a sunny quiet afternoon and there was no danger so I hung up an anchor light, locked the hatch and the two of us rowed ashore to the funky little bar/resort named Buck's Landing where I could call Jane for a ride home.

While waiting for Jane to arrive Anne and I had a coke and chatted with the bar patrons. Soon a young deputy sheriff arrived in a jeep, entered the bar and inquired who owned the boat which was now leaning well over. When I explained that it belonged to me and that it was quite safe and would be retrieved that night, he relaxed and joined the conversation. When he mentioned that he had lived all of his life around there, I asked if he knew what sort of vessel was sunk near the channel where there was a sign on a post advising "Caution – Wreck". He said he thought it was just some old wooden barge. At this, one of the patrons laughed and said "That is my father's old ship, the barken-tine, *City of Papeete."* He explained that his father, a Frenchman, had owned the vessel during World War I but had lost it when it was in-terned during the hostilities. He said it had turned up on San Francisco Bay in the 1920's where it was to be used as a gambling ship and eventually was towed to San Pablo Bay and left to rot on the mud. I learned later that none of this tale was probably true but it made a good story.

About midnight Jane drove me up to Buck's Landing for the sail home. The tide was very high and I could see from the shore that

Vim was floating nicely and riding quietly on her anchor so I rowed out to the boat and got the motor started. It was calm but a very dark night with no moon. It dawned on me that there were no lights or even reflectors on the channel markers and I had only a very dim flashlight aboard. Within minutes of getting underway I could feel the keel touching the mud as I groped my way along the channel. I got off easily and made further progress but realized that it was hopeless to try to find my way slowly along the marked channel. Since the tide was so high, I believed my best chance was to go full speed directly over the shallows toward the center of San Pablo Bay by heading for the lights on the opposite shore. I was doing fine and was sure I would reach deep water before the tide dropped when suddenly a huge black mass suddenly loomed in front of the boat. I almost had a heart attack until I realized it was a big foliage-covered duck blind. I had seen these blinds on the horizon but had never paid any attention to them until now. Eventually I reached deep water and arrived home in the wee hours.

The next day I read in the Marin County newspaper that I was not the only boat having an adventure on that dark Sunday night. It seems a couple of guys in a small sailboat had anchored off Red Rock, the small island between the Tiburon Peninsula and Richmond. Apparently when their anchor dragged, they had been set ashore in the same ebb tide which had left Anne and me on the mud. Lacking a radio, they had waved at passing boats in vain for hours for someone to rescue them. Finally long after dark, they decided to light the ultimate flare--they set the island on fire. According to the newspaper, observers on shore said the brush burned so fiercely that it looked like molten lava flowing down the sides of the island. Well, that got the attention of the authorities, especially since it was quite near the Chevron Oil wharf, and soon the Coast Guard came to their rescue. Although I passed fairly close to Red Rock that night, I didn't see anything of this drama as it had apparently taken place earlier

Bill Hickman was a good partner but in a couple of years he decided to relocate on the East Coast because of a family crisis and I was back on my own again. I must have been getting restless because in the fall of 1977, I actually made a foray into the world of motorboats. I noticed an antique cruiser tied up at the yacht club and then saw an ad in the local paper for what was obviously the same boat. It was a 30', 1930 Richardson cruiser named *Limelite* and the asking price was $2200. Since I had a place to keep her at the dock behind our rental house on Gallinas Creek, I bought her thinking it would be an interesting project to improve her cosmetics over the winter.

Limelite, an old 1930 Richardson cruiser I bought to repair as a winter project, moored in Gallinas Creek

The boat had a massive 6 cylinder Chrysler "Crown" engine which barely ran because of a rusted-out exhaust manifold. I was able to fix this problem with the help of my friend, Doug Duane, one of the New Zealanders who had arrived in Sausalito on *White Squall* in 1960. He was an expert metal worker who applied his skill by brazing up the holes in the manifold. With this done, I was able to move the boat up the creek and happily spent many hours over the winter working on the exterior painting and varnishing and on the interior with more painting and upholstery. What I didn't touch in any significant way were the structural items including lots of broken frames and rot here and there. By spring she looked quite nice, but I really didn't want to keep her so I turned her over to a yacht broker in San Rafael who specialized in older boats, especially wooden ones. In the end I sold her for a pittance more than I paid for her, an outcome which, I am sure, could have been predicted by any knowledgeable yachtsman. Still, I enjoyed my winter project and came closer to realizing that I am probably happiest when working on a newly-purchased boat, getting it into the shape I want.

In the summer of 1979 Pete Passano returned from his three-year stint in Algeria. He had been corresponding with me when he arrived on the East Coast and started looking around for a boat to buy. He had in mind a large, classic wooden boat in the 55' range which would be big enough for him and his family to live aboard and go cruising. He was unsuccessful in finding what he wanted for a reasonable price so he temporarily gave up and came back out to Marin County. I told him I would be happy to be in partners again with him but only in a boat of a more modest size. When I took him down to the Corinthian Yacht Club and showed him a 36' Ohlsen sloop which I had seen there, his wife, Brooke, said, "This looks wonderful and it certainly seems plenty big." By checking the ads in *Soundings*, an East Coast yachting publication, we spotted at least four of them for sale. Pete returned east and sought out the best of the bunch, a boat named *Torfin* which we bought for $27,000. The plan was for Pete and his family to cruise New England the next season (1979) while I sold *Vim*. The following season our family would take over for a similar cruise.

Selling *Vim* was not as easy as I thought it would be, but early in the spring of 1980 she was purchased by Steve Gann, the son of the author, Earnest K. Gann. It was a happy deal all the way around. Steve loved the boat and we were pleased that someone with his experience and enthusiasm would be the new owner. He took her to Monterey and embarked on a series of upgrades which put her in top condition. She had been a grand boat for us—such a fine sailing craft and just the right size for Jane and me and our young family. I still consider her to be the most satisfactory boat I have ever owned considering what we needed and how we used her at the time.

Torfin, an Ohlsen 36, under sail in Long Island sound

CHAPTER 12

TORFIN

By September, 1979 Pete Passano and his family had completed their summer cruise on *Torfin*. They had sailed along the coast of New England from Essex, Connecticut to Maine and now the boat was lying at Camden, Maine. It was agreed that when Pete's family left to return home, my brother Skip and I would come back and help him sail her back down to Essex for a winter layup so that she would be in position for Jane and me and our two children to do a New England cruise the next summer. I hadn't sold *Vim* yet, but I was eager to see my new boat and have a spin down the coast on her.

In mid-September Skip and I caught a red-eye flight to Boston then took the bus to Maine and eventually arrived in Camden the next evening, thoroughly exhausted. The boat was anchored out in the middle of the harbor and it was dark by the time we got aboard. We all hit the bunk almost as soon as we got aboard. The dinghy with the small outboard attached was tied off astern. Sometime in the wee hours or very early in the morning I awoke out of a sound sleep thinking I could hear someone rattling the oarlocks in the dinghy, but I was just too tired to rouse myself and take a look. Anyway I was wearing contact lenses at the time and I wouldn't have been able to see anything without them so I went back to sleep. Pete was the first one up in the morning and quickly noticed that our dinghy had been stolen!

Being without a dinghy in California, with marinas all around, is no big deal, but in New England at that time, where the boats were all at anchor or on moorings, it was a serious loss. Also starting a coastwise passage with no "lifeboat" or means to get off the boat or ashore was an important safety issue. We moved *Torfin* over to the town dock and tried to figure out what to do. Within minutes we learned that yet another dinghy and motor had been stolen from a mooring that morning. I recalled that I heard what sounded like a fishboat getting underway shortly after hearing the dinghy being stolen. We called the Coast Guard on the VHF radio and told them all this and asked them to be on the lookout for a boat towing two dinghies with outboards attached. The locals who soon heard all about the thefts were outraged. That kind of thing just wasn't done in Maine!

By good luck, Pete had a friend in Camden named Clive who lived aboard his boat and offered to loan us an inflatable dinghy for our trip on the understanding that we would bring it back from Connecticut. By midmorning we were underway on a lovely fall day with a nice light northerly breeze in our favor. The trees were ablaze in their autumn colors as we slipped out of the harbor. Normally getting back to Long Island Sound from Maine is a long, tedious beat to windward, but we carried our favorable breeze all day and by evening we were off Monhegan Island, where we decided to stop for a look around and possibly spend the night. After a stroll around the island it was getting dark, but our northerly breeze was still holding so we decided to sail on through the night.

The moon was full, the air was crisp but not cold and the following wind was perfect. Except for a few afternoon sails on the bay, Skip had never done any serious sailing so I was pleased that he was getting a pleasant introduction to ocean sailing. He quickly got the knack of following a compass course and it was obvious that he was having a grand time. I was also pleased to see how nicely *Torfin* slipped along, without effort, in the ruffled, moonlit sea. By the next morning we were somewhere in the middle of the broad expanse of Cape Cod Bay. About noon, with binoculars, we spotted the upper part of a tall tower appearing over the horizon to the east which we figured was the Pilgrim Monument at Provincetown at the tip of Cape Cod and which confirmed our dead reckoning position. By nightfall we entered the canal through the arm of Cape Cod leading to Buzzard's Bay and the eastern entrance to Long Island Sound. It had been a remarkably fast and easy passage.

Three days later, after stops at Onset, Cuttyhunk Island and Stonington, we entered the Connecticut River with Essex a few miles ahead. We had set the spinnaker to take advantage of the light sea breeze behind us and were running toward the railroad drawbridge which, as usual, was in the open position (it only closed when a train approached). As we got close to the bridge we were horrified to see that it was beginning to swing shut in front of us even though there was no train in sight. Of course, a "Chinese fire drill" ensued as we spun the boat around and endeavored to douse the spinnaker as it tried to wrap itself around the rigging. As soon as we got things more or less under control, we saw the bridge starting to open again! Maybe the bridgetender was just playing games with us, but I think it is more likely that the boredom of his job just made him a little crazy.

We arrived at the Essex Boat Works to find the process of winter layup in full swing. It was the last week of September and the boating season was clearly over. Even though the weather had been superb, we saw few boats underway on our trip from Maine. The yard was pulling them out of the water and storing them as fast as they could. We arranged for a few jobs to be done over the winter and for the boat to be put in a huge covered shed with the mast placed on a rack. On our arrival at the yard we were pleased to learn that our dinghy had been found outside Camden Harbor floating upside down with the motor still attached. It had been taken to the local boatyard who flushed out the motor and stowed the dinghy for us to retrieve. We surmised that the culprit had heard our broadcast to the Coast Guard and had flipped it over and cast it loose. Pete returned to Maine with the borrowed dinghy while Skip and I returned to California.

By the following spring we had sold *Vim* and were eagerly looking forward to our summer cruise. *Torfin* was an Ohlsen 36, a very handsome boat with lovely, classic lines and having made our little trip down from Maine, I knew she would be a joy under sail. She had been built in Gothenburg, Sweden in the late 1960's and was constructed in the typical Scandinavian fashion with edge-glued planking riveted to bent oak frames. She had teak decks, laminated mahogany cabin sides and cockpit coamings with attractive, curved corners and lots of varnish. Below decks she was equally pretty with intricate joiner work and lots of charm. Her only obvious shortcoming was the underpowered auxiliary motor, an "Atomic 4" with an improperly pitched propeller.

We planned to fly east as soon as school was out and spend a little over two months cruising. Pete and his family would take over the boat for a couple of weeks in Maine at the end of our cruise after which Pete would arrange to have the boat trucked out to Sausalito. There would be four of us aboard plus Wallace, Bill Hickman's westy (West Highland white terrier), which we had been taking care of for the past year and a half. Anne was 14 and Robby was 12 years old. Both had spent enough time aboard sailboats to be good crew but probably approaching the maximum age when they would be content to leave their friends behind and spend an entire summer cooped up with their parents on a boat. Once they got the message that daddy was captain and his word was more or less law all was well, although it took them about a week to figure out that scrapping among themselves was not a good idea. We had high hopes for an interesting summer in an area where we had not traveled before.

On June 15, 1980 we boarded a night plane for New York with Wallace in the cargo compartment then drove to Essex in a rental car. We arrived at the boatyard to find *Torfin* already rigged and in the water, looking very smart in her fresh coat of dark green paint. As promised, a new bow pulpit had been installed, the home port on the transom had been changed to San Francisco and all the other tasks assigned to the yard over the winter had been taken care of. In spite of our exhausted state, we set to work to get the boat ready to sail.

*In June 1980 we arrived in Essex CT to fit out Torfin for
a 2 ½ month cruise in New England*

By afternoon the next day we had groceries aboard, the water and fuel tanks full and things mostly organized below decks. We shoved off and sailed a few miles up the Connecticut River to a perfectly sheltered spot called Hamburg Cove where we gratefully anchored and took in our surroundings. It was a weekday and still fairly early in the season so we had the cove to ourselves. The trees surrounding the cove were in their lush green colors of early summer and on one side of the cove was a picturesque little graveyard of obvious antiquity with a small, steepled church in the background. Our first taste of New England couldn't have been nicer.

Anne and Rob were determined to sail to New York so the general plan was to sail west down Long Island Sound, spend a day or two in the City then travel back up the Sound and on to Maine. After two days of plodding slowly to windward we arrived at the wealthy community of Darien, Connecticut where we had an introduction to the family of our friend, Walter Crump in Belvedere. With some trepidation we approached the modest-looking but obviously exclusive, Norotan Yacht Club, home of such sailing luminaries as Bob Bavier. When we inquired if a mooring could be found for us, they couldn't have been nicer and commented that they seldom had visits from distant cruising boats. We had dinner that night in the splendid waterfront home of Walter's sister and brother-in-law.

At this point it occurred to me that our kids really didn't want to *sail* to New York, they just wanted to *go* to New York. With this revelation, it was easy to decide to just take the commuter train to the City the next morning and play tourist. It was a wonderful day. We arrived at Grand Central Station, took the subway to lower Manhattan where we went to the top of the World Trade Center, then took the boat to the Statue of Liberty. After seeing Times Square and the Empire State Building and a short shopping spree at Macy's at the insistence of our kids, we caught the evening train back to Darien with everyone completely satisfied and happy. Now we could begin our cruise to Maine.

We retreated up back up Long Island Sound with the light westerly breeze now in our favor. One memorable overnight stop was at the Norwalk Islands where we anchored behind a low offshore island which was the home of a group of friendly trumpeter swans who quickly came over to see us and beg for handouts. We found their presence a charming addition to the scene but we learned later that they were rather controversial because they were not native to the area and being rather aggressive, they had displaced much of the local sea-fowl.

After a brief return to the boatyard in Essex and an overnight stay at Block Island, we sailed for Cockles Harbor, a shallow anchor-age at the extreme east end of Long Island. The entrance was via a short but narrow channel with sandbanks on both sides. The currents are strong in this area and, in this case, the flow was at right angle to the channel. In no time we were set out of the channel and hit the sand about halfway in. Luckily, we were towing the dinghy so it took only moments to lower the outboard motor and attach it then scoot up to the bow, drop the anchor down to the dinghy and carry it out to deep wa-ter. It was a good thing all went like clockwork because the tide was dropping fast. We quickly put the anchor warp on a sheet winch and we were off! Things don't always work out this nicely, but this time we got lucky.

We were fortunate in getting a reservation to tie up in Mystic Seaport for a few days and it was surely a high point of our cruise. A short trip up the Mystic River, through a drawbridge and we were in the middle of the finest historical maritime setting in the nation. We tied up to the CCA dock with a dozen other visiting yachts in the cen-ter of a miniature 19th century seaport complete with a pair of square rigged ships, a working shipyard, and functioning workshops of all kinds including a sail loft, boatbuilding shop, a cooper's shop, black-smith shop, a rigging shop and many others. The library and collec-tion of ship models and carved figureheads alone took hours to browse through. It was a nice break to return to *Torfin* for a beer or lunch then set off again to take in more of the collection.

While there I noticed a wood sloop named *Curlew* from San Francisco. It was obvious that she had been on a long sailing voyage because of her weather-beaten condition and the chafing gear on her rigging. The owner, Berto Nevin, said he was on his way to Maine and mentioned that he had sailed to British Columbia from San Fran-cisco a few years before and that it compared favorably with Maine. When I asked what boat he had sailed on he said, "A big 67'yawl named Athene." I was surprised by this because I had sailed up the coast on the *Athene* and I knew he must have been referring to the same trip. After comparing notes we realized that we were both on the same boat at the time! She was a big boat but not *that* big! It turned out that we were on opposite watches, Berto now had a big bushy beard and I was now wearing contact lenses instead of my usual horn-rimmed glasses. Since then we have become good friends and always get a chuckle out of our meeting at Mystic without recognizing each other.

Anne at Mystic Seaport where we spent three days enjoying the ships and exhibits

Our next port-of-call was Newport, Rhode Island where we anchored off the Ida Lewis Yacht Club. It was a spectacular setting with magnificent mansions (summer cottages) from the "Gilded Age" of the late 1900's, on the waterfront opposite our mooring. This happened to be a year for an America's Cup Race regatta and it was to take place here in Newport in late summer. Now, in early July, we saw the 12 meter boats out for practice daily and we visited the docks where the boats from the local syndicates and the challenging countries were tied up. It was a lively, interesting scene.

The town of Newport had promised to shoot off a million dollars worth of fireworks for the 4th of July, so we extended out stay to see the show. Unfortunately, as evening approached a dense fog rolled in and the event was canceled, a real disappointment for Anne and Rob. It seemed unlikely that they would spend a million celebrating the 5th of July, so we sailed next morning for the Elizabeth Islands, about 30 miles to the east. It was clear and calm when we got underway but soon a very fresh northeast wind began to blow and it got stronger as the day went on. Within an hour or so a moderate gale was on our stern and it took some careful steering to keep the boat steady on her course while the steep, cresting seas tried to shove her stern aside as they passed under the counter. We were towing the dinghy which was a very unseaman-like thing to be doing in such conditions, but to our surprise it skittered along behind us without showing any signs of capsizing. It was a miniature version of a Boston Whaler with a square bow which seemed to suit the conditions. In any event there was no room to stow it on deck, so we just hoped she would survive.

*Sailing in a fresh northeaster across Buzzards Bay on
our way towards Martha's Vineyard*

While all this was going on poor Wallace was definitely not feeling well. He climbed into the pilot bunk and looked miserable. On deck *Torfin* was tearing along while the sun shone brightly on the white-capped seas all around us. Suddenly we spotted a nearly new Avon inflatable dinghy near us on the top of a wave. My first impulse was to spin the boat around into the wind and attempt to capture it. This idea got an instant veto from Jane in the form of "don't even think of it!" She was absolutely right, of course, because we would have been thrown on to our beam ends, doused in spray, possibly torn a sail and maybe even have lost our dinghy if we had done so. So we carried on with our wild ride and by late afternoon slid under the lee of the islands and anchored in Tarpaulin Cove at Naushon Island. That night, after dark, we faintly heard the boom of the fireworks 30 miles away back in Newport.

While anchored at Tarpaulin Cove, we were hailed by a Cruising Club member who told us that his mooring at Edgartown on Martha's Vineyard Island would be vacant and we were welcome to use it. This was good news because we were now well aware of how crowded the harbors in New England were. We found the mooring the next day after some hunting around and within minutes the harbormaster's launch came by to inform us that we were tied to a private buoy. When we told him we had met the owner and had been offered the use of it, he cheerfully welcomed us.

Edgartown was in full summer tourist mode. The harbor was packed with boats, the main street was thronged with vacationers and there was plenty to see ashore in the way of quaint New England style houses and shops. It was a colorful scene. The next day we accepted an invitation to go out to the center of the Island to spend the day with friends from Belvedere who had rented an old farmhouse for the summer. This apparently is a fashionable thing to do as reflected in the exorbitant rent they paid for what was not much more than an unattractive old house in a flat uninteresting district. Luckily they had brought along their maid who had her work cut out to make the place habitable. For us it was a nice break to be away from the boat for a day.

Our cruise continued toward Cap Cod by braving the swirling currents at Woods Hole and finding a nice anchorage at Hadley's Harbor, one of the snuggest and prettiest places we had seen. It was here that I began to see the advantage of being a member of the Cruising

Club of America. Hugh Jacks had proposed me for membership 15 years earlier with the explanation that it was no big deal, in fact almost unknown on the West Coast, but on the East Coast a member flying the burgee at the masthead would have a chance to meet many interesting people and would enjoy a certain status. As we entered Hadley's Harbor I noticed two boats flying the CCA burgee, one of which was a good-sized motor yacht. Shortly the skipper came by in his dinghy and introduced himself as "Dick." It took me a few minutes to realize that it was Richard Bertram, president of Bertram Yachts. The other CCA yacht, a transatlantic veteran named *Guilemot*, became a buddy boat for several days as we headed north

I think the home port designation of San Francisco on our transom was a bit of an asset, if not entirely an honest one. A typical comment by a passing boat was, "My! You have sailed a long way." Usually we would explain that we had purchased the boat on the East Coast, but not always. When we sailed into Gloucester, MA we anchored off the prestigious-looking Eastern Yacht Club, a stately structure located in the corner of the harbor. We rowed ashore to the club hoping that we could possibly get a shower. As we entered the clubhouse we realized that there was a rather formal cocktail party in full swing. When we explained that we were off the green San Francisco sloop in the anchorage, they instantly insisted that we join the party. We could hardly refuse.

Just north of Cape Ann, off the coast of New Hampshire lay the Isles of Shoals, an intriguing group of nine small, rocky islands with a well-sheltered anchorage and tons of history. It was one of our favorite stops on our New England cruise. Apparently the name comes not from shallow water but from the shoals of fish formerly seen around the islands. The bounty attracted fishermen from Europe, before the Pilgrims, in the early 1600's and was shown on Captain John Smith's map of 1617. Supposedly Edward Teach (Blackbeard) spent his honeymoon here in 1717 but scrammed leaving his bride and buried treasure when the British navy came after him. In the 1700's it had a population of 1000 souls and a township named Gosport. Today it has one private home and a Unitarian Church conference center housed in an old Victorian, wooden hotel building. One of the island's claims to fame is a sensational ax murder of two women in 1873 described in lurid detail in the popular little booklet sold on the islands named "Moonlight Murder at Smuttynose" (the name of one of the islands). We enjoyed wandering over the treeless islands and pondering the history of the place. From there we sailed for Maine.

The crew aboard Torfin in Cape Cod Bay including Wallace, Bill Hickman's Westie, on loan to us for 1 ½ years.

The weather had been fine ever since we left Essex and continued to be nice for the remainder of the summer. We were surprised at how warm the seawater was right up until we reached Maine, at which point it turned not just chilly, but downright frigid. Also surprising to us was how placid the ocean was. With the weather patterns moving across the U.S. from west to east and out into the Atlantic, there was no big persistent swell system like we have on the Pacific coast and the breezes were generally in an offshore direction. We were frequently asking ourselves, "where are the waves?" It was not at all unusual to have a smooth anchorage in full view of the open Atlantic Ocean. The sailing was nice too in the generally gentle breezes. We sailed almost exclusively with our biggest genoa jib. The usual pattern was a flat calm in the early morning with a light sailing breeze coming up just as we started to get underway after breakfast and continuing through the day. *Torfin* was such a fine sailing boat that we used the engine very little. It was not unusual for us to stop at a fuel dock to fill our 30 gallon water tank and buy only a few gallons of fuel.

Once we reached Maine, the crowds of boats we saw in Long Island Sound and Cape Cod were gone. There were cozy anchorage everywhere with lovely wooded scenery and quaint towns to visit. Having Wallace aboard was a nice thing too, since it gave us the perfect excuse to go ashore a couple of times a day and look around while giving him a walk.

Our cruise in Maine was mostly centered on Penobscot Bay, a large complicated cruising ground on the central coast of Maine. It was a wonderland of islands, fjords, bays and waterways of amazing complexity. It tested our navigation skills since we had no radar and a sizable error in our magnetic compass. Added to this was a certain amount of fog, large tides and plenty of current in places. To add additional spice to the problem were rocks and ledges of solid granite everywhere. Fortunately, there were lots of buoys marking hazards to navigation. Common wisdom in these waters when one missed a buoy in the fog is to head for a bold shore where one can creep along the shoreline until a known point is found, then lay out a new course. We tried to follow this strategy one foggy day while crossing a wide stretch of water as we headed for Winter Harbor on Vinylhaven Island. We missed the buoy about halfway across so we altered course a bit to the right to head for the shore adjacent to the deep inlet of the harbor. When we had "run out our time" and still had not made out the shoreline, we slowly and cautiously continued on the same course. After much too much time, just as panic was about to set in, the fog "scaled up" revealing our position in middle of and far inside the long, narrow confines of Winter Harbor by sheer luck.

It was at this place we encountered one of the students of the Outward Bound School from nearby Hurricane Island. We had been told how each student is dropped off at a small island or point of land to undergo his four-day survival test and that we should just leave them alone. They are given only 8 matches, a square of plastic tarp, a tin can and a knife and left to survive on whatever berries, clams and mussels they can find. We spotted a girl on the point opposite our anchorage and made a point of ignoring her. Unfortunately (for her) the night of our arrival, we fired up the grille on the stern and cooked a batch of fried chicken which produced a plume of fragrant smoke leading directly to her camp. Four days later just before she was picked up, Anne, Rob and I took the dinghy over to have a chat with her. She said the area where she was marooned had been picked clean of berries by the previous students. She had spoiled her eight matches and could not stomach raw mussels and clams so she simply starved for four days. She said she was awfully weak and sleepy but otherwise was amazed that she was quite all right. Her biggest crisis she said was the night we arrived when the smell of our fried chicken just about killed her!

One of our favorite areas was Blue Hill, Maine, a spacious harbor with a nice little town and a congenial club named the Kollegewidgwok Yacht Club. Our friend, Hal Roth, well known cruising sailor and author, was living here with his equally well traveled wife, Margaret. We had known them well when they lived in Sausalito and were pleased to see them again and learn of their latest travels on their sloop, *Whisper*. We had dinner together and spent a pleasant afternoon picking blueberries on the hill behind the town. When we first arrived in Blue Hill we passed a boat with a young boy aboard who took a look at us and casually said, "Hi Rob. What are you doing here?" It turned out that he was a school mate of Robs back in Tiburon, whose family had as summer place in Blue Hill. Also we reconnected with Berto Nevin, the former shipmate with the bushy beard I had met in Mystic. It is truly a small world around cruising folk.

In all, it was a grand summer. *Torfin* was a perfect boat for job—she was roomy for the four of us, pretty enough to gather complements everywhere and lots of fun to sail in the gentle breezes of the area. Rob and Anne had a good time too after they settled into life aboard a 36' boat. About a week before the end of the trip they went back to their usual bickering and rivalry, but they really got along well during almost the entire summer. Rob had a particularly fine time using the dinghy and outboard motor. He discovered that if he got the boat perfectly balanced it could actually plane with the little 1 ½ HP motor. He had fun being our "ambassador". He loved to invite interesting cruisers from other yachts over for drinks. I must admit we met some remarkable people that way. Even Wallace was a good addition to the crew until Bill Hickman got his life back in order and drove up to Maine to reclaim his beloved pooch. It was wrench to see Wallace depart.

Finally, on August 18th my boat partner, Pete Passano and his family arrived at Camden, Maine to take over the boat and begin a two week cruise of their own before shipping *Torfin* by truck to California. Pete and I had heard many horror stories about trucking a wooden boat across the country. We had been told how the varnish can be blasted off by the highway grit or how the boat can become so dried out the seams will all be gaping open at the end of the trip. The truck driver, an old experienced hand, told Pete to paint the teak deck with dish-washing detergent, wipe the dark green hull with plenty of car wax to turn it white and to seal up the hatches with duct tape with the rugs, blankets and sleeping bags soaking wet inside. The boat arrived six days later in Sausalito with her hull looking in perfect shape and when the deck was scrubbed and the hull polished, she never looked better.

The following summer we sailed *Torfin* to Southern California for a cruise in the Channel Islands with Pete and I taking turns having two-week cruises with our families out of Santa Barbara. The sail down the coast was uneventful and the sailing around the islands was fine. The trip back, however nearly cost us the boat or worse. Pete and I together with a pair of sailing friends left Santa Barbara in mid-morning for the typically smooth 40 mile segment to Point Conception. We were not surprised to find a very strong northwesterly wind blowing beyond the Point so after sticking our nose out into the gale briefly, we retreated back around the Point and anchored in Coxo Anchorage to wait for things to calm down. After dinner and a snooze the wind appeared to have dropped altogether so we got under way again about 11:00 PM.

When we rounded Point Conception again it was obvious that there was still plenty of wind blowing and the farther offshore we went, the harder it blew. Hoping to get less wind and sea closer inshore, we tacked back in on port tack (with the wind on the left side) and tried to work our way up the shore. It was very dark although we could get a glimpse of the occasional star overhead. Soon it was obvious that even though the mainsail was reefed we were carrying way too much sail. We decided we needed to get the jib down and Pete clawed his way forward to do it. I was steering the boat through the rough seas with spray flying all over the place and visibility just about nil. I couldn't see how close we were to the shore and was concerned because I couldn't see the light on Point Arguello which should have been clearly visible. Suddenly I saw the wash of a wave on a huge rock directly ahead of us! I instantly put the helm down to throw the boat onto the other tack which caught Pete, up on the bow, unawares and nearly caused him to go overboard. It was a terrifying moment. Later we realized the reason I couldn't see the shore or Arguello light was because there must have been a shroud of fog right along the shoreline.

We worked our way offshore by motorsailing and toward dawn the wind eased and the sea smoothed down. Amazingly, we had been towing our aluminum dinghy through all of this drama. When we checked it the next morning, it had only a teacup of water in it. The rest of the trip up the coast was definitely an anticlimax.

Pete and I owned *Torfin* for a total of 8 years. We took her on summer vacations up in the Delta, on weekend cruises, and day sails and other activities, including a burial at sea. One day a recently widowed friend phoned and asked if we would be willing to help her dispose of her late husband Bill's ashes from our sailboat. We willingly agreed to take her, her three grown children and a couple of friends out on the Bay for the ceremony. It was a typical windy summer Sunday when we arrived at a spot near Alcatraz where Bill had loved to sail. The waves were big, the wind was strong and there must have been a couple of regattas going on as there were boats all around us yelling at us that they were racing. The sealed plastic box of ashes, which seemed quite heavy, was produced, some appropriate poetry was read, flowers were strewn on the water and the box was reverently cast over the rail. But damn! It floated!

Retrieving the box was not easy, as we had the mainsail up and no scoop net or other means of grasping the darned thing before the bow wave washed it away from us. We madly circled around with the sail flapping wildly as we tacked and gybed amidst the traffic. Meanwhile Bill's wife and kids were shouting with laughter about how much he would have loved the crazy scene. At last we got the box back, pried it open with a hammer and a screwdriver and finally consigned the contents to the deep.

Later I was describing the fiasco to a yachting friend. He asked, "Was it one of those tough brown plastic boxes?" When I confirmed that indeed it was the same sort of container, he laughed and said the same thing had happened on a burial at sea he had attended. The skipper of the boat resolved the flotation problem my slipping down into the cabin and retuning with a revolver which he used to shoot the box full of holes!

Each year we made a trip 50 miles up the coast to Tomales Bay where Pete's father-in-law owned a cabin at Shallow Beach, an enclave of ten family properties inside the California State Park. These trips were always combined with a CCA cruise to Tomales Bay. Usually we would leave *Torfin* at anchor or on a mooring for a couple of weeks so that our families could spend time at Shallow Beach. I thought our little cruises to Tomales Bay were always especially nice. The place is invariably shunned by the cruising guides because of the shallow, sometimes dangerous entrance but once inside, it is delightful. The CCA cruise get-togethers were fun and I always enjoyed the trip up and back.

The only time I can recall when we had a bit of difficulty in Tomales Bay was the time an extremely low tide temped us to try an alternative channel on the way out to avoid a shallow patch inside of, but near the entrance. Partly we did this to help our friend, Doug Duane, who had been invited to join us with his boat, *Hinano,* which drew 7 ½ of water. The channel took us around a big shoal inside of Tom Point then down the inside of the beach at the entrance. The fast-flowing current over the partly submerged beach quickly set both boats out of the channel and put us hard aground on the sand. It was a scary situation because there was enough swell coming over the beach to make us thump heavily on the hard sand and the current was running so fast that it was almost impossible to row an anchor out to kedge off. After a lot of agony and effort, we got a small fishing boat to help us get our anchors out and managed to get afloat again.

Once we got back in the main channel we crossed the bar, but to our dismay found a strong southerly wind and a very rough sea outside. *Torfin* was making heavy weather of it and leaking pretty badly so after short while we decided to go back inside Tomales Bay and leave the boat for another week. As we neared the entrance we noticed that the wind was blowing directly *out* of the bay. I suggested to Pete that it might be a good idea to start the engine just in case we had to go head-to-wind to get through the narrowest and shallowest part of the entrance. We were close-hauled and barely making it over the bar when the engine stopped cold! Talk about the perversity of inanimate objects! That bloody motor could have stopped anywhere, but it chose to do so right at the worst possible moment. Luckily we were able to point high enough to get inside and sail to safety. Later we found out that the condenser on the ignition had failed just at the wrong time.

It seemed like *Torfin* was always having narrow escapes. We didn't have a permanent berth at the San Francisco Yacht Club but were usually in a temporary berth. When we had to leave the harbor for lack of an available berth, we would put the boat on a mooring out in Belvedere Cove if it was summer or put her up in Gallinas Creek behind our little rental cottage if it was winter. We always made sure that we had the boat safely up in the creek by November 1st. On year I was unable to move the boat until after the first week of November because of very low tides during the day. To be safe I added an extra 40' length of rope to the mooring. On November 3rd an unexpected southerly storm came up. I received a phone call at the office from a Club member who lived on Belvedere Cove informing me that *Torfin* was loose from its mooring and was headed for the rocks. Jane received a similar call at her job in Sausalito. We both headed for the scene of the shipwreck. It was blowing like the dickens straight into the Cove and there was a wicked sea running. The boat was lying near the shore but by good luck, the rising tide was still low enough that her keel went aground before she got up against the rocks. Jane was there ahead of me and was furious because the Coast Guard had just left without giving any help. They could have easily pulled the boat out to deeper water but refused, saying no lives were in danger. Thanks a lot! I managed to get to the boat in a dinghy and was able to carry out an anchor with some help from friends who were on the scene. With the tide coming up, we were able to winch the boat out to safety before any serious damage was done. The new piece of mooring line I had added had parted right in the middle of its length. I never could figure out why.

A final near-disaster took place when poor *Torfin* sank at the dock one winter while she was tied up in Gallinas Creek. I had heard a major storm was coming so I drove up to the creek, checked the mooring lines, took off the big canvass cover and pumped out the bilges. We had a rather large electric pump which discharged into a "tee" right under the sink drain. The pump worked so well that it tended to fill up the sink in which case I sometimes put the plug in the drain until the pumping was finished. As I was driving away, I wondered if I had remembered to remove the plug. I thought "sure, I must have," and kept on driving home. Early the next morning, at the peak of the storm our tenant phoned to say that maybe our boat had sunk because he could only see a part of the stern sticking up out of the water. I knew exactly what had happened and it had nothing to do with the storm. By leaving the plug in the sink I had allowed water to siphon back into the boat through the pump. Damn!

We drove up to scene of the disaster. It was an extremely high tide, the storm was going full force with driving rain and the water was muddy brown from all the wind and runoff. The boat's hull was completely underwater except for some of the railing around the stern. It is very shallow at the dock so I knew she was sitting on the bottom and that her cabin house would undoubtedly be exposed at low tide later in the day. I went off and rented a gas-powered pump then went back and rented another one for good measure. It was all very depressing and it seemed to take forever for the tide to drop. Finally by afternoon the deck was just about level with the water except for the bow. After plugging up the chain hawse pipe with rags, we started the pumps and within minutes poor *Torfin* floated up to her normal waterline.

The mess below decks was a disaster. When the boat sank, all the oil in the engine came out via the dipstick hole and deposited itself over the entire surface of the boat as she was pumped out. The mattresses were sodden, everything in the lockers was soaked in oily water and everything electrical was ruined. We set to work to empty the boat then went after the motor to try to salvage it. The starter and alternator were removed and washed and later dried in the oven at home. We washed and flushed the engine as best we could then poured oil in the cylinders and cranked it over by hand. It survived just fine. The next day we completed stripping everything out of the boat and began the laborious process of cleaning and scrubbing the interior. In the end we scrubbed it three times and later still found places where oily residue remained.

The next step was to paint and varnish the interior, replace all the electrical equipment and fixtures, replace the galley surfaces and then make new cushions and upholstery of pretty blue fabric. It was a lot of work but when complete, the boat looked better than ever. Pete and I had never carried insurance on the boat so the clean-up and repair was all done at our expense. I think the total cost was probably less than $500. I am sure if we had been insured and had called a boat yard to float and repair her, the cost would have been in the range of ten thousand dollars. You can be sure that one of the repair items I did was to install a check valve in the bilge pump hose.

Later in the spring, Pete and I scraped down all of the brightwork on the cabin sides, rails and cockpit and refinished them with many coats of varnish. Next we hauled the boat for her annual bottom job and gave her an especially nice paint job of dark green on her topsides using a sponge pad for applying the enamel. She looked absolutely gorgeous.

We had decided that the time had come to sell *Torfin* so we placed an ad with a photo in *Latitude 38* for the asking price of $32,000, quite a large sum for a wooden boat with a gas engine. On the first day the ad appeared a couple came over to the yacht club to have a look. We took them out for a short sail and when we got back to the dock they gave us a check for the full price.

Sea Bear, our home-built, steel 39' cutter

CHAPTER 13

SEA BEAR

We sold *Torfin* in the spring of 1987. It was part of my master plan to retire early. Actually my ambition had always been to retire at age 55. I had already missed that target by a couple of years, but it was close enough. Anne was in college at Hayward State struggling to get a degree in business. Robby had graduated from high school and had decided that he could use a bit of discipline in his life so he joined the Army. Jane was working part time at Scanmar in Sausalito, where they made windvane steering gears for sailboats, when I abruptly resigned from my career job at URS/Blume Engineers partly because I got fed up with the corporate style when URS, a holding company, took over the firm, but actually because I wanted to. I had a lot of sailing in mind and decided it was time to get started.

I was 57 years old so I had a few years to go before I would get Social Security and I had no company pension or retirement benefit except for a little money from a modest profit sharing plan. My ace-in-the-hole was that we had invested in a few bits of real estate in Marin County which produced some income. I figured we could get along. Jane, God bless her, went along with the plan. It was a wonderful feeling to suddenly be free. I had apparently been under more stress than I realized because now I was no longer having indigestion and began to sleep well. I had a couple of jobs to finish up at the office, which I did on a consulting basis, but otherwise I was able to plan ahead for a life of nautical adventure.

My boat partner, Pete Passano, was also wrapping up his career, not necessarily because he wanted to, but partly because his employer, Bechtel, was going through a dry spell and people, including Pete, were being put on furlough. Pete and I had talked a lot about

getting a boat suitable for some serious ocean cruising. We settled on
the idea of a disposable steel boat---a simple but rugged boat which
could be built inexpensively and sailed hard for some years and then
sold cheaply. To be truthful, I wasn't sure I wanted to embark on a big
boatbuilding project---I had seen too many of them turn into 10 or 15
years marathons. I told Pete OK but only if we did it in a way that it
could be completed in two years and no more. This meant keeping it
super simple.

We knew about a diesel engine built in China, sold by a dealer
in San Diego, for only $1500, so we decided we would start there and
find a design to match it. A hard chine steel hull with a full keel and an
outboard rudder would be the easiest to construct. After quite a lot of
looking around we found a design we liked called a "Departure 35" by
Charles Whitholz, an East Coast designer. The style was what we had
in mind but it was a bit small, so I contacted him and asked if he had a
similar design in a larger size. He said he had a 42 footer with a
counter (overhanging) stern but offered to give us some blue prints
plus a supplemental drawing with the stern bobbed off for an outboard
rudder all for the modest sum of $400. We now had a design.

She was to be a 39' cutter, a true cutter, with the mast stepped
right in the middle of the hull with a jib and large overlapping fore-
staysail and a modest-sized mainsail. Mr. Whitholz had given us the
lines and offsets for laying out the hull plus a variety of drawings
showing various layouts and rigs for several of the 42 footers. I began
drawing a set of drawings for our boat showing the sail plan, deck layout and interior we intended to build. It was an interesting process,
especially arriving at an interior layout we were both happy with.
About this time we paid $300 for a broken aluminum mast (in three
pieces) from a large racing boat we found lying at Anderson's Boatyard in Sausalito. It appeared to be suitable for our new cutter but was
a few feet short, so I modified the rig, keeping the same sail area but
spreading the sail plan out along the base by adding a short bowsprit
and a longer boom. The mast had come from a boat named *Fujimo*,
which, as the story went, derived its name from the owner getting such
a hard time from his wife for spending so much money on the boat that
he changed the name to mean F*** You Jane, I'm Moving Out!

Pete and I owned a pair of adjacent small cottages on Gallinas
Creek in San Rafael and the plan was to build the boat in the backyard

of Pete's house then move it over to a little dock behind my house after it was launched. The creek was very shallow so just how we would launch the boat was a bit vague, but we figured we would solve that problem when we got to it.

In the late summer of 1997, after I had returned from a sailing trip from Victoria, BC to Alaska, Pete got a call from a friend telling us about a nicely constructed steel boat which had arrived in Sausalito from Puget Sound. We went over to see it and were impressed. The design wasn't so great, but the construction and details were superb. We made a point of getting to know the owner, Gary Webb, who was living aboard with his wife, Patty and little son, Spike. We could see that they were living in an expensive marina on a shoestring, so we made them the offer of a free dock behind my house on Gallinas Creek, and if things worked out, perhaps he could work for us helping build the new boat. Gary said, "I'll think about it." We even dragged him up to the place one evening to see it, but we still got no commitment. A couple of weeks later we heard from a friend that Gary planned to move his boat that weekend somewhere up a creek. We knew there was only one creek he could be going to, so we went to see him and offered to pilot his boat across the shallows. When we arrived at the dock, Patty was delighted---the dock was located across from a lovely wooded island but best of all, it was only a block away from her beloved Kingdom Hall of the Jehovah's Witness Church. Poor Spike was dressed in his little tweed suit, out with his mother selling copies of *The Watchtower* the next evening.

Pete and I bought some simple metal working tools including a "stick" welder, oxy-acetylene outfit, abrasive cut-off saw and a drill press and built a small tool shed in Pete's backyard. One of the advantages of a steel boat is that it can be built outdoors with minimal equipment. Meanwhile I had laid out a floor of plywood sheets in my backyard in Tiburon and started to loft the full-size lines and sections of the boat and had placed an order for a truck load of steel to be delivered from Petaluma. On the first of December, I had completed my obligations at the office and Pete was out of work so we were free to begin. We stared construction with Gary as the boat builder/welder and Pete and I as the helpers. Within a couple of weeks the keel was in place and the fabricated frames were erected. On January 2nd we had a big "keel laying" party at the backyard boat works, but actually the boat was almost a fully-formed skeleton at the time. It was amazing how quickly the boat took shape. Within a couple of months the hull was plated and the deck and cabin were begun. Gary kept Pete and me busy grinding all the welds smooth, moving steel into place and helping to fabricate many minor pieces and fittings. Gary had a lot of clever ways to round off all the corners and edges of the boat using pipe, "weld ells" and segments of hollow truck drive shafts. It was soon obvious that we were not building a disposable boat. She was going to be a beauty.

Sea Bear framed up in our backyard boatyard on the banks of
Gallinas Creek in San Rafael, December 1987

We had picked up our Chinese diesel and set it up on blocks near the boat. It was a very heavy two-cylinder, 20 HP brute with top revs of only 1600 RPM and had already acquired the nick name of "Tu Lung Bang". One Sunday, a day when we ordinarily didn't work on the boat, we were all three messing around in the backyard and decided to try running the engine. Gary was not satisfied that the reverse gear lever was operating smoothly and suggested we take a look inside the gear box before we started it. When we opened it up, we were surprised to find a steel angle bracket sitting on top of the gears in spite of a nice little chrome-plated strip on the side stating, "Inspected to satisfactory by Z". We were puzzled and could only surmise that someone had been putting something over on Mr. Z. A few weeks later I saw an article in the paper telling that the Commerce Department was concerned that convict-made products were coming in from China. One of the products was diesel engines! Regardless of its origins, that engine is still in the boat after 16 years and over 100,000 of travel and still runs fine.

After only six months all of the steel work was complete including the engine installation, hatches, anchor rollers and lifeline pulpits and stanchions. Gary and his family sailed away toward Mexico and Pete left for a Bechtel job in Tennessee. I was left to complete the boat and began by setting to work to paint the boat, a laborious job involving sandblasting and many coats of primer and paint. In August Pete returned for a short while to give a hand to melt 5000 pounds of lead ballast into ingots and to help launch the boat. I had already removed the shoring holding up the boat and had it lying over on its side on a plywood sled which rested on wooden rollers. The rollers would roll down a pair of wood plank rails resting on the ground and extending down the bank to the water. It was much too shallow to launch the boat upright in a cradle in the usual fashion.

On August 28th we invited about 150 of our friend to witness the christening of *Sea Bear* and her launching. Our unorthodox method of getting her into the water caused a bit of anxiety, but all went well. At precisely high tide the winch on the front of a truck took a strain on the rope which led from the boat, across the creek to a tree and back to the truck. The boat slowly moved forward then gained speed as she rolled down the slope and into the water. A great cheer went up as she seemed to shake herself and settle back on her lines. A wonderful moment! Later in the afternoon, after much beer had been consumed, a "bucket brigade" was organized to move all 2 ½ tons of ballast down and into the boat.

Sea Bear ready to roll down the ways and into the creek
Shallow water precluded the use of a launching cradle

In early October I motored the boat down to a boat yard to step the mast and on January 2nd, only a year after the start of construction, Pete came out from Tennessee to help take *Sea Bear* for her first sail. She was just a shell below, but on deck she looked like a real sailboat and she sailed beautifully---nicely balanced and surprisingly fast. To say I was delighted would be an understatement, especially after having taken some liberties with the design of the rig. I spent the following year building the interior of the boat. I have to admit I was a bit intimidated at the outset because of my lack of experience, but as I got into the work I found it was not as difficult as I had imagined and was extremely rewarding. Afterward, while cruising, I would find myself gazing around the cabin and admiring the curved moldings and details and reflecting on the satisfaction and pleasure which flowed from their creation by my own hands. Our promise to keep the boat simple was kept. Refrigeration, roller furling, water pressure, opening ports and various other luxuries were left out of the program. Much of the equipment including winches, anchors, compass, pumps, stove, etc. came from the well-stocked basements and garages of the yachting community and marine flea markets. We liked to think that *Sea Bear* was equipped with the very latest in 1950's technology. By April, 1990, a little less than 2 ½ years from the start, the boat was complete and we hosted a big "Commissioning Party" complete with a live band. The boat looked fine and we were eager to take her on her first real sea trial, a voyage to Hawaii.

A year after launching the interior shapes up

*   *   *   *

We set off for Hawaii on June 26th with a crew of four aboad — Pete and I plus our daughter, Anne and her fiancé, Steve. Jane had opted out of another long trip at sea and would join us later for some cruising in the Islands. Anne had been sailing with us all her life on various boats, but Steve was a complete novice. He quickly "learned the ropes" however and soon became a good crew. Normally a voyage to Hawaii from San Francisco is characterized by a rough, cold spell getting away from the coast followed by increasingly warmer and more beautiful sailing as one nears the islands. This time, however, it was lovely from the very first day and remained so for the remainder of the 15 ½ day crossing to Hilo. I vividly recall the first night as Anne sat silhouetted in the moonlight after the last lights of the California coast disappeared astern. A fast-flowing stream of foam emerged into the silver path of the moon as it rose higher in the eastern sky. Below a cabin lamp turned very low cast a mellow light on enamel and varnished trim. *Sea Bear* slid along without effort on an easy beam reach, steered flawlessly by "Mortimer," our Monitor windvane gear. Ahead lay three months of cruising to Hawaii and return, the culmination of probably the most rewarding effort of my life.

June 1990, we are ready to sail for Hawaii
with Anne, me, Pete and Steve Camby, Anne's fiancé

For the entire trip the wind simply varied from 12 to 18 knots, with very few squalls and a nice moon most of the way. Within a few days the wonderful routine of a yacht at sea on an easy passage was established with the nights and days occupied with the usual round of watch keeping, cooking, cleaning and sleeping. To our surprise, Loran coverage stopped on the 4th day, which gave us the additional pleasant task of celestial navigation.

Sea Bear ambled along at an easy pace under her downwind rig of poled-out genoa, mainsail and watersail under the main boom. Except for one breezy day when we made 180 miles, the gentle conditions held our average speed to a modest 138 miles per day. But with dry decks, hatches wide open and shirt-sleeve weather during the night watches, we weren't complaining. Anne seemed to catch the spirit of the passage one night when she said, "Well I guess it's time for me to go on deck and pretend I'm on watch".

Pete and I were delighted with our new boat. She was steady and perfectly well balanced and so easy to steer that she felt like she was traveling on rails. Her insulated hull was amazingly quiet and seemed cool as a cave even in the tropical sun. About the only little problem we had was the complete failure to bring along even a scrap of sailcloth to fix the leech of the old cast-off genoa jib which kept coming apart because of its sun-rotted condition. In the end, the best we could do was to cut up a small bag holding the spare parts kit for our windvane.

The trip across was truly a "lazy man's vacation." Other than a few mild squalls at night, the weather was about as close to perfection as one could wish. We had a small sailing awning which we would rig between the boom gallows over the companionway hatch and the twin backstays. It provided a cool patch of shade for the cockpit, which combined with the pleasant trade wind breeze, made life on deck downright luxurious.

We had hoped for a dramatic landfall in the form of an approach to the majestic shape of 14,000 ft high Mauna Kea, but instead all we saw on the 15th day was a bank of clouds on the horizon. We never did recover Loran signals, but we were confident of our celestial position and after dark we began to see lights along the shore beneath the clouds. About midnight we crept into the little basin called Radio Bay in the corner of Hilo Harbor. It had been a remarkably smooth and pleasant voyage and a grand affirmation of the success of our new boat.

Hilo has no marina, but the snug anchorage at Radio Bay is a good substitute. It has a short concrete quaywall where a dozen boats can lie stern-to and space for a few more to lie at anchor. It is the usual point of arrival for ocean cruising yachts coming from the coast or Mexico or coming up from Tahiti, and thus is an interesting place to meet new yachties, compare passage notes and swap sea stories. Hilo is a very pleasant little city and the main street is a reasonable walk away. I had first seen Hilo on the trip over to the Islands on *Tai Fung* in 1952. At that time it was still recovering from a disastrous tidal wave which swept over the breakwater and destroyed all of the buildings along the waterfront. Wisely, they never rebuilt the structures on the water side of the street, making it a fine esplanade with a grand view of Hilo Bay. It was also at Hilo where we found the mother lode of pilot biscuits, those big, round, unsalted crackers which, to my mind, are the basic staple of boat food when the bread had been eaten or gone to mold. They are almost impossible to find nowadays in our grocery stores, but here we found the *Hilo Saloon Pilot* factory where they could be purchased in cellophane packets, boxes and even in big white, 5-gallon buckets. Oh joy! I admit, however, that not everyone has my enthusiasm for them.

We were in need of water and had our eye open for an opening in the line of boats tied to the quaywall. At last a boat pulled out from a spot alongside of a very spic-and-span sloop flying the British red ensign. We had noticed the owner carefully washing his decks, polishing the metalwork and even cleaning his fenders each day and had heard the other yachties joking about how fussy he was about the condition of his yacht. Pete and I knew that in England there are varying grades of ensigns, with the red ensign being the lowest rank, so as we were maneuvering carefully, very carefully, to slide into the spot alongside him, we were joking about how we should kid him about not having a more prestigious ensign such as the blue one which only members of special yacht clubs can fly. We were expecting him to be rather nervous about having a tough steel boat sliding in next to him, but to our surprise he jumped ashore and took our lines and helped us tie up. Next he invited us over to his boat for a cup of tea with his wife. Being totally tone deaf to social niceties, Pete and I persisted in kidding him about his red ensign by asking why such a nice boat didn't sport a blue one. His reply was a perfect put-down. "Oh yes, I could fly a blue ensign, in fact I can fly the Saint George's Cross, but that is because I am a duke".

The Hawaiian Islands do not have a great reputation as a cruising ground because of the strong trade winds and the lack of natural anchorages. However, we had a delightful and interesting cruise during the six weeks we spent in the Islands. In traversing the Islands from east to west we stopped at 17 different locations, in many of which we were alone or in the company of only one or two other boats.

While moored at Hilo we drove up to Volcano National Park to see the activity at Kilauea Crater. It was in a state of relative inactivity; however we had the pleasure of seeing the glowing streams of lava at night as we sailed along the east coast of Hawaii a few days later. After rounding Ka Lae, the southern tip, we enjoyed several anchorages while ghosting along in the smooth waters of the Kona Coast including our favorite, Kealakekua Bay, where Captain Cook met his fate.

The passage across the notoriously rough Alenuihaha Channel between Hawaii and Maui was delightfully benign. We continued along to the popular anchorage in the roadstead at Mala Wharf near Lahaina, an awkward place to anchor because of the excessive depth, but which features a spectacular view of Maui's mountainous topography. While here we had a crew change with Steve going home and with Jane plus John and Judy Sanford joining the boat. Pete had left earlier from Hilo to return to work. He would return at the end of the Island cruise for the sail back to the mainland. The Sanfords had agreed to join us in a spur-of-the-moment decision.

We visited the island of Lanai, and then returned to Maui to spend a few days at Honolua Bay, a delightful keyhole-shaped cove on the northwest corner of the island, with colorful reefs on both sides and a nice beach at the head of the bay. Next we sailed close inshore along the windward coast of Molokai to gape at the unreal sight of 2000 foot cliffs with waterfalls tumbling straight down into the sea. Also on Molokai we anchored off the old leper colony at the Kalapapa Peninsula then spent time off Ilio Point, a good anchorage with small sandy beaches at the northwestern tip of the island.

Honolulu was a nice change of pace. We enjoyed the week moored "Med-style" at the new transient dock at the Ala Wai Harbor. After another change of crew when Anne and Jane, who both had jobs to return to, had left the boat, we sailed for the island of Kauai via Pokai Bay on the leeward coast of Oahu. Visiting Kauai at the end of a Hawaiian Islands cruise is saving the best for last. Our son, Rob, and a couple of his friends were able to join us for this part of the cruise.

Following a couple of days at the small port of Nahwiliwili, we sailed for Hanalei Bay by sailing around the island clockwise. We stopped at the pretty little cove of Wahiawa Bay on the south coast then a spectacular anchorage on the west coast named Polihali, where the Napali Coast meets the Barking Sands Beach. A sunrise passage along the awe-inspiring Napali cliffs brought us to Hanalei bay, by far the most beautiful spot in the Islands and a spacious and secure anchorage as well.

Sea Bear moored near Five Needles on the southwest side of Lanai

On August 26th we headed for Bellingham, WA, where we intended to keep *Sea Bear* for the winter and the next season. Pete Passano and our old crew from the *Armorel* trip, Phil Price, had come to Kauai and the three of us would be the return voyage crew. As anticipated, the first week was pretty rough beating into the trade winds. *Sea* Bear loved this kind of weather even if the crew didn't. She was very stiff and could carry a lot of sail partly because we had given her more ballast than the design called for and also because all of her water and fuel tankage was down in the keel. She slammed, banged, and punched her way to weather with 'nary a groan or worry while we mostly sat below and let the Monitor windvane do the steering. As we got into somewhat higher latitudes the wind eased until it became almost calm at times then picked up from the northwest, and at one point strengthened into a moderate gale. Near the end of the passage we were running very fast one night in Force 7 conditions when we almost ran down a yacht which was hove-to. The boat was well lit, but our helmsman, Phil, had been sitting under the dodger reading a book and didn't see it until Pete, the relieving watch tender, came on deck and yelled a warning as we swept by a hundred yards away. Yikes!

We completed the passage to Cape Flattery in 20 days, not bad for a heavy cruising boat. After a brief stop in Victoria we sailed for Bellingham and found a berth in the municipal marina. Pete was working for a construction company nearby and would take over the boat until the next summer when we would both use her for various short cruises in the islands nearby. She had more than fulfilled all our expectations. In her simplicity and strength, her plain beauty and honest virtues we were pleased and rewarded.

*   *   *   *

With *Sea Bear* berthed in Bellingham for the summer of 1991, we planned several cruises in the nearby superb cruising area. First a week in the San Juan Islands with my little half sister, Jan, and her family in the San Juan Islands, then a week with our friends, Emily and Stuart Riddell, in the Gulf Islands and finally, a 10 day CCA national cruise in Desolation Sound and Princess Louisa Inlet. It was all lots of fun, but our focus was on a cruise to Alaska the next year.

In the meanwhile, life went on. Anne graduated from university in June and was married to Steve in a ceremony on Mount Tamalpais in August. Rob was out of the Army and began a career as a plumber. In November I began a big remodel of our rental cottage in Santa Venetia, where we built the boat, and in February 1992 Jane's mother Theresa, died. She had lived contentedly in a small unit I built in the back of our house for five years until she suffered a stroke and eventually had to be moved into a nursing home.

By spring our plans for a three month cruise to Alaska were in place. Pete had been seeing a gal who lived on Orcas Island named Carlyn Stark who was the granddaughter of Henry J. Kaiser and a very interesting person as well as an accomplished sailor with her own 42' cutter named *Pandemonium*. The plan was that I would take *Sea Bear* and Pete would sail with Carlyn on *Pandemonium* and we would more or less "buddy boat" in company for most of the way. I intended to break the trip into three one-month segments with crew changes in Prince Rupert, B.C. and Juneau Alaska with Jane joining the boat for the middle segment.

After a busy week in which the boat was hauled out and a radar was installed, we shoved off on schedule on June 15th with Evan Pugh, an old friend from Belvedere, and Bob Alderson, an old family doctor and sailor from San Rafael, aboard as crew. We entered Canadian customs by phone at Sidney and then proceeded up the delightful waters inside Vancouver Island in company with a mass of fishing vessels, all headed for the fishing grounds of Alaska. The weather was beautiful and we had high hopes that it would stay that way.

One feels that an Alaskan cruise is really underway after crossing Queen Charlotte Strait and entering the maze of channels in northern British Columbia. Although frequently rough and worrisome to motorboaters, Queen Charlotte Strait was one of our few nice sailing days and was climaxed by a night in an interesting bay with the intriguing name of Schooner Retreat.

Within a few days we had left the main "inside passage" route to Alaska by simply moving over to a parallel set of channels to the west. In doing so we had departed from the traffic and found ourselves mostly alone in anchorage after anchorage except for our "buddy boat," *Pandemonium*. About this time we also began to appreciate the full value of having a steel boat. One morning we weighed anchor in Oliver Cove and departed at speed whereupon we hit a rock so hard it sounded and felt like a train wreck! *Sea Bear* ended up on top of the granite but was soon was lifted off with the rising tide. Later we pushed through ice with impunity and on the return trip during a windy sail across the Strait of Georgia we hit a large log so hard we rolled it under the full length of the boat. I shudder to think what that log would have done to a boat with an exposed propeller and a separate skeg and rudder. With our full length keel and steel hull we laughed and suggested the helmsman keep a better lookout.

Before continuing on to Prince Rupert, we decided to make a side trip to the Queen Charlotte Islands for a week. The 75 mile passage across Hecate Strait from Camano Sound was made overnight to insure a daylight landfall. We had a fine sail and found the narrow entrance to Ikeda Cove in heavy overcast and mist with the help of our radar. It was all exactly as I had imagined it would be—remote, mysterious, beautiful and sad as we considered the vanished Haida Indian life which had flourished there. We encountered an old tugboat named *Gillcrest,* owned by our friend Bob Coe from Seattle and shared several anchorages with her.

We also visited two former Haida villages and were given tours of the sites by friendly and informative Indian guides. Sadly, however, little remains to be seen—only a few rotted and split totem poles and decayed lodge timbers. An overnight passage in misty rain back to the mainland via Otter Pass and we rejoined *Pandemonium.* Along the way we had the excitement of almost running over the long tow wire between a tug and a barge on which a tiny, dim light was almost obscured by the mist. Reentering the channels via Otter Pass looked like a nightmare to me with rocks all over the place, but we got through without difficulty and soon found our "buddy boat" with a VHF radio call.

At Prince Rupert, B.C., a pleasant little city bustling with fish boat activity, we exchanged crew for Jane, Wink Smith and Jim and Lynn Hurst. We then headed for the Alaska border and Ketchikan. Normally famed for its heavy rainfall (165 inches per year), Ketchikan was enjoying such a sunny spell that one store had pasted up a sign saying "Welcome to the Ketchikan Desert."

One Alaska resident we met mentioned that it was impossible to hold a conversation lasting longer than 15 minutes without the subject of bears coming up. Everyone has bear stories. We all read a hair-raising book named *Alaska Bear Tales.* We began to imagine big bears behind every tree when we landed on the beach. We soon saw our first black bears at Anan Bay, from a bear observation spot on a salmon stream. The ease with which the bears could catch fish was amazing. Later we would see the famed Alaska brown bears as well. A resident pointed out that one could easily distinguish black bear from brown bear droppings by observing that brown bear droppings were the ones with hiker's bear bells in them. Joking aside, the wild-life was everywhere to be seen—bald eagles, porpoise, whales, sea otters—and was a highlight of the trip.

Shortly after leaving the fishing town of Petersburg, we caught our first glimpse of glacial ice in the mountains and then our first real glacier at Thomas Bay. Two days later we entered Endicott Arm and saw yacht-sized pieces of blue floating ice. It was here we entered a fascinating fjord named Ford's Terror. It took a bit of doing to figure out just how the entrance worked because our cruising guide had it all wrong, a problem I solved by climbing to the top of the mast and get-ting a good look. To get in, one waits until the very moment of slack water, then shoot through the narrows and into a veritable water-filled Yosemite Canyon with an anchorage in front of a splendid waterfall. Nearby Tracy Arm then provided us with a display of sheer cliffs, floating ice, bergy bits and glaciers that was the high point of the voy-age. We were so enthralled we rammed *Sea Bear* into the pack ice in front of South Sawyer Glacier and sat motionless for hours, listening to the groans of the glacier and taking in the awesome show.

In the ice at Tracy Arm, Alaska, in July 1992

To complete this middle segment of our Alaska cruise we made a circuit of Admiralty Island, visiting a number of interesting places. Our favorite was the quaint little village of Tenekee Springs which boasts a community hot springs with special hours for the ladies, the men and the families. Because there is a perpetual water shortage in the village, the entire town takes their baths there. No clothes allowed. There were no motor vehicles on its miniature "main street," except for one or two tiny tractors for offloading the supplies that are boated in every once in awhile. Near here we were able to make contact via VHF radio with *Truly Fair* our friend, Fritz Warren's boat from Sausalito. We arranged to meet at a nearby cove named Chaik Bay and raft up for and afternoon and swap stories of our Alaskan experiences

On August 13th we had another crew change at Auke Bay, a convenient harbor about 10 miles north of Juneau. Jane and our friends flew home, and I was joined by my old shipmate, Phil Price, and Walt Mestrovich, another sailing friend and former colleague from my working days. By this time the weather seemed to be telling us that summer was about over in these parts because we began to have a series of lows passing through with only occasional fine days.

As required, we had made reservations at Glacier Bay National Park for a visit starting on August 21^{st,} and with great good luck we had a four day spell of perfect weather while in the Bay. Glacier Bay is a huge place—it takes two days of traveling to get from Bartlett Cove (where one must register)—to the first glacier. But we were treated to magnificent views of the Fairweather Range of mountains with 13,000-foot, snow capped peaks along the way. We anchored on the shallow moraine in front of Reid Glacier, hiked to its base and back, and spent the night. The next day we viewed Lamphugh Glacier in early morning sunlight, spent hours in front of Margarie Glacier and saw tremendous icefalls and finally from our last anchorage saw bears and moose along the beach. It was all a great experience and a fitting climax to our long voyage north.

Sea Bea exited the inside passage via Lisianski Strait (another nightmare-looking pass) without difficulty and sailed mostly against moderate southeasterly winds and occasional rain through an intriguing area at the northwesterly tip of Chichigoff Island to Sitka. Here we reprovisioned, showered and fueled then set forth to sea for the passage home. On the second day at sea, the barograph started to drop rapidly and by sundown we were bucking into a rapidly rising south-east wind under reefed staysail and double reefed mainsail. By 0300 we were in proper gale and decided to heave-to. I tried to do so in the traditional manner by backing the staysail and sheeting the mainsail tight with the tiller lashed to leeward, but the boat was just too power-ful and insisted on making too much headway. Once I dropped the staysail, however, she settled down and sat comfortably like a duck until things improved later in the day.

At the end of a 5-day passage we were in Port Hardy, having made the decision to seek better weather by returning via the inside of Vancouver Island. It was a wise decision and we had a delightful re-turn cruise with several fine sailing days down Johnstone Strait and Desolation Sound, arriving in Orcas Island, WA on September 13th. Here I turned the boat over to Pete Passano who wanted to try a single-handed passage to San Francisco. It had been a super summer.

*   *   *   *

Peter completed his solo passage down the coast without diffi-culty (except for a spell on the mud in Bodega Bay) and arrived with the boat at the San Francisco Yacht Club. We then turned our atten-tion to getting ready for a lengthy cruise to the South Pacific starting the following spring. When we were building the boat, people would sometimes ask just how it would work with two owners. Pete and I had, of course, been partners for years in two previous boats on the Bay, but we had always used the boats in a similar fashion, day sailing and short, local cruises, with or without our families, often with both of us aboard. Now we were starting to use *Sea Bear* on a full-time ba-sis with possibly conflicting long-range plans. I would tell everyone, "I'm not sure how it will all work out. All I know is that I plan to cruise plenty hard for about five years and not worry beyond that." Shortly after the boat was launched I sat down with a piece of paper and outlined a series of cruises including sailing to Hawaii, Alaska, New Zealand and back to San Francisco. Since I never seemed to get any feedback from Pete, we just started down the list. I think Pete's conception, since he was now single, was to use the boat as a full time, live aboard life style for long-distance cruising. This was to lead to some unhappiness later on, but it was eventually resolved to our mutual satisfaction.

During the winter we made some minor improvements for the forthcoming voyage. We had found that the manual anchor windlass was not satisfactory. We had a scary time once in Hawaii when the excessively slow speed of the windlass almost got us on the reef as we were trying to get under way from a windy lee shore. Later in Alaska where we frequently had to anchor in very deep water, it was so difficult to lift the long length of chain along with the anchor that we gave up and changed over to rope with a short piece of chain. With some help from Bill Hickman, who was in the hydraulic tool business, I devised a way to power our windlass with a hydraulic motor using a pump belted on to the engine. It was a great success and provided a big safety factor for us.

During the winter we installed a short wave radio. Meanwhile, I worked hard to pass the code and radio theory tests and get a General Class Ham license (KC6UXZ). We also installed a nice GPS unit which had become quite affordable by this time. It was a wonderful thing but, sadly, rendered obsolete all of our celestial navigation skills. In fact it virtually eliminated navigation as a skill altogether. Still, who would want to be without one?

As planned, Pete and I and our friend, John Sanford, departed from Belvedere on Easter Sunday, 1993. It was a lovely day but by afternoon the northwesterly wind was blowing strong. The first couple of days were rough with *Sea Bear* sailing under storm trysail and reefed staysail, the wind blowing 35-40 knots and the seas high and confused. The first night just as dinner was about to be served a big wave struck the side of the boat sending a cascade of water down the slightly cracked-open skylight and dumping dinner all over the cabin sole. At that point no one felt much like eating anyway. By Tuesday the seas were down and the boat was no longer taking water aboard, but she was tearing along at up to eight knots, surprisingly fast considering she was heavily laden with all tanks full and a seven month supply of stores aboard. Two days later we had found the northeast trades and were romping along under blue skies and all was right with the world as it continued to be until we approached the doldrums.

We spotted a ship in the middle of the night which was bound from Panama to the Philippines and passed about a half mile behind her stern. It was our only sighting during the passage. At about 7 degrees north we encountered the usual unsettled weather and calms of the doldrums. Reluctantly, we ran the diesel to keep going but were happy when we could get a bit of breeze and turn it off because it was hot (80 degrees plus) in the cabin. During this period of calm, glassy seas, a brown bird about the size of a seagull landed on deck sometime during the night. Eventually identified as a sooty shearwater, it was nursed by an attentive crew and fed a diet of fresh-caught tuna. I tried to examine it for broken bones/wings but got nipped for my trouble. Apparently it was tired and was just resting, since it flew off the next night when a breeze came up. *Sea Bear* crossed the equator about noon on April 29, our 18th day at sea. King Neptune (me) came aboard and presented Pete and John with scrolls proclaiming that they were now Shellbacks. I had attained that exalted status 40 years before during our race to Tahiti on *Mistress*. We celebrated with a bottle of 40-year old Cuban rum.

It took only a couple of days to get through the doldrums, but afterwards the southeast trades never did come on and blow strong and steady as advertised. Mostly it was light airs and changeable, squally conditions for the remainder of our 24 day passage to Hiva Oa in the Marquesas. With our GPS, the landfall was a bit of an anticlimax—we knew exactly when and where we would arrive. Gone was the satisfaction and excitement of sighting land and the relief of knowing that one's navigation had been successfully carried out. Nevertheless, it had been a very nice voyage with no problems of any kind.

Our point of arrival was at Atuona, the main (and only) town on the island of Hiva Oa. It had a tiny artificial boat basin which was jam packed with yachts and more arriving every day—the class of '93 on their way to Tahiti and beyond. We checked in at the *Gendarmerie*, bought a some fresh veggies and fruit, topped off the water tanks and sailed on a little four-day, clockwise cruise around the island. It was spectacularly beautiful and everything I had hoped for.

We cruised in the Marquesas for about three weeks, visiting all of the six major islands—each one more lovely than the last. Anaho Bay on the island of Nuka Hiva was our favorite spot with a secure anchorage, a fine beach and a backdrop of fantastic cliffs fronting a range of jagged mountains. Although we had been warned about the rolly anchorages and no-see-ums (nono flies), we found neither to be a serious drawback. Because we didn't know any French, our biggest problem was making contact with the locals on any thing but the most superficial level.

Blessed by a full moon and an easy beam reach, *Sea Bear* had an idyllic four-day passage from the Marquesas to the Tuamotu Islands. We made land fall at Makemo atoll on the east end of the group and proceeded to visit eight islands as we worked our way west. We eventually departed for Tahiti from Tikihau.

Nearly every boat on the "Milk Run" visits at least a few popular atolls in the northern part of the Tuamotus such as Manahi, Ahe and Rangiroa, but when we went to several of the less well-known atolls, we found we were the only boat there. I think these atolls are the perfect "South Sea Islands," with lovely colors, smooth lagoons, charming little villages and wonderful people. True, the passes take a bit of getting used to, but we soon learned that the fearsome-looking breakers in the pass really weren't all that dangerous. The waves caused by the swift currents meeting the swells on the outside mostly just tumble you around.

The "Dangerous Archipelago" was great—and thanks to GPS, it's no longer difficult to navigate through, even at night. One must keep in mind, however, that the charts are not necessarily all that accurate, especially with regard to the charted longitude. We found errors of up to 1½ miles in the Marquesas, and in the Tuamotus we heard first hand of a typical "GPS assisted wreck." Because of a need to get to the airport in Tahiti to pick up an elderly parent, a Dutch yacht left a Tuamotu island on a rainy night and headed on a course between a couple of islands and then around a third island. The course required a change in direction to miss the last island and the owner said he arrived at the course change waypoint spot-on according to his GPS. Just as he was changing direction he crashed onto the reef. He said the chart must have been in error by close to a mile. Luckily there was group of islanders collecting coconuts in the area who saved the Dutch couple the next morning, but not the boat.

John Sanford left the boat in Fakarava Atoll and thus missed a savage little storm Pete and I encountered on the way to Tahiti. Locally known as a *maraamu*, it had winds of more than 60 knots. Once we got *Sea Bear* shortened down and hove-to, we were fine. And with GPS we had no worries about getting past the small atoll of Tetiaroa (owned by Marlon Brando) which was under our lee. The storm only lasted for about eight hours but, oh my, how it blew! On the radio we heard a woman's distressed voice on a nearby 42' boat named *Silkey,* saying they were in terrible winds and pleading, "We need INFOR-MATION!"

We arrived in Papeete on June 14th, and a couple of days later we were joined by Jane who was to sail with us for three months. Our daughter, Anne, and our son-in-law, Steve, who were to spend a couple of weeks with us, also arrived. Jane had just retired after 15 years at Scanmar where they made Monitor windvane gears and sold assorted other selfsteerers for sailboats. She was the first employee after Hans Bernwall and Carl Seipel organized the firm after their voyage around the world in the 1970's. She had loved the job partly because there were always lots of cruising sailors hanging around and was so appreciated that Hans and Carl called her "the president."

Tahiti, of course, couldn't possibly have lived up to my memories of it from my previous visit on *Mistress* 40 years before. Papeete is now a big city with lots of traffic, tourists, boats and very high prices. Still it was kind of exciting in a chaotic sort of way. One of the first items of business was to see a doctor about nasty skin infections on my legs and my arm. These had originated from some abrasions I had received when I fell from the mast in the Tuamotus. I still wince when I think about it, but here is what happened: I had climbed up the mast steps for some reason and was about half-way to the top when my foot slipped off the edge of a step when the boat rolled. I had a good hold on the step above me but I was unable to keep my grip when the full weight of my body suddenly came on it. Pete and John, who were watching from the cockpit as I came down, were horrified. Amazingly, I landed on my feet and was mostly unhurt because my fall had been broken by the lower diamond shroud. These were additional shrouds (rigging wires) I had installed to stiffen the mast in the athwartships direction. I had slid down the wire, losing some skin in the process, but other than feeling a bit shaken up, I was fine (and extremely lucky). A big dose of expensive antibiotic and I was soon good as new.

Within a week of our arrival in Tahiti we left for the other Society Islands. Moorea, especially the spectacular anchorage in Oponohu Bay is lovely and was a very perfect change of pace except for the stormy weather which plagued the South Pacific that year. We had a bumpy overnight sail to Huahine, which turned out to be our favorite island of the group. It has snug anchorages inside the barrier reef, a reasonable number of boats, only a few tourists and a whole lot of charm. Anne and Steve left us here and we were joined by Evelyn, a Swiss lady-friend of Pete's who cruised with us for the four months. Next we sailed to Raiatea, where we had a bit of engine trouble in the form of a broken water pump shaft, a problem we remedied by having a new shaft made for us on a machine lathe. We also had to replace a blown head gasket with a new one from our big wooden box of spares which came with Tu Lung Bang. Then it was on to Bora Bora, which we found to be beautiful, especially from a distance, but overrun with tourists and beach resorts.

June 1993, Sea Bear anchored in lovely Opunohu Bay, Moorea

We set out on our next passage, the 800 mile jump to Suvarov Atoll, a little dot in the Northern Cook Islands which is uninhabited except for the a family who act as caretakers on behalf of the government. The entire island is a bird refuge and a national park and is lovely, but has a rather worrisome anchorage because of all the coral heads and the unsettled weather which could, and did, send wind and waves all the way across the lagoon. This put us on a lee shore with our anchor chain snubbing on the coral, an unsettling and dangerous situation. Nevertheless, we loved the place and the wonderful family in residence. When we first arrived they gave each of us a refrigerated coconut with a straw in it (there was a generator on the island). There is nothing more delicious than ice cold coconut milk, particularly considering that we had no refrigeration on the boat! They were eager to visit, take yachties on spear fishing expeditions and put on big BBQ feasts at frequent intervals. After five days, however, our nerves couldn't take the strain of the dicey anchorage anymore, so we bailed out in a gale of wind and headed for American Samoa.

Pago Pago was a bit of a mess as there are several big tuna canneries which foul the harbor water and make a big stink, but it's in a spectacular setting and in our opinion, a lot of fun because it is full of yachts and the prices of food, booze, postage and phone calls are all cheap. Hot showers are handy and the funky little Pago Pago Yacht Club had a good happy hour *every* night. With the local Samoans being very friendly, we ended up enjoying our week there. I had made a number of trips to Pago Pago in the process of carrying out a couple of engineering design projects on the island and had learned to like the place.

We skipped Western Samoa and headed next for Tonga, stopping first at Niuatoputopu in the northern end of the group. Its charted location is out by several miles, an important fact when navigating by GPS, but it had a fine anchorage inside a reef with a shallow but easy entrance. It was an appealing, rather primitive place with lots of pigs running around and the added attraction of having an interesting salvage operation going on. A group of guys were trying to raise a big three-masted schooner named *Golden Dawn* from 50 feet of water and thus provided endless entertainment and gossip for the half dozen yacht anchored there. The yacht had sunk about 9 months before when it touched the bottom in the shallow entrance and started to leak. Being unable to get into the anchorage, it had backed out of the channel into deeper water where it went to the bottom.

It seems the owner of the sunken schooner and his crew had madly set to work to strip the boat when they realized that it was doomed. They shuttled back and forth to the beach with all the fittings, sails, rope and everything else they could remove as it slowly went down. Next they arranged for all of the stuff to be stored in a big empty shed owned by the village chief. They also got the village police to agree to guard the wreck from looting divers while they returned to California and fitted out a 55' ketch with salvage gear. When they returned 9 months later the warehouse was empty and the wreck was stripped to the bare bones, even including the steering wheel. When confronted, the villagers shrugged and reportedly said, "We needed the things." (An old Polynesian philosophy). We also heard that the village policeman and his pal, the customs man, were the first divers to hit the wreck. Things weren't going well with the ship-raising effort either. Each day we heard that the next day would be the one when the buoyancy bags would bring it to the surface, but it never happened. To make matters worse, the diving crew from California all acquired pretty Tongan girl friends who helped themselves (and their families) to the stores. Well, you get the picture. It was a soap opera.

A 2 ½-day beat to windward brought us to Vava'u, the main cruising ground for Tonga. It is a great area with many nice islands and dozens of good anchorages—all within protected waters and just a few miles apart. The weather still wasn't very good, but we had a wonderful time doing lots of daysailing, snorkeling, beachcombing and visiting with the other yachties. There were 60 boats at the main harbor of Neiafu, but not too many in the other anchorages. Several times we had anchorages to ourselves. There is an active charter business there that puts out a useful cruising guidebook including a chart with all the anchorages designated by a number. It was common to overhear cruisers telling their friends "We'll see you tomorrow in number 15". The Tongans are very religious and take church-going seriously. They are also wonderful singers, making our visit to a Sunday service a special treat with some of the finest close- harmony singing we have ever heard. They also like to put on native feasts as a means of earning some hard currency but also because they simply love to do it. From time to time the word would go out via VHF radio that a feast would take place at a certain anchorage and all yachts were welcome to come and enjoy the food for a modest price.

Most all yachts avoid the Ha'apai Group—between Vava'u and Tongatapu in the south—because it is full of shoals and reefs and the charter boats are not allowed to go there. Having a steel boat, we decided to take a look anyway and it turned out to be a wonderful area!

We visited five islands and would have seen more had it not been for a combination of being storm-bound for two days and then having to keep moving to get Jane to her plane home from Nuku'alofa on September 8th. All things considered, we enjoyed Tonga the most of all the places we visited.

An easy three day sail from Nuku'alofa took us to Fiji where Pete, Evelyn and I spent a month cruising. After enjoying the nice yacht club and assembled yachties at Suva for a few days, we headed for the Great Astrolabe Reef and Kandavu Island. Later we sailed around to the west of Viti Levu island and cruised among the Yasawa Group. Fiji is a huge place and has about three hundred islands, so we didn't even scratch the surface of the cruising possibilities there.

The Fijians were about the nicest people you could hope to meet. On the other hand, the elaborate customs paperwork was a bit of a pain, and the necessity of seeking permission from the chief of each village to anchor and visit ashore, while interesting, can get tiresome, particularly if you don't care for kava, the slightly pixilating local grog that is required by custom to be consumed by newcomers.

We gave the boat a quick haulout at the crude little boatyard at Lautoka, then sailed for New Zealand in mid-October to escape the approaching cyclone season in the tropics. We made the 1,050-mile trip in nine days of mostly easy sailing to windward and entered at Opua in the Bay of Islands. New Zealand and its friendly people are a delight! After a week in the Bay of Islands we made our way to Auckland and took advantage of an arrangement which our friend Doug Duane had made for us to moor in front of the Panmure Yacht Club in the Tamaki River on the south side of Auckland. We had sailed 8,638 miles in seven months and had a wonderful experience.

* * * *

I returned home for the Christmas holidays, then Jane and I flew back to New Zealand for six weeks of coastal sailing on *Sea Bear* with Pete during January and February in the spring of 1994. We returned to the Bay of Islands for more cruising, including sailing up to Monganui in Doubtless Bay to visit our old boat *Armorel*, which was under the loving care of Bob ("have-a-chat") Diecks and his wife, Caroline. The old boat had been almost completely rebuilt including a new skin of double-diagonal planking and was in wonderful shape. Oddly, neither of us could seem to reconnect emotionally with her, I suppose because her appearance had changed but mostly because our love of her was largely based on the grand adventure we were having at the time, 35 years ago.

By November 1993, Sea Bear was in The Bay of Islands, New Zealand

Jane and I left the boat back in Auckland. I would rejoin *Sea Bear* in July in Fiji for more cruising which would take us to Australia. Pete prepared the boat for the 1994 cruise and on April 27th, shoved off from Opua for Fiji, with a pair of Swiss friends a couple of weeks ahead of the disastrous "Queen Birthday Storm" which claimed a number of lives and half a dozen boats on their way north from New Zealand. On July 2nd I joined the boat for three months of cruising between Fiji and Australia. After a haulout and bottom paint job in Lautoka we shoved off for Vanuatu with Pete, me and his daughter, Paige and her boyfriend, Greg, aboard.

There was plenty of wind for the run to Santo Island in the north of Vanuatu (formerly the New Hebrides), and we knocked off the 525-mile distance in only 3 ½ days. The main port of Luganville, where we anchored on arrival, was the scene of furious activity during WWII where it was the center of the build-up for the Solomon Islands campaign. The harbor at that time was full of ships and floating dry-docks and there were 17 airfields nearby. Now almost no evidence of this activity remains except for some rusty Quonset hut buildings around town and fences made of perforated landing mat. The shore where we anchored was lined with hundreds of rusty blocks from GM 6-71 landing craft engines. The hulk of the troop ship, *President Cleveland,* which sank when it hit an American mine, is now a popular dive site.

The anchorage at Luganville was not the best, so we stayed only a couple of days before moving 12 miles north to lovely Paikulo Bay. The Santo Yacht Club maintains a little outstation on the beach there complete with BBQ, water, shade and garbage pick-up. One day we were exploring a big old wrecked tugboat on the beach when a 7.4 magnitude earthquake struck. The wreck rolled around and shed a ton of rust—while all of us just about went into cardiac arrest!

We proceeded south to Malekula Island, home of the last re-corded cannibal feast. Most of us would think the last "long pig" feast was probably 100 or 200 years ago, but it was in 1967! We heard that some of the participants went to jail afterwards. Our favorite stop here was a small anchorage on the southwest coast, Caroline Bay, which we were able to enter because of the smooth sea and fine weather prevail-ing at the time. We were apparently the first American boat to have ever come into the bay and we were treated like honored guests. They insisted we attend a large lunch at the chief's house at mid-day, and then in the evening, since it was Sunday, we were seated at the place of honor at a community dinner and afterward had to give a speech of thanks to the congregation at church. We tried to reciprocate by invit-ing everyone to come to *Sea Bear* in the afternoon for cookies and Kool-Aid. It was a huge success. Our visit reinforced our opinion that, in spite of their fierce appearance, the Vanuatuans were the sweetest people we had ever met. Although rather shy, they were in-variably friendly and very courteous.

Port Vila, the capitol, is a compact and charming little city with a lovely anchorage, a nice public market and a good yachtie hangout at the Waterfront Bar. It isn't all that modern, but it was a different world from the outer islands. Our visit to Port Vila included enjoying the week-long Independence Day celebrations, entering *Sea Bear* in the Independence Day Regatta (we sailed well but didn't win), taking a side trip to Havannah Bay, driving around the island and careening the boat on a nearby beach to change the sounder transducer. We also said goodbye to Paige and Greg who had sailed from Fiji with us.

While in Vanuatu we made a short cruise to Tanna Island. It was a bit of a nuisance because you have to backtrack to Port Vila later in order to clear out, but it was still well worth the extra slog to windward. There is an excellent landlocked anchorage at Port Resolution which isn't a real port, but rather a lovely little bay with hot springs on the beach and easy access to Mt. Yasur, the fantastic active volcano. We took a truck almost to the top of the mountain, and stood on the edge of the crater while Volkswagen-sized blobs of lava – accompanied by frightening explosions – were thrown hundreds of feet into the air. After looking around and seeing big solid chunks of lava on all sides, we realized that not all of the lava blobs landed back in the crater! One night the wind changed and caused the boat to be coated with a thick layer of black gritty ash from the volcano, with some of it even finding its way below decks. It was mess to clean up, but we wouldn't have missed visiting the volcano for anything.

One evening we were informed that there would be native music and songs at the "Cargo Cult" village at the foot of Mt. Yasur. Pete and I joined a group of yachties who arranged for a pickup to take us to the village by crossing over the lower slopes of the volcano. It was dark by the time we arrived and were deposited in a smoky hut lit by a single candle and adorned with odd WWII memorabilia and a large board describing the tenets of the Jon Frum Movement (Cargo Cult) in Pidgin English. It seems they believe when Jon Frum returns someday, largess will arrive from the sky (including jeeps and refrigerators) -- obviously a legacy of the Pacific War which must have seemed a fantastic, inexplicable time for these people. Eventually, we paid our modest contribution and were led to an outdoor pavilion and seated on low benches while two teams of performers strummed guitars and sang what seemed to us like the same song over and over for a couple of hours. The strangest part was that there was no eye contact or interaction with us at all. Meanwhile, the volcano was thumping and banging away in the background. It was about as weird a night as I ever hope

to see. In Paul Theroux's book, *The Happy Isles of Oceania,* he describes Tanna as the strangest island in Vanuatu. He wasn't kidding.

The passage to New Caledonia was a 2 ½ - day punch to
windward. We entered at Havannah Pass on the east side at night
without difficulty and dropped the hook – unofficially – at Baie de
Prony then continued on to Noumea the next morning to check in. We
liked New Caledonia immediately; it's a nice combination of modern
conveniences in town and great cruising inside a barrier reef between
various anchorages along the coast.

We sailed out to the Isle of Pines, a former French penal colony with some interesting but gloomy prison ruins on an otherwise
pretty island. Unfortunately, the weather decided to turn windy and
squally, so we didn't see it at its best. We did, however, enjoy other
fine anchorages in the Baie de Prony and Ille Quen area along the
south coast. After picking up our friend, Jim Algert, who was to sail
with us to Australia, we sailed up the west coast to Baie St. Vincent
and enjoyed exploring the many arms of this large shallow bay. There
was nary a boat in sight.

On September 9th, we headed for Australia and had a smooth 5
1/2 - day passage with nice breezes on the beam. In spite of stories to
the contrary, we had an easy entry and were met by pleasant officials
upon our arrival at the Customs dock on the Brisbane River. The sail
up the river to the city of Brisbane was a delight, and upon arrival, *Sea
Bear* found an excellent berth between pilings off the Botanical Gar-
dens right in the heart of town. Brisbane is a lovely modest-sized city
and we had a grand time exploring it and a bit of the surrounding
countryside during our week there.

We had reserved time for some coast hopping toward Sydney,
and we stopped at seven ports, each quite different and interesting.
Most of the small harbors along the east coast have shallow bar en-
trances, so decent weather is necessary to enter in safety. We crossed
the bar at Port Macquarie nervously one midnight and got caught by a
breaker which came over the stern and gave *Sea Bear* a goose. Otherwise we had no trouble. Our favorite harbor was Camden Haven, a
pretty little town on a small river. We got a scare here when our engine overheated just as we were crossing the bar and forced us to anchor quickly as soon as we were inside. Once safely moored we found

a friendly Aussie with a machine shop in his garage who fabricated a new water pump shaft for "Tu Lung Bang."

Sailing into Sydney Harbor in October 1994
where I sold my half of Sea Bear to my partner, Pete

We enjoyed our cruising down the coast of Australia, and it climaxed wonderfully on October 5, 1994 with our entry into the spectacularly beautiful harbor at Sydney. It was so inspiring, we sailed around the harbor for a while admiring the city skyline, the Harbor Bridge and the Sydney Opera House before seeking a temporary berth at the Cruising Yacht Club. Here I bid a fond farewell to *Sea Bear*, having made the decision to sell my half to my partner, Pete. It had been a wonderful cruise in the South Pacific in a boat which was perfect for the job. It was also the end to an excellent 20 year partnership.

As I left the boat, Pete mentioned that maybe he would go uptown and put up a notice for crew at the backpacker's hostel. When he returned to the boat there were already two Canadian gals ready to sign on. Together with Herb Recktenwald, a friend from San Francisco, *Sea Bear* sailed to Tasmania then back to Sydney, up to Papua New Guinea and back to New Zealand. Pete then sailed singlehanded across the Pacific, around Cape Horn and on up to Maine. Since then he has crossed the Atlantic six times and sailed to South Georgia Island, and Cape Town, putting a total of over 100,000 miles under her keel and still going strong. Not bad for a "disposable boat."

Misty, our Aries 32 sloop in a fresh breeze

CHAPTER 14

MISTY

I returned home from Australia in October, 1954 without a clear idea of what was ahead. For the first time in many years I was without a boat (and without a boat partner, except for Jane, of course). At the annual Cruising Club Christmas dinner Jane and I were named the "Cruisers of the Year" and received a similar honor from the San Francisco Yacht Club for our ramblings aboard *Sea Bear.*

There was plenty to do. Jane and I had self-published a book written by Marjorie Petersen, our old cruising friend, who together with her late husband, Al, had sailed their gaff-rigged cutter *Stornoway* on a two year circular cruise around the Pacific about 20 years before. She was an excellent writer and had a previous sailing book published, but had never found a publisher for her story of their latest voyage. The book, *Red Sky at Night,* came out just about the time I came home, and suddenly we had 1500 copies in our basement. We managed to sell all of them and a second printing as well with a considerable effort. We had hoped to make some money for Marj, but it turned out to be a break-even proposition, but Marjorie seemed rewarded just to see her book in print. It was an interesting project and we had no regrets about giving it a try.

After the Petersens returned from their last voyage, they continued to live aboard *Stornoway* in the harbor at Sausalito. On Christmas Day 1983, Anne and I went over by boat to visit them and deliver a pumpkin pie only to discover that Al, weakened by cancer, had died aboard the boat during the night. Marjorie continued to live aboard for a couple of years but emotionally she was in pretty bad shape and the boat got that way too. Eventually I was able to find a buyer for the boat and located a small apartment in San Rafael for her. She had her up and downs in succeeding years and had to be relocated in various situations providing care. I was sure she wouldn't last long but I was wrong. Jane and I and a group of her old, loyal friends helped to keep her going financially to the end, 18 years after leaving the old cutter.

I built dory number eight to add to the fleet on the yacht club dock, and in July Jane and I went to England where we had accepted an invitation to make a three-week cruise with Bill and Joyce Hickman on a 60'x 7' "narrowboat" on the English canals. It was a lovely vessel, a sort of showboat for the builder, and the cruising was fun. It truly was life in the slow lane with the speed limit being "the speed of a walking horse". One could stop anywhere simply by driving a pair of stakes in the bank and tying up or by mooring in front of one of the many pubs along the waterways. Pretty tame stuff after our adventures at sea but very enjoyable -- all except the part where Jane broke her wrist when she tripped on the towpath.

Also, to keep out of mischief, I volunteered to act as resident engineer on a project to build a new 1500' concrete breakwater to replace the old timber one at the San Francisco Yacht Club. It was a major undertaking for the club and involved a cost of about $1.5 million. My job was to make daily inspections of the work, keep technical records of progress and assure strict adherence to the plans and specifications or approve any minor changes. It was interesting work, even if it did drive some of the residents of Belvedere nuts with several months of noisy pile driving. Fortunately we had a capable and cooperative contractor (Dutra Construction Co.) and had no problems of consequence. In the end the work was finished on time, within budget and without a dollar of extra costs. It was also a beauty to behold, if your taste in architecture runs to massive, straight concrete walls.

While the breakwater job was going on during the late summer of 1995, Jane and I were looking around for a little cruising boat to buy with the proceeds from selling my half of *Sea Bear*. About the only criteria were that it be a pure cruising boat and that it didn't cost too much. We finally settled on an Aries 32 named *Mitzy* which was for sale for $28,000 at a yacht brokerage in Sausalito. I recognized the boat from having seen it at the Corinthian Yacht Club, and since our son, Rob, was working at the club at the time fixing things around the harbor, I asked him to find out from the owner, a nice man named Wen Lin, what he really wanted for the boat. It turned out that that Wen had taken his wife on a club cruise up the Delta and on the way back encountered the usual nasty, windy conditions on San Pablo Bay. As I got the story, the wife was so frightened that she made a *Mayday* call to the Coast Guard. To their credit, the Coasties figured out the situation immediately and soothingly told her to calm down and then came out and took her off the boat. The result was that when she vowed never to go out on that dinky sailboat again, Wen put her up for sale and then went out and bought a big Swan sloop. Well, no one ever needs to own two yachts at once, so he was happy to deal and readily accepted our rather low offer of $21,000.

Since the previous owner's daughter was named Mitzy, we figured it was a sort of private name and we really ought to give the boat a new one, even though we were well aware that changing a ship's name is a serious taboo which can bring all sorts of bad luck, a concern that never stopped us from renaming a boat in the past. Nevertheless, we started making a list of possible new names, a process which went on for months. In the meanwhile I had stripped off some very classy graphics on the hull which spelled out her former name. I should have left them alone since in the end we settled on *Misty*, which was only one letter different. A national boating organization conducts an annual survey of the most popular boat name each year—of course it turned out to be Misty. We have seen boats named Misty everywhere, ranging from big motor yachts to scruffy fishboats and everything in between. But *Misty* she is.

The Aries 32 is a design by Tom Gilmer, a specialist in cruising boats, probably best known for his design of the both of the *Pride of Baltimore* schooners. She is a traditional double-ender with a full length keel, an outboard rudder and a short bowsprit modeled roughly on the style of the famous Colin Archer-designed, Norwegian lifesaving boats of the 19th century. She has a rather modest rig and isn't likely to win any races, but she is tough, an excellent sea boat and is very easily handled, with surprisingly comfortable accommodations, but best of all, Jane loves her and gets very upset when I make critical comments about her lack of speed. Perhaps her best attribute, to my mind anyway, is her pretty design -- a real classic in traditional style.

Far more important than boats or breakwaters that year, however, was the birth of our first (and only) grandchild, a sweet little girl named Lacey, born November 14, 1995. The product of an oil & water relationship between Rob and his lady friend, they wisely decided that they would forgo marriage in favor of a sharing of custody. Jane and I have certainly been the beneficiaries, since we have had the inestimable joy of seeing a lot of Lacey, watching her grow and sharing wonderful times ashore and afloat with her, which continue to this day after 11 years. In spite of what would seem a rather chaotic childhood between two households, she is a bright sensible child with a passion for reading and sports and seems happy and well adjusted to her life. May it always continue to be so.

*Fall 1996. Our newly purchased boat
and our new granddaughter, Lacey*

Near the end of the following year, I received an invitation to help wind up the two-year circumnavigation of Jerry and Suzie Knecht's 42' sloop, *Night Watch,* by sailing with them and their crew, John McVey, from Panama to San Francisco, a voyage of 3500 miles. I joined the boat in Colon, Panama on Feb. 1, 1997 where *Night Watch* had been waiting her turn to transit the Canal.

By good fortune, a senior Panama Canal pilot named Doug Finley, who was a good friend and a member of our yacht club, was on hand to assist in our passage arrangements. We had a day to spare, so Doug offered to take us on a jungle river trip. He met us at our berth at the Panama Canal Yacht Club early in the morning and took us to a small US Army jungle warfare training base where he had arranged to use an aluminum skiff with an outboard. With our lunch, cameras, hats and bug repellent in hand, we set off up the lower end of the Chagres River. In no time we were enveloped in the jungle, with the canopy of the immensely tall trees shutting off all sign of the sky. At one point, with some trepidation, we followed Doug as he leaped ashore and ran off following a troop of howler monkeys which were making a great commotion far above our heads. We wound around gigantic buttress roots supporting huge trees and pushed aside long liana vines which hung from branches far above our view—all the while wondering if we could find our way back to the boat. We stopped at a mysterious grotto in a side stream of the river then eventually reached the dam which impounds the waters of the Chagres to form Gatun Lake, the source of the water to operate the locks and a major part of the pathway between the seas. It was an amazing day capped off when we saw a strange creature very slowly crossing the road back at the little Army base. It was a large, three toed sloth, which Doug calmly picked up and carried to the base of a tree. Suddenly it shifted out of low-low gear and easily climbed high into the branches.

The next day we were up before dawn to meet the launch which brought our pilot-trainee and his understudy who would guide us through the Canal. The Panama Canal Co. now runs a training school for Panamanians to become pilots, a part of the curriculum being to start by taking yachts through. Our friend Doug explained that nowadays, with the Canal booked solid 24 hours a day, yachts present a problem because they represent very little revenue but cause about a 15 minute delay in lockage time for the set of three locks on each side, time which they can ill afford to lose. We were scheduled to transit with a "panamax" ship, one designed to barely squeeze into the locks. We were the only yacht going through in our cycle so we were to lie alone in the center of the chamber, a potentially difficult situation with the turbulence of the water entering the chamber from huge orifices in the bottom but made even more so with such a large ship in front of us.

In order to move ahead when the chamber is full, the ship must use her engine in addition to the pull of the towing locomotives, because with only about a foot of space on each side of the ship, it is difficult for the water to pass alongside of the ship. The prop wash can easily cause the boat to get out of control if the four long lines are not kept securely snubbed and tight. Either because of good crew work or good luck, all went well.

A three-toed sloth in the hands of Doug Finley, Panama Canal pilot,
who took us on a jungle river trip

If the boat can meet the same ship at the far end of Gatun Lake, it is possible to complete the transit in one day without a layover at Miraflores Lake. We managed to do this because we had good speed under power and because we had a nice fair wind on our route via the "Banana Cut", a shallow water shortcut. By evening we completed the last of the down-locks and were in Pacific waters where we proceeded to the Balboa Yacht Club and picked up a mooring. I maintain that a transit of the Panama Canal is about as interesting a day one can have.

As we started up the west coast of Panama, it brought back memories of our voyage on *Armorel* some 37 years earlier. In that earlier trip I was filled with apprehension about the coming difficulty of the trek up the coast (which turned out to be relatively easy). This time, as a crew member on a modern yacht with an affable and highly experienced skipper and crew, it all seemed like a lark. We stopped at Honda Bay and Parida Island in northern Panama, a couple of beautiful anchorages in a cruising ground I scarcely knew existed. In Costa Rica we anchored at Drakes Bay in Corcovado National Park where we arranged for an eco-tour with a young Costa Rican guide who led us on a hike through a jungle filled with exotic birds and flowers.

Since we had not legally entered Costa Rica, we decided it would be prudent to get underway upon our return to the boat after the hike even though it was now quite dark. The next morning while motoring along in calm weather we saw a lot of bees buzzing around the boat, then noticed that the radar dome on the backstay was a solid mass of swarming bees. Yikes! Killer bees! This started a long discussion about how to deal with them. Since we had no bug bomb aboard to exterminate them, my idea was to fill a soap pump-bottle with outboard motor gas and spray them. I would climb to the end of the boom and give them a volley of squirts then quickly retreat as they went into a mass agitation followed by some of them dropping to the deck. After half a dozen forays we had the boat to ourselves. I was rather proud of my technique but Suzie, the owner's wife, was upset with the brutality of it all – a Mars vs. Venus view of the situation I suppose.

I had recalled reading a letter to Latitude 38 sometime earlier from a young couple who discovered a swarm of bees on their boat while sailing across the Gulf of Tehuantepec. Naturally they assumed they were dreaded killer bees so they barricaded themselves below decks behind their hatch screens as the boat continued on its way under autopilot. Being true Americans, they did the logical thing—they called the US Coast Guard on their shortwave radio. Surprisingly, the Coasties were up to the task—they contacted a professor of entomology at UC Berkeley for advice. He simply suggested they kill them all with a bug bomb. End of problem.

Other than a delay of a couple of days in Acahutla, El Salvador, to let a strong northerly gale in the Gulf of Tehuantepec blow through, we traveled easily up the coast, stopping at various ports in Mexico including Acapulco where we fueled and restocked the boat. Continuing north, we stopped at more cruising locations including one of my favorites, the anchorage at Tenacatita, which has a lovely beach and an interesting little jungle river. Even the trip up the coast of Baja was not difficult. Instead of the proverbial "baja bash" we had quite smooth sailing, although it was very chilly as usual. We spent several days at the Coronado Yacht Club as guests of my friend and shipmate, Jim Algert, then sailed the last lap up the California coast and under the Golden Gate Bridge on March 21st at the end of an extremely pleasant, 11 week, 3850 mile voyage for me and the end of a perfectly executed, two year circumnavigation by *Night Watch* and her skilled owners, Jerry and Suzie Knecht and their stalwart crew John McVey.

*   *   *   *

Up until now we had used *Misty* only for daysailing, overnight cruises and short vacation trips up the Delta and to Tomales Bay, all the while making minor improvements in the boat and gaining confidence in her ability as a sea boat. It was now time for some serious cruising. The plan was to get up the West Coast and spend two seasons cruising the waters of Puget Sound and British Columbia. With summer cruising in the Northwest in mind, there are two ways to get one's boat up there – the smooth way (by truck) or the bumpy way (by water). We believed that *Misty*, our little double ender with a brave heart, demanded at least a try at the 800 mile passage along the often hostile coast between San Francisco and Cape Flattery at the entrance to the Strait of Juan de Fuca.

On April 25th three of us, SFYC member Bob Alderson, Evan Pugh of Belvedere and I shoved off from the club harbor. We left early in the season while it was still cool because if we had waited until later, the heat in the Central Valley would have established a thermal low which typically results in strong winds blowing down the coast. We also planned to stick close inshore, motorsailing along the 20 fathom line, if possible, which my experience has shown to be often dramatically less windy than offshore even a few miles. It also offers the chance to duck into the occasional anchorages along the coast in the event of really strong headwinds.

Small craft warnings were posted the day we departed, but we figured we could at least get as far as Drakes Bay. By pushing on past a rough patch at Point Reyes we won the first 50 miles to Bodega Bay. Next day we tried to press on but had to turn back near Fort Ross when rough seas and fresh northwesterlies made further progress doubtful. We remained in famously windy, "Blowdega" Bay for the next three days waiting for things to ease down.

Underway again at last, we got past Point Arena shortly after sundown, but at midnight a serious problem with the propeller shaft and gearbox developed. We drifted around all night wondering if the cruise was at an end, however next morning we discovered that we could run the engine very slowly and thus crept into the narrow and shallow Noyo River entrance. Luckily, there was very little swell and a slack tide. *Misty* moored amongst the fishing boats and with help from a local mechanic and a diver we removed the gearbox and the propeller shaft, rented a car and drove to Sausalito. Miraculously, in one day the gearbox was repaired, the prop shaft straightened, a new coupling fitted and we returned to Noyo by nightfall. By the next afternoon we were on our way again.

Soon we were rounding the loathed and feared Cape Mendocino, then St. George Reef and were intending to stop at Brookings, Oregon, when a south (!) wind began to make up. We quickly changed our plans and ran past Cape Blanco in rough seas and patchy fog with the main boom on the shrouds and the genoa jib on the pole. The southerly left us near Coos Bay, but we carried on toward Newport, Oregon for fuel and a night's rest.

Next day we sailed close to the beach along a spectacular shoreline, however increasing headwinds forced us to anchor under the sheltering cliffs of Cape Lookout. By early morning the wind had gone into the south, making our anchorage untenable but giving us a welcome fair wind for about half a day, which lasted long enough for us to cross the latitude of the Columbia River on a moderate, sunny afternoon. Unfortunately the nice weather gave way to a rough, overcast night off Willapa Bay and Grays Harbor. Next day as we neared the northwest corner of the Washington coast, *Misty* tacked past Destruction Island and the towering rocks of the Giants Graveyard near La Push. By nightfall we could see Cape Flattery.

At 2:00 AM, using radar, we were taking a short-cut between Tatoosh Island and Duncan Rock, a gap of about a mile at the entrance to the Straits, when the engine stopped. It was déjà vu with the perversity of inanimate objects. The motor could have stopped anywhere but, no, it had to pick this spot. I paid dearly for my bad planning in letting a fuel tank run dry by spending a wretched half hour bleeding the fuel system while waves crashed on the island rocks and the lighthouse beam swept over the boat and the windless waters. I simply could not get the blasted diesel engine to start until I remembered a trick told to us by the man who sold us Tu Lung Bang, the Chinese engine in *Sea Bear*. It was to keep spraying some gasoline into the air intake as the engine tries to start. Bingo.

Early the next morning we entered the snug harbor of Neah Bay for a well earned rest. Two more days in the relatively smooth waters of the Strait of Juan de Fuca and we were at the end of our 17-day journey. We had reached Port Ludlow where *Misty* would wait for us to join her later in the summer. A good crew, a seaworthy little boat and a bit of luck with the weather had spelled success for *Misty's* first sea voyage.

Jane and I returned to Puget Sound in August for a couple of weeks of cruising in the San Juan Islands, then joined a national CCA cruise in Desolation Sound starting in Sidney, B.C. on September 8th. At the end of five weeks of sailing, we put *Misty* on the hard at Canoe Cove near Sidney for the '97-'98 winter. For some reason Canadian Customs discourages Americans from leaving their boats in Canada except to have major boatyard work performed. Thus one goes through a big charade by giving the yard a long list of expensive work items to be undertaken over the winter. When I handed the yard owner the list I told him, "Now don't do any of this unless I expressly authorize it." His reply was, "Relax. We know what's going on." It all worked out fine and we found the boat ready to go when we returned the next spring.

The plan for 1998 was to spend a full three months in British Columbia -- including a circumnavigation of Vancouver Island -- before returning to San Francisco Bay. Vancouver Island is 280 miles long and, in the words of one Canadian we met, serves as the "world's biggest breakwater". Thus the waters east of the island are wonderfully sheltered and have lots of delightfully smooth passages and anchorages. The west coast of the island, however, is another matter. It all promised to make for an interesting summer.

Misty at anchor in Melanie Cove during the 1997 CCA Cruise in Desolation Sound, British Columbia

Jane and I flew up to the boat on June 1, and, as was promised, found her already in the water. She needed only a wash down, groceries, ice, and a few more charts before we were ready to go. For the first week while cruising through the Gulf Islands, we were joined by Bob Petersen, our old crew from the *Armorel* trip and his wife, Toshie, who lived in the Northwest. For the rest of the next two months, Jane and I cruised alone.

An incident early in the cruise tested our ingenuity. Our engine starter failed on an absolutely windless day, and the nearest anchorage where we might find a telephone - let alone a mechanic - was about six miles away. After some thought, we tied our inflatable - with its little 2 hp motor - alongside *Misty* and slowly but surely pushed her to safe harbor. By late the next day we were back in business!

For the first couple of weeks of June, the weather wasn't ready to settle down. We found ourselves wind-bound in Nanaimo for several days - which was all right since we were anchored off a large island park with lots of hiking trails and a snug anchorage. But at our first opportunity, we moved across the Strait of Georgia and up the mainland coast to Desolation Sound - while the weather steadily improved. We enjoyed revisiting some of the places we had seen the previous fall and were pleasantly surprised to find that there were few boats in the popular anchorages during the month of June.

By July we had moved north to the maze of channels and islands opposite the northern part of Vancouver Island. It was all new territory for us, and we found it absolutely fascinating. The Canadian charts are excellent, but the aids to navigation are few and far between. We found it very important to keep careful track of exactly where we were amidst the jumble of islands, reefs and rocks. With 12 to 18 foot tides, the landscape changes dramatically and islands seem to appear and disappear as they blend into the solidly forested background. But after threading our way through the aptly named Beware Passage, Jane exclaimed, "Hey, this is fun!" It reinforced what I already knew. I had married a suitable mate for what I loved to do best.

Other highlights in this wonderfully, complex cruising ground were watching a bear that swam right across our bow at Lagoon Cove, visiting the abandoned Indian village at Mamalilaculla; piloting into beautiful and well-protected Waddington Bay on a stormy day, anchoring below a 2,300 foot high cliff in spectacular McKenzie Sound, observing Roaring Hole Rapids live up to its name, mooring at a zany little floating village in Sullivan Bay, and engaging in an unexpected and intricate bit of navigation in pea soup fog into rockbound Cullen Harbor. With the dense forest behind most of the anchorages making access ashore virtually impossible, it was always a treat to find a trail and stretch our legs, and occasionally it happened.

All too soon July had passed, and Jane headed for home from Port Hardy near the northern tip of Vancouver Island. There I was joined by John Nooteboom of Tiburon and Jim Algert of Coronado, two very experienced sailing friends who would complete *Misty's* crew for the more arduous cruise of the coming month.

In spectacular McKenzie Sound in the summer of 1998

On August 3, we set off for one last anchorage before rounding Cape Scott which is the northern tip of Vancouver Island. The cape we were about to round is almost exactly the same latitude as Cape Horn. Happily, the weather at 52° north is far warmer and less stormy than at 55° south. Still, we were excited to make our way past the turbulent sea at the tip and out onto the restless Pacific swell which is ever-present along the west coast of the island.

Our first anchorage on the west coast of Vancouver Island was Sea Otter Cove, which requires that you enter between breakers crashing on the rocks along each shore. We anchored carefully inside the deserted cove, set our crab pot, than ventured ashore to take a brief hike along a muddy trail through the forest, keeping an eye out for bears. The cove was typical of many we visited along the northern part of the island: good protection, but without habitation or other boats, and having a wild and brooding aspect.

At Nootka Sound on the west coast of Vancouver Island

A major obstacle on a passage down the west coast of Vancouver Island is the Brooks Peninsula, which juts out about ten miles from the coastline and is notorious for stormy conditions. The weather didn't look promising the first day we attempted to get around, so we holed up just to the north in Klaskish Basin. This place is so snug that fishing boats would have to raise their trolling poles to clear the entrance. We tried again the next day, but gave up near the end of the peninsula when we were flattened by rainy blasts of wind from the southeast. We retreated back to the basin and were completely stormbound the following day. We didn't see another boat or human during the entire time. We finally managed to round the peninsula without incident on the fourth day, and in quite nice weather.

From Brooks Peninsula south we enjoyed fairly good weather – but without the nice northwesterly winds we had hoped for. We visited a new interesting cove nearly everyday in the four huge inlets along the coast. As we progressed south, we began to encounter more pleasure boats, lots of kayaks – we began to call them sea lice – particularly in Barkley Sound, a large, island-filled cruising ground not far from the Strait of Juan de Fuca. Because of severe restrictions by the Canadian Government, fishing boats were noticeably absent everywhere we went.

By the third week of August, we had to face up to the fact that it was time to sail south to San Francisco. We crossed the strait and cleared US Customs at Neah Bay. The next morning we set off in a calm to round Cape Flattery, and headed south on what was to be a six day passage. After two days of motoring, we passed Cape Blanco and for the first time picked up a northwesterly wind. By sundown we had much more breeze than we needed and spent most of the night running at high speed under a scrap of jib winged out on the spinnaker pole.

We caught our breath for a day at Crescent City, then set out for the last lap home. The notorious Cape Mendocino was rounded in light air, but off Point Arena – about 100 miles north of the Golden Gate – the wind came back with a roar. We had a wild night of running under storm canvas before ducking into Drakes Bay. After a pleasant day's sail we were back in the bay and were welcomed by friends and family at the San Francisco Yacht Club, bringing *Misty's* two-season northwest cruise to an end.

*   *   *   *

To me and Jane, poking around in the backwaters and gunk-holes on a leisurely schedule is not a bad form of cruising. With this in mind, we shipped *Misty* to the East Coast for a three month cruise up the Intracoastal Waterway and Chesapeake Bay, winding up the trip at Cape Cod. Maybe it didn't have the excitement of a voyage around Cape Horn, but the route was all new territory for us and was great fun.

On the advice of various cruising friends, we decided to skip the Florida portion of the ICW because it had too many boats, houses and bridges, so *Misty* was trucked to a spot near the northern border of Florida. A boat trucker from Jacksonville, FL picked up the boat in Richmond, CA and delivered it one week later to Fernandina Beach, Florida. They did an excellent job for a very reasonable $3,850 and delivered it right on schedule at 9 AM, Monday, April 17, 2000. We had her rigged and in the water by 4 PM the same day! We spent the next day getting organized and putting stores aboard and then we were on our way.

April 2000, Misty is ready to head for the East Coast

A big advantage of cruising north on the ICW is that the pre-vailing wind is in the southerly quarter thus giving lots of running and reaching. We sailed far more than we had expected and by the end of three weeks of traveling, we had used only 15 gallons of fuel. Another advantage was having the sun behind us as we stared ahead for the next waterway marker. Also, being early in the season, the weather was quite cool and pleasant. Other than the no-see-ums early in the cruise, bugs weren't a major problem either.

Sailing through the waterway in Georgia seemed to us a lot like sailing near our home waters, in the delta of the Sacramento and San Joaquin Rivers, but with no levees and with endless marsh grass on each side instead. Without the waterway markers you would be hard pressed to know where you were! Much of the ICW passes through wildlife reserves and is quite beautiful if your taste in nature runs to marshy flatlands with lots of birds. We would usually go only about 15 to 25 miles a day, although one day we went 40 miles because the an-chorage we were headed for turned out to be off our ICW strip chart.

We anchored out nearly all the time, usually trying to find a spot with a stand of trees nearby. We could always find an anchorage in the many creeks, nooks, and rivers along the way. Frequently we were alone, although sometimes we shared a spot with one or two other sailboats. The powerboats always headed for the marinas at night. We saw very little commercial traffic on the ICW but far more sailboats than we had expected. We judged the ratio was about 40% sail and 60% power. It was a pleasant surprise to find that almost always the powerboats would slow right down when passing us.

One afternoon we anchored off a nice grove of trees in Cane Patch Creek, GA. About 2 PM the storm clouds moved in and within minutes the rain was torrential, accompanied by a spectacular lightning and thunder show-- both exciting and kind of scary. This went on for hours with only a short respite around dinnertime. The pyrotechnics didn't stop until midnight. And I thought this trip might be dull!   After about a week we stopped at our first marina at Thunderbolt, GA for some stores, a little boat work and some much-needed showers. We took a taxi into nearby Savannah to see the historic sights, including the locale of the book and movie, "Midnight in The Garden of Good And Evil." Another favorite stop was in Beaufort ("beau"as in beautiful), South Carolina, a lovely little city with a nice waterfront park and lovely old houses and a good library with e-mail facilities.

Sailing up the Intracoastal Waterway in South Carolina

Contrary to my expectations, there was plenty of depth in the ICW -- generally about 9 or 10 feet at low tide. We managed to go aground once in a while, but it was always while wandering around off the waterway.   One day we misjudged the entrance to Tom Point Creek, SC, and went up on the putty on a falling tide. *Misty* showed her pretty bilges nicely for quite a while until finally, the rising tide floated us off with a bit of help from a kedge anchor. It was so nice once we got in the creek we lay over a day, while I, at last, got the propeller shaft aligned to stop the annoying chatter it had been making.

The contrasts of the trip were part of the charm of it. While at Charleston, SC, we stayed in the modern Ashley Marina lying along-side a shiny 145' power yacht, enjoying all sorts of luxuries like hot showers, dining ashore and viewing the historic district. The next day we were anchored in the marshes of the Cape Romayne Nature Pre-serve where the banks of the creek were absolutely carpeted with mil-lions of oysters. Great flocks of terns were feasting at low tide and making a huge racket when not eating.

We liked Georgetown, SC, an interesting little harbor at the confluence of the Sampit, Waccamaw, and Great PeeDee Rivers. We had aboard a biography of General Francis Marion ("The Swamp Fox*")* who raised hell around here in the American Revolu-tion. Lots of history. We met some interesting cruising characters too, including an old chap nicknamed "Captain Seaweed" who sailed around the waterways in an old sloop he rescued from the dumpster. He told us about the big cottonmouth water moccasin which climbed up his boomkin and slithered into his cockpit one day while at anchor here. He was afraid it might get down below and was trying to whack it with a winch handle but kept getting his aim spoiled by hitting the awning.   Eventually the snake decided it was in un-friendly territory and slid overboard.   He also told us about Sweetie, a large alligator that habituated the place for a number of years.

After departing Georgetown a real highlight of the trip was our passage up the Waccamaw River in the heart of a huge cypress swamp. Beautiful! The scenery went a bit downhill as we passed Myrtle Beach and entered North Carolina where we encountered stretches of the waterway with few trees but many houses with little wooden piers jutting out into the water, some still unrepaired from the latest hurricane. But it all got prettier again when we reached Beaufort (as in "bow"), NC. This was a nice historical town with an excellent maritime museum, and a lively waterfront filled with boats transiting the ICW and using the excellent entrance from the Atlantic. As usual, we met some interesting cruising folks.

Some very nice sailing followed for the next few days as we passed through large, shallow, open water areas that form parts of Pamlico Sound. We were reminded of our nearby San Pablo Bay, but on a gigantic scale and with crab pots. Before crossing the last bit, Albemarle Sound, we anchored in the wide Alligator River and had the fun of riding out not one but two big electrical storms. The wind blew, the rain came in sheets flattening the water and the dinghy filled. Thank goodness I had increased the size of *Misty's* anchor!

The final section of the ICW began with our arrival in Elizabeth City, NC and an amazing display of southern hospitality. Cruisers are greeted by the "Rose Buddies," a welcoming committee who give the ladies a rose, provided free dockage and put on a little wine and cheese party for the new arrivals. From here we entered the Great Dismal Swamp Canal. It belied its name and was gorgeous -- a very long narrow "ditch" with lush trees on both sides. It has locks on both ends with a limiting draft of about 5.5' and a speed limit of 6 knots, so most powerboats take the less scenic Virginia Cut route.

Our arrival in Norfolk, VA at the bottom of Chesapeake Bay on June 1st marked the halfway point of our cruise. We suddenly found we had to make choices as to our route as we entered this huge and surprisingly shallow cruising ground. The weather was getting quite warm and the breezes were definitely on the light side. We were also surprised at the continually hazy (smoggy?) condition of the atmosphere.

We wandered up the west side of the Bay, stopping at the little port of Hampton with its impressive aviation museum, then several pretty creeks, in the first of which we went aground upon entering, because its only aid to navigation looked like a broom handle that was about to fall down. We were en route to the mouth of the Potomac where we planned to sail to Washington DC. It took us three days to get to the Capitol, but it was good cruising along the way and definitely worth it. There is an excellent anchorage, which we shared with only a half dozen other boats, within walking distance of the Mall. A five dollar a day charge by the nearby marina gave us access to the dinghy dock and showers. The 94-degree weather was too hot for us, but we enjoyed seeing the monuments, museums and the National Cathedral which were shown to us by Dick and Joan Underland, a college mate of Jane's. Dick had recently retired from the State Department which had kept him posted during his career in the Middle East. It made for some interesting conversations.

We had some very good sailing on our way back down the Potomac and some excitement in the form of a real Chesapeake Bay line squall one evening while anchored opposite Mount Vernon. Suddenly the wind was upon us which broke the battens in the awning and nearly knocked Jane overboard while we were trying to get it down.

The final portion of our cruise on the Chesapeake was spent poking around the creeks on the East Shore in the vicinity of Oxford and St. Michaels, both lively little yachting centers surrounded by nice anchorages in the many creeks nearby. Except for the occasional, brief late afternoon thunderstorm, the weather was sunny and it was too early in the season for the nasty "sea nettle" jellyfish to spoil the swimming, so we enjoyed ideal lazy cruising.

On July 1, Jane swapped places on *Misty* with our old friend Bill Hickman and his brother-in-law, Bud Monaghan, my crew for the trip to Cape Cod. We went via the Chesapeake and Delaware Bay Canal to Cape May, NJ, then a two day passage to Block Island and on to Cotuit, MA where *Misty* lay on a mooring for the remainder of the summer pending her layup on the hard for the winter at Barnstable, MA. Both Jane and I agreed that the three-month, 1800 mile trip had been one of the easiest and most interesting cruises we had ever made. I would do it all over again in a minute.

*   *   *   *

In the October of 2000 I went back east and fetched *Misty* around to the north side of Cape Cod to Barnstable where she spent the winter on the hard. The plan for 2001 was to sail into the Great Lakes and keep going west until the water ran out at Duluth, Minnesota, another three month cruise of 1800 miles.

The route would take us down Long Island Sound to New York City, up the Hudson River and into the Erie Canal. About half-way along the Erie we would turn right into the Oswego Canal, go across

Lake Ontario and into the Canadian Trent-Severn Waterway to Lake Huron. Finally, we would traverse Lake Superior and wind up at its western tip in Duluth. It promised to be a cruise of great variety and indeed it was!

Misty got underway on June 4th with sailing friends, Bill Hickman and Bob Smith of Cape Cod, as crew. Jane would spend a week in Cape Cod with Bill's wife, Joyce, and then join the boat in Tarrytown, NY with a car for the crew to take back home. Our smooth start was rudely interrupted when *Misty*, riding a swift current through the Cape Cod Canal, bumped into to the usual strong wind and sea blowing up Buzzard's Bay. We bucked into one sea so hard the weld on the spreader light snapped and sent it crashing to the deck. After that, things got smoother and we had a pleasant, four day trip to New York City, climaxed by a fascinating ride down the East River and around the tip on Manhattan Island.

With Jane now aboard, the two of us started up the broad Hudson River which provided interesting scenery especially where the banks rose steeply around West Point and Storm King Mountain. Nice anchorages can be found along the river. We especially liked one behind a little island surmounted by Bannerman's Castle, a crumbling replica of a medieval castle built by an arms dealer who made tons of money selling Civil War surplus munitions around the world a hundred years ago. At Kingston, NY, we pulled the mast at a funky little boat yard for $50 and laid it on sawhorses we had prepared for this purpose. We were to remain in "African Queen" mode until we emerged onto Lake Huron a month later.

At Troy, NY, we paid our $75 transit fee and entered the historic Erie Canal. Immediately we began to climb a "stairway" of five high-lift locks, which raised us a total of 169 feet to the level of the Mohawk River. We would continue to travel along the route of the Mohawk River almost until we branched off into the Oswego Canal 150 miles later, and it was beautiful. Both sides of the river were wooded with big trees and almost no houses or buildings were to be seen. For that matter very few boats and no commercial traffic were to be seen either. The locks were at about five mile intervals and were fully manned and operated by mechanical or hydraulic power. Generally, the area around each lock was nicely landscaped and provided a pleasant place to tie up along the lock approach walls. We seldom shared a lock with another vessel. To tell the truth, I marveled that the State of New York could afford to operate and maintain the canal system when it was so clearly underutilized.

Misty in a lock in the Erie Canal, summer 2001

At Oswego, NY, we were on the southern shore of Lake Ontario and facing a 45 mile lake crossing with our heavy mast on not-too-stable sawhorses. A couple of days before, in our efforts to better stabilize the heavy mast, we nearly lost it overboard and had a very dicey time getting it back in place, so we were praying for calm weather. Our wishes were granted and we rejoiced in a glassy smooth trip across. By late afternoon we entered a gap taking us into the Bay of Quinte, a string of spacious waterways leading to Trenton, Ontario and the start of the Trent-Severn Waterway. First, however, we found Prinyer's Cove, where we entered Canadian Customs (by telephone) and reveled in the lovely surroundings for an extra day.

At Trenton, Ontario we were joined by Bill and Joyce Hickman who were our crew through the Waterway. The Trent-Severn is 240 miles long and connects an irregular string of little lakes (and one big lake) that form a passageway between Lake Ontario and Georgian Bay on Lake Huron. It passes through lovely countryside, nice little towns, many waterside cottages and contains 45 locks, several of which are absolutely amazing. We paid a transit fee of $76 (US) plus a small fee each time we tied up for the night at one of the attractive lock walls. Each lock also provided nice rest room facilities although no showers. Unlike the Erie Canal, there was lots of recreational boat traffic and a lively atmosphere all the way along. Unfortunately, boats drawing over 5' 6" cannot get through.

The trip through the Trent-Severn took 10 days and provided a wonderful variety of scenes. Of special interest were two high "lift locks" which consist of a pair of balanced ascending and descending boxes of water big enough for several boats at once. One enters the box, the end closes, a little extra water is let into the upper box, you rise (or descend) about 65 feet, the opposite end of the box opens and you go on your way. Incredible! Equally incredible was a huge marine railway carriage, which took several boats each time out of the water, across a road, then down a steep grade to the water 57 feet below!

At Midland, Ontario, we pulled into a marina where we stepped the mast, a do-it-yourself operation costing $50 US. We were a sailboat again! We sampled an anchorage on Beausoleil Island, but decided we had followed enough buoys and markers so we forsook the rock-strewn, 30,000 Island portion of Georgian Bay in favor of the wide open sailing route along the southern shore. After wiggling our way out of the rocks, we had a grand sail across to the Bruce Peninsula and the nice little town of Meaford. A couple of more hops and we were at Killarney and the start of the pristine cruising grounds of Lake Huron's North Channel.

The North Channel is a complex maze of islands, coves and inlets all set in a stunning mass of pink and white granite. There are endless snug anchorages surrounded by wooded shores but with plenty of easily navigable water and good sailing breezes in between. It is no wonder that it is the destination of choice for the cruising boats of Lake Huron and Lake Michigan. Surprisingly, by far the majority of boats are sailboats and we usually shared our anchorages with several of them. The weather was mostly very nice, the water was quite warm (and fresh) so we often enjoyed swimming.

Long Point Cove in the North Channel of Lake Huron

We had selected Duluth as the terminus of our cruise because it is as far west as one can go by boat but also because Jane's family roots are there and it still is home to her cousins. It also gave us a good reason to recruit, Herb Recktenwald, proud alumni of Duluth East H.S. class of '51, Navy jet fighter pilot and sailing friend on San Francisco Bay. Herb managed to find us in Sault Saint Marie even though the airline managed to lose his duffel bag in the wilds of northern Michigan. While waiting for their unification we spoke with a pair of large sailboats who had just returned from Lake Superior. When asked about their adventures, they admitted that they had only gone to the first anchorage around the corner at Batchawana Bay and were now on their way back to Lake Michigan, having had their "Lake Superior experience."

While cruising in Lake Huron, when we mentioned that we were bound for Duluth in Lake Superior, the usual reaction was "Geez. Don't you know that big ships break in half and sink there?" Indeed Lake Superior seems to have such an evil reputation for big, steep waves, icy water and sudden thunderstorms that cruisers from the other Great Lakes don't even consider going there. Luckily, we had been briefed on the cruising conditions on Lake Superior by an experienced couple who knew the area well, so undeterred, we passed through the Canadian Lock at Sault Saint Marie and emerged onto the bosom of Gichi Gumi, the "Shining Big Sea Water".

As *Misty* sailed along the east and north shores of the Lake we realized that we just might be enjoying the last frontier of cruising areas. It was magnificent. And better yet, there was hardly anyone around, either ashore or afloat. We found nice anchorages about every 20 or 30 miles. Our second stop was one of the best, a place called Sinclair Cove, a tiny round cove with a nice beach, spectacular pink rocks, prehistoric Indian pictographs on the outside cliffs and water warm enough to swim in -- an idyllic spot, but only one of many.

We stopped at several other lovely anchorages, then hit the jackpot with a two and a half mile trip up the uncharted White River to the "pool" just below some impressive rapids. We would never have attempted this except for the excellent directions in our Lake Superior Cruising Guide by Bonnie Dahl. We hiked above the rapids then crossed the 200' deep canyon on a suspension bridge reminiscent of the one in "Indiana Jones and the Temple of Doom." Not for the faint of heart, but Jane crossed it anyway.

The weather during our three-week cruise on Lake Superior was quite good except for one rainy day and a partial day of fog. It was also surprisingly warm and on several days we went swimming (always in a shallow cove). To test the notion that Lake Superior has especially big, steep waves we tried to judge if they were bigger than any normal ocean waves in the same wind. Since waves anywhere are governed by depth of water, fetch, and air-water friction, we were unable to distinguish a difference between them and our home-grown variety. If anything, they seemed to be smaller because there was no accompanying ocean swell.

A day was spent in the oddly named, CPR Spit, a snug little basin that was almost impossible to locate along what looked like an unbroken coastline, it had modest improvements built by the local Canadian boaters including some floats, a fire pit and a sauna. Based on the advice of the friendly locals (but contrary to our cruising guide) we set off next day with cloudy skies, headwinds and choppy water to take a short cut to Nipigon Bay via Blind Channel. We had been advised that it was buoyed informally with red and green Clorox bottles and after touching the gravel bottom lightly once, we managed to get our 5 foot deep keel safely through and into the huge bay beyond.

We found a small marina at the lumber mill town of Red Rock and set off in search of groceries. Being Sunday, the store was closed, but we bought a couple of blocks of ice and started to walk back to the boat in the warm sunshine. A man cutting the lawn at a church jumped off his mower and insisted on giving us a ride in his pickup. In response to his query as to what brought us this little town, we mentioned that we were out of food. Less than an hour later he was back at the boat with a large bag of sandwiches and a big can of soup prepared for us by his wife. It was a charming incident and one which will long remain in our memories of the cruise.

We continued along the north shore of the Lake stopping at the Slate Islands, then at some of the many little islands in the Rossport area, an idyllic cruising area with snug anchorages everywhere. Finally, with time running out before our truck hauling date in early September in Duluth, we visited Isle Royale and the Apostle Islands, both national parks and fine cruising grounds. Then it was on to Duluth and the end of a unique voyage.

In terms of the unusual character of the cruise and the great variety of experiences we had, the cruise had been wonderful. We were still on a high when we returned, only to be brought down to earth in shock as we watched the events of 9/11 which took place within a few days of our return home.

* * * *

It seems like our routine had become one of having two-year cruises with a year off in between. 2001 was such a year, a time to enjoy a cruise up the Delta with Lacey and various other sailing events. It was obvious we had enjoyed our Great Lakes cruise because we signed on for a CCA National Cruise which would take us back to the North Channel of Lake Huron. We chartered a boat together with Bob and Marlene Allen, old friends from Tiburon, a little 35' trawler named *Chocolate Monkey* (a cocktail whose ingredients seem to be a bit of a mystery). The weather was grand and it was a joy to return to this pristine cruising ground in company with a pack of interesting cruising friends. It was all perfect except for the Commodore sailing up on a granite reef and smashing the rudder of his chartered sailboat.

By the next spring I had turned my attention to our upcoming two-season cruise to Alaska on *Misty*. The plan was to sail up to the northwest early in the season then leave the boat for a month or so to let the weather improve before continuing on to Alaska. At the end of the summer we would leave the boat for the winter in Ketchikan.

The sail up to Canada was a rough, cold trip which was not surprising since by then the weather on the West Coast that spring had been very windy, wet and unsettled. We left from the San Francisco Yacht Club on April 26th in a break in the weather which didn't last long. For crew I had my friend, Dr. Joe Alderson and a gal named Sharon Smalley who also owns an Aries 32 like *Misty* and wanted to get some experience at sea (she succeeded beyond her wildest dreams). I was 72, Joe was 80, but in good shape, and Sharon was a 66 year-old grandmother, so it was kind of a geriatric crew, but despite our combined age of 218 years, we all survived and had fun to boot.

We sailed with a nice little southerly breeze and by evening we were doing fine, so we went right on by Bodega Bay. Early the next morning off Noyo the wind began to increase rapidly and soon we were in a genuine storm with driving rain, lots of wind and very rough seas off Cape Mendocino. I think the wind was up to about 40 knots in the gusts and we were running fast with a double reefed main and a scrap of jib on the pole. Just as I was about to call Joe up so I could get the main down, we gybed and broke the boom. It was a bit of a mess, but we got the boom secured then carried on through the night with plenty of speed under the mostly rolled-up jib on the pole. During the night the wind eased up somewhat and by mid-morning the next day we reached Crescent City, near the northern border of California.

There was a good-sized boatyard there but they said they no longer did work on wooden boats and couldn't help us with the boom, but luckily, since it had split apart at the gooseneck, it looked repairable with enough epoxy and hose clamps. The biggest problem was that it was so cold and rainy, I wasn't sure the epoxy would cure. It did harden overnight and by the second day the weather was a bit better so we put things back together and got underway. We carried a nice south wind and a north-going current past Cape Blanco and beyond as far as Coos Bay where the whole system reversed following a heavy squall. We reached Newport, Oregon the next afternoon and struggled in against a very strong headwind and an engine which kept overheating. After disassembling the water pump and inspecting the seawater strainer, I concluded the problem was being caused by excessive heeling while motorsailing on port tack in the rough seas and sucking air into the engine sea water intake.

Joe Alderson steers Misty in a southerly blow
as we head up the coast towards Alaska

My little sister, Jan, and her husband live just down the coast, so they came up and hauled the crew off to showers and a nice hot dinner at their house on the evening of our arrival. The next day it was still very windy from the northwest, so we laid over a day to let the wind ease up while we enjoyed lunch at the brewery near the harbor and played tourist. We had a mixture of wind on the next leg past the Columbia River and managed to break the end of the spinnaker pole. By morning it was getting pretty rough so we went into Grays Harbor for shelter. The harbor has a scary, shallow entrance and a rather dismal appearance, particularly in the cold, rainy, windy weather, but it served the purpose and allowed us to fix the pole with more of the epoxy-and-hose clamps treatment. In this case, we insured the epoxy would cure by cramming the 14' pole down into the cabin overnight. About this time I had pretty much made up my mind that the weather was just too bad to continue up the west coast of Vancouver Island, but by the time we got to Cape Flattery the next night things looked better, so we crossed the Strait of Juan de Fuca and continued on up to Barkley Sound on Vancouver Island. In fact, the weather was quite nice for several days and since we now had some extra time in hand, we visited a number of the interesting anchorages we had visited in this marvelous cruising area when we had *Misty* on the west side of Vancouver Island five years before.

We had warning that a gale was coming so we got ourselves into Sea Otter Cove just below Cape Scott. It was well protected and quite shallow with good holding, so we had no problem riding it out for a day. Getting around Cape Scott the next morning in the big left-over seas was exciting, but by noon we got over the shallow and sometimes dangerous Nawitti Bar and into Bull Harbor on Hope Island. Next day we sailed down to Port Hardy where the 1060 mile, three week trip ended on May 15th.

The best thing we had on board was our new Dickinson diesel heater which we had going a lot of the time. When we left Port Hardy for home Saturday morning, *Misty's* deck and the dock were coated with ice! I hoped that it would be a lot more like summer when we got back up in mid-June to continue the cruise to Alaska.

In mid-June Jane, our good friend, Carl Seipel, and I flew up to Port Hardy and started north with the general plan of sailing as far north as the Ketchikan area on a three month cruise with Carl along for the first month. After wintering *Misty* in Alaska we would continue the cruise in 2004.

The weather was reasonably good when we departed to cross Queen Charlotte Strait. North-bound cruisers, especially motor-boaters, often spend a lot of time fretting about this passage, but for sailors it is frequently the only lively sail on a trip to Alaska. We stopped at a snug little anchorage in the Walker Islands about halfway across and at misnamed Fury Cove opposite the south end of Calvert Island and were now out of open water. From the north end of Calvert Island we exited Pruth Harbor, which nearly bisects the large island, crossed blustery Hakai Passage, and entered the southeastern portion of Queen Sound. For years Barry Arnett, a sailing friend in Seattle had been telling me about the joys of Queens Sound, the area between Calvert Island and Bella Bella, but to seaward of the normal "Inside Passage." We explored only a few channels and anchorages in this fascinating and seldom-visited area and vowed to do more cruising here next year on our return trip.

Continuing up the B.C. channels we visited many delightful anchorages and made brief stops at the "First Nation" (indian) villages of Bella Bella and Klemtu. Contrary to some cruisers' comments, we found the folks at both these places to be friendly and helpful although somewhat reticent. At Klemtu an elder proudly showed us their handsome new long house and another local generously gave us a replacement for our dead battery. At this point we made a jog to the west via Meyers Passage, a circuitous, shallow, shortcut to the outer channels leading north. By this time the weather had settled into a prolonged rainy spell, but with the aid of our little blue tarp and our diesel cabin heater we managed to enjoy our poking about in this endlessly interesting area. In Dunn Passage, an extraordinarily intricate nest of tiny islets, Carl almost completely lost his way while rowing about on a rainy afternoon.

At Prince Rupert we stopped at the Yacht and Rowing Club for our first major pit stop in nearly three weeks for groceries, water, ice, fuel, laundry and showers. Before crossing the loathed and feared Dixon Entance, the only bit of exposed water on the trip north of Queen Charlotte Strait, we found such a delightful anchorage at Dunira Island that we stayed awhile to enjoy the solitude and scenery. It was tricky enough to get into that we were guaranteed to have it all to ourselves. Then it was on to Ketchikan and the shock of seeing multiple huge cruise ships and hoards of tourists. Here Carl left us to return home leaving Jane and me to explore Prince of Wales Island for the next month.

Prince of Wales Island is very large with a circumference of about 300 miles, and because it is off the usual itinerary of an Alaska cruise, is seldom visited by cruising boats. In our month there, we saw only one sailboat and three motorboats and a handful of fishboats. It is a splendid cruising area with no end of scenic coves and anchorages and a handful of quaint settlements. Except for our first foray into Kasaan Bay in rainy conditions, the weather had turned fine and remained that way for the remainder of our cruise in Alaska. Jane was convinced we would never get all the way around Prince of Wales Island in a month, so we hustled along up Clarence Strait to the top of the island where we found the funky but delightful little floating village of Point Baker. Read Joe Upton's book "Alaska Blues" for an insight into life here a few years ago. His little cabin is still there and we visited it and its current owners, who had come with their family for a holiday.

With time now in hand for a more or less leisurely cruise, we started down the west side of the Island, including a two day trip down El Capitan Passage, a scenic and sometimes exciting waterway through a portion of the Island including a section called "Dry Pass." Guess what that means! Highlights on the west side of Prince of Wales Island: a climb up 385 steps for a guided tour a large limestone cave, a stop at the nice little town of Craig, meeting the master totem carver, Mr. Marsden and his grandson at the indian village of Hydaburg, having a whale surface about three feet off the bow of *Misty*, seeing three bears on the beach at Breezy Bay on Dall Island, and finding the perfect anchorage in the Barrier Island group. The south and east sides of the Island also provided plenty of wonderful places to explore and too soon it was time to get back to Ketchikan and for Jane to fly home.

Our daughter Anne arrived the day after Jane left and we wrapped up our 2003 Alaska season with a two week cruise to Anan Bay to see the bears gorge themselves on salmon, then a delightful circuit of Misty Fjords National Park (Behm Canal) with its spectacular, Yosemite-like scenery. Finally, at the end of August we took *Misty* to a little boatyard about 6 miles north of Ketchikan to be hauled out and put on the hard for the winter. She was propped up with oil drums (the Alaskan version of a jack stand) and covered with a polytarp cover I had made at home. We left her without heaters or dehumidifiers but

with as much ventilation as we could devise, with the promise of a fellow sailor who lived nearby, to keep an eye on her, and hoped for the
best.

*   *   *   *

Our 2004 cruise began with my arrival in Ketchikan the first
week in June to get *Misty* in the water. Jane was to arrive a couple of
days later with Carl Seipel, who was to cruise with us for a month between Ketchikan and Port Hardy, B.C. The boat had survived the winter quite well with only a small amount of mildew down below. The
only damage seemed to be the varnish on the railcaps. The varnish
was fine; it just wasn't touching the wood anymore. Another job was
to replace the gearbox with the new one I had sent up to the boatyard.
By the time Jane and Carl arrived we only needed to put groceries
aboard and get underway.

Misty enters Walker Cove in Alaska's Misty Fjords National Park in June 2004

We started off with another little one-week cruise through Misty Fjords Park in weather which had suddenly turned fine. This area is a pleasure to see in any conditions, but in such sunny, clear conditions it was a wonder to behold with waterfalls everywhere and 2000 foot granite cliffs soaring above our boat. A few days later we checked into Canada at Prince Rupert and were ready to return to the outer channels of the northern British Columbia coast. While exploring the large sound in the center of Porcher Island the weather became rainy and, like last year, pretty much stayed that way until we reached the northern tip of Vancouver Island.

Of course it didn't rain all the time and we enjoyed returning to some of the anchorages we had visited on our way up last year as well as finding new ones. We considered sailing out to the Queen Charlotte Islands but were discouraged by the new bureaucracy now that it is a Park with requirements for reservations, daily visitor fees, boat fees, orientation lectures, etc. Instead we decided to save our time for a detailed cruise in Queen Sound which we entered from the north via a skinny waterway named Rait Narrows. We now found ourselves in solitude amongst a veritable maze of islands with snug anchorages everywhere, not all of which are perfectly charted. In one spot named Potts Island we anchored at high tide and to our dismay at low tide the next morning, we saw a huge uncharted rock only a few feet behind our rudder. Piloting in this area was both challenging and very interesting. Jane particularly enjoyed that aspect of cruising in these waters. Of special interest was Goose Island, the relatively large, uninhabited island which forms the outer barrier of Queen Sound. It had a superb fine- sandy beach which totaling disappeared with the tide about three hours after we had enjoyed walking barefoot on it. Jane and I would have liked to spend the night there, but Carl had a plane to catch and found it kind of spooky anyway, as did one of the writers of our cruising guide. Just as well we left, as a nasty stormy day came up the following day, but by then we were in a very snug landlocked anchorage. After a few more days we made a rough but short offshore passage to Calvert Island and returned to the "Inside Passage" and Queen Charlotte Strait.

At Port Hardy Carl left us, and Jane and I proceeded down the inside of Vancouver Island in weather which remained mostly sunny for the rest of the trip. Starting with a delightful sail back across

Queen Charlotte Strait to Blunden Harbor, we cruised amongst the
channels between the lofty mountains in Broughton Sound then on
down to join the crowds of boats in Desolation Sound.   Jane flew
home from Sidney (she doesn't do oceans anymore) and I was joined
by my down-the-coast crew Bob Vespa and Jack Hetherington, a pair
of gray-haired salts from Marin.

A peaceful and spectacular anchorage in Simoon Sound, British Columbia

We decided to make a bit of a cruise of the trip back and it was
a good thing too, since the wind remained fixed in the south for the
first ten days.   It didn't blow real hard but enough to raise a nasty chop
and get the current setting to the north. After Sidney we made stops at
a number of little places on the Washington and Oregon Coast. At last
the wind got back into the northwest where it belongs which allowed
us to have a good non-stop sail to Drakes Bay and home.   In all, a
grand two seasons in the Northwest.

Cloud Nine in the ice in the Northwest Passage

CHAPTER 15

CLOUD NINE

When Roger Swanson, owner of a British-built Bowman 57 ketch, phoned in April 2005 to ask if I was interested in joining him and his wife, Gaynelle, on an attempt at the Northwest Passage in July, he really got my attention. Actually his call didn't come as a complete surprise—I had heard from friends who had just returned from sailing with him that he was on his way to Greenland and a possible shot at the NW Passage. They also mentioned that he was looking for crew and that when my name had been suggested; he said he was really looking for younger people. I guess he was getting desperate and decided to call me anyway in spite of my age of 74. I knew I wasn't likely to get another chance at an adventure like this, so after a day to think it over, I said yes.

Roger also asked if I could suggest any additional experienced crew. He already had one person in mind, Doug Finley our Panama Canal pilot friend who had sailed with him recently on a short cruise in the Caribbean and was very keen to go. I confirmed that Doug would certainly be an excellent crew and suggested he consider taking Carl Seipel, our Swedish friend who had sailed around the world on his own boat and who had crewed aboard *Misty* with us in Alaska. I also suggested Chris Parkman, a tall, affable sailor in his 50's who had sailed with a close friend on a voyage across the North Atlantic and on a voyage from Scotland to Iceland and beyond before being forced back by brutal weather. Roger was agreeable to this group as crew so we all began to prepare to leave Marin County on July 8th to join *Cloud Nine* in Greenland for an east to west voyage over the top of Canada and Alaska, which we hoped would end in San Francisco 5900 miles later.

Roger Swanson, who describes himself as a pig farmer from Dunnell, Minnesota, is no stranger to ocean passages, having made three circumnavigations in *Cloud Nine*, plus two voyages to Antarctica and a previous (unsuccessful) attempt at the Northwest Passage in 1994. Apparently he got interested in sailing with E-class scows on the lakes of Minnesota then took up serious ocean cruising in his 50's. During WWII he had been the executive officer on a destroyer. He was short of stature but tough as they come and had a nice sense of humor. A bit set in his ways of doing things perhaps, but a skilled, no nonsense sailor nevertheless. Perhaps as a result of his farming days, Roger was a master of equipment repair and carried a ton of spare parts (new and old) for the purpose. Roger was a member of the Cruising Club of America and was affiliated with our San Francisco station. I had met him on several occasions and was sure that we would get along fine. He had been a recipient of the prestigious Blue Water Medal in 2000 in recognition of his 160,000 miles of ocean voyaging.

Gaynelle, his wife of recent years, was as one of those rare commodities, a gal who was a sailor in her own right who enjoyed the life of long distance cruising at sea. She had owned her own boat on the Great Lakes and had completed a circumnavigation on *Cloud Nine* the previous year. She was in charge of all the provisioning and took care of the communications and much of the navigation.

The boat was built in the 1970's and was a good looking yacht, typical of racer-cruisers of the era. Like other early fiberglass boats built around that time she was very heavily constructed of solid fiberglass with timber stringers molded into the hull. She had an odd deck layout with two cockpits each having a separate steering system. Being of fiberglass and drawing 9 feet with no inside steering, she was not ideal for the trip, but was quite strongly built, and with her skipper's considerable experience in ice navigation we felt we were reasonably well set up for the endeavor. A steel or heavily built aluminum boat would have been better especially if it was properly insulated and had provision for inside steering but as Roger said, "*Cloud Nine* is the boat we got."

I collected every account I could find of the previous 25 or so passages by yachts through the Northwest Passage, and I quickly learned that although two or three boats get though in most years recently, by no means do most of them make it in a single season. It is not unusual for boats to have to winter over one or even two seasons at one of the few small harbors along the two thousand mile length of the passage. My reading indicated that the possible time during which the ice would be open was limited from about August 1 to September 1, although some knowledgeable people argue that the navigable season can extend to the end of September. One thing for sure, it all depends on whether it is a good "ice year" or a bad one. The movement of the ice depends almost entirely on the direction the wind blows. Although global warming has thinned the Arctic ice pack, there is still plenty of the stuff up there most years to block the passage.

In the interval between my phone conversations with Roger and our date for departure in July, the four of us in Marin scrambled to assemble the arctic clothing, sleeping bags, and other gear we would need. I had met a man named Winston Bushnell in British Columbia who had taken his little 27 footer, *Dove III,* through the NW Passage in 1995 with two companions. I immediately phoned him and received much good information of what we probably needed. The first priority was to get an exposure suit, a one-piece, foam insulated outfit which was super warm and provided water proof protection and flotation at the same time. Winston also advised that we get Canadian "Kamik" boots, rubber boots with thick, removable felt liners. Arctic sleeping bags, mittens, face masks and woolen hats also went into our kits.

Our Marin County group met *Cloud Nine* on July 13, 2006 at the small Eskimo town of Aasiaat on Disko Bay, about half way up the West Coast of Greenland. Just getting there turned into something of an adventure in itself what with cancelled flights and lost luggage. Roger and Gaynelle were mighty glad to see us since they had come close to losing the boat the previous night in a severe gale while anchored in the small rock-bound harbor when the anchor failed to hold. The boat had begun this trip in Trinidad in the West Indies in March with various crews (three sailors from Marin were on the leg from Trinidad to Bermuda) and was now ready for the final leg. Baffin Bay, between Greenland and Canada was still full of pack ice and icebergs but was slowly becoming clear as we worked our way up the coast, stopping at several picturesque little settlements. Huge icebergs of stunning beauty were everywhere.

The Marin County contingent of Carl Seipel, Doug Finley Chris Parkman and me (not pictured)join Roger and Gaynelle Swanson in Aasiaat, Greenland

Our first stop was at the village of Upernavik, where we were forced to shuttle between an unsatisfactory anchorage, a large ship wharf, a quaywall and a moored tugboat to find a suitable mooring amidst the floating ice in the harbor. Our principal concern was the total failure of our shortwave radios (we had three of them plus several antennas). Roger hired a local technician who struggled along with him to find the problem but to no avail. After several days we moved up to the village of Kullorsuaq and the nearby rock spire named "Devil Thumb," a famed landmark for early explorers and whalers. Unfortunately the anchorage was so choked with floating ice we had to retreat 30 miles south to the little harbor at Kraulshavn which had good protection and only a moderate amount of ice. More work on the radios continued but still no success.

There was enough ice in the harbor that it was necessary to stand anchor watches to insure that a floe didn't catch on our anchor chain and dislodge the anchor. This was not much of a hardship since it was broad daylight all night. Ashore the "night" was made interesting by the sound of innumerable dogs, chained up on a small ledge nearby, sporadically going into mass howling contests. Also the local kids played noisy games at all hours on the stacks of cargo ashore near the boat. One of the locals told us that in the summer, people just never went to bed. I could believe it.

A fantastic iceberg in Greenland

By July 27 our ice information indicated that, by sailing as far north as 75 degrees latitude, we had a clear path above the pack ice in Baffin Bay for the 400 mile transit to the mouth of Lancaster Sound and the entrance to the fabled Northwest Passage. A further 200 ice-free miles took us to Erebus Bay on Beechy Island, the scene of much of the 19th century drama in the exploration the Passage and the searches for the lost Franklin Expedition.

At Erebus Bay we met up with Skip Novak on his new 72 foot aluminum sloop, *Pelagic Australis,* which was specially built for high-latitude sailing and usually based in Antarctica. He had a group of six wealthy Italians aboard who had chartered the boat for the summer to try for a transit of the NW Passage (they failed). We pooled our information and concluded that the ice situation in the Passage was still so bad that it was too early to even attempt to get through. Skip also explained that sun spot activity in the high arctic was especially bad this year and was undoubtedly the cause of our radio problems. He recommended that we should push on to the settlement of Resolute on Cornwallis Island where we could probably acquire an Iridium satellite phone. To be without communication in these waters was too much of a risk.

While at Erebus Bay we went ashore to have a look at the many artifacts left by the early explorers. The ruins on the beach included hundreds of barrel hoops and staves as well as innumerable rusty, square, hand-soldered tin cans from the earliest experiments in tinned meat. Lately there had been much investigation of possible lead poisoning of the explorers by lumps of solder in the cans. On the beach are three graves of crew members of the Franklin expedition of 1845. One body (frozen and in perfect condition) was exhumed recently and found to be badly affected by lead poisoning although the death was apparently caused by tuberculosis. While on excursions like this, we were *always* armed with a pump shotgun loaded with big slugs as protection from the polar bears which frequent the shore. We were well aware of their propensity to stalk humans, and why not? They were certainly at the top of the food chain up here.

We wiggled through bands of relatively loose ice and arrived at Resolute Bay just in time to be pinned down by a three-day easterly gale with winds up to 45 knots. We rode it out on 200 feet of ½ inch chain on a 66 pound Bruce anchor. Finally the wind eased and we got ashore, officially entered Canada, and looked around at the tiny Inuit village and the incredibly bleak background of raw rock. Because Resolute is a jump-off point for arctic expeditions, we were able to acquire an Iridium telephone, along with water and diesel fuel which we jerry-jugged out to the boat, a tough job in cold, wet, windy conditions. One of the crew, Carl Seipel, decided to leave the boat in Resolute for various reasons including being uneasy with the idea of a being on a fiberglass boat in ice filled waters and a feeling that we were ill prepared for possible disaster in the form of sinking or winter survival. Roger was upset with his defection but happily he was able to recruit a young man named Judd Reed, who had just finished working on a simulated Mars landing project up in the Arctic. Tells you something about the landscape up there! Judd had never done any sailing but was an intelligent, interesting person and turned out to be an excellent crew.

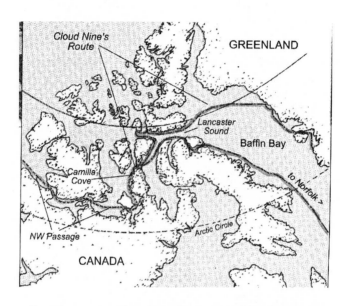

Cloud Nine's route from Greenland to the Northwest Passage
until we were stopped by the ice and retreated south

When we attempted to leave Resolute on the fourth day we found our way blocked by ice which had accumulated during the gale and forced us to retreat back to Resolute. After surveying the situation from the top of a high hill next day, we tried again and managed to get around the ice and back to the entrance of Prince Regent Inlet, 110 miles to the east, where we anchored at Port Leopold, a bleak windswept refuge which had been an important rendezvous point for exploring ships in the 19th century. We made one foray ashore to check out the lonely, abandoned cabin on the beach which was obviously of considerable age and the artifacts scattered about including a boulder with "E+I 1849" neatly carved on it. Checking our history books aboard, we learned it stood for the ships *Enterprise* and *Investigator* which had wintered over here under the command of Sir James Ross in 1849 while searching for the lost Franklin Expedition.

This was the beginning of three weeks of waiting in three different locations for the ice to open enough for us to proceed. We had been advised by the Canadian Coast Guard ice officer that our location at Port Leopold was likely to become untenable because of a possible movement of ice into the bay so we retreated 75 miles back to Erebus Bay. The weather during this period was a mixture of reasonable days and severe gales, one of which blew from the east for three days with winds gusting to over 50 knots. During our wait at Erebus Bay we saw as many as four polar bears at on time on the beach which, in addition to the wind, discouraged trips ashore. Mostly our time was spent going through the extensive library we had aboard, cooking and working on various minor maintenance jobs. It was usually too cold to spend much time on deck and below decks it was impossible to see through the cabin windows so the atmosphere was a bit claustrophobic. Fortunately we had an excellent little Dickenson diesel heater which kept the saloon at a reasonable temperature. All things considered, our morale was quite good in spite of the fact that we had scarcely begun our transit of the Northwest Passage and were getting nowhere fast. Finally on August 24th the wind eased and the sea had been mostly cleared of ice by the easterly gale so we got under way toward Prince Regent Inlet and further progress. The ice reports still weren't good but things seemed to be improving.

Our last anchorage was at Fort Ross, at the eastern entrance to Bellot Strait and the gateway to the heart of the Passage. Here we had the company of *Jotun Arctic* a 42' Norwegian sloop with a sled and 3 dogs aboard and which had already failed to get through and had overwintered twice. We were the first sailboat they had seen in two years. In addition to the owners, Knute and Camilla, they had aboard temporarily four young Canadians they had met in Arctic Bay, the site of their last overwintering. The Canadians were skilled at netting arctic char, a salmon-like fish which they shared with us as well as the dogs.

We impatiently listened to radio reports of several yachts attempting to proceed eastward, plotted information on the ice maps, and hiked to the top of the hills to see if Bellot Strait was still blocked by ice. We knew that the season was rapidly coming to a close and Point Barrow was still 1600 miles away and Dutch Harbor in the Aleutians a further 1200 miles away. Night travel would be slow or impossible with ice in the water so it could be late October or November before we got out of the arctic even if we got through. Not a happy thought.

Camilla Cove, our safe little haven where we were trapped by ice along with Jotun Arctic on September 4th

Finally, on September 2nd it seemed that there was a chance, with ice blocking only about 50 miles of the Passage ahead and prospects for further improvement in the next day or two. *Cloud Nine* and *Jotun Arctic* got underway and easily passed through Bellot Strait only to find increasing amounts of floating ice as we proceeded south. By evening, only 20 miles south of the Strait, we were stopped by nearly solid ice and retreated a couple of miles to a patch of clear water in the lee of a pair of small rocky islets. After pushing small ice floes away from our anchor chain all night and re-anchoring a couple of times we found a tiny, almost landlocked harbor. This little haven, which we christened "Camilla Cove" after the wife of the skipper of *Jotun Arctic*, was discovered when I went to the top of our mast and could see over the islet. When Knute sounded it, he found it had 25' of water inside but only 11' at the entrance, a factor which would keep it nearly ice free or at least free of ice pressure. Roger had been very concerned that the if the wind changed it would bring the ice pack down on us and force the boat onto the rocks, a factor which I had not fully appreciated. We wasted no time in getting our anchors up, moving into the blessed little refuge. Meanwhile, however, ice began to accumulate solidly outside and soon we were trapped.

I was quite sure that with the season this late, there was little chance of *Cloud Nine* getting out before a solid freeze up. I expected she would survive a winter alone while frozen in but Knute was not so sure because she had a fairly serious leak around the rudder stock. In any event a crew would have to wait aboard until the boats were solidly frozen into the ice. Then they could be taken out by helicopter or snowmobile from an Inuit village about 100 miles to the south. Roger was obviously worried but seemed to remain confident that we would get out somehow before freeze-up.

About 30 miles south of us, two boats which has been heading our way had become beset in the pack ice and were in serious trouble as the ice closed up and began to exert pressure. One boat, a Canadian 57' aluminum motorboat named *Idlewild* was pushed by the ice right up onto an ice floe. She was undamaged but remained high and dry. The other boat, an Australian 40' steel sloop named *Fine Tolerance*, was being squeezed by the ice and heeled over in both directions until her rail was in the water. Fearful that the boat would be crushed and sunk, the couple aboard abandoned her and dragged their dinghy and hiked over the ice floes to *Idlewild* for safety.

Nanook pays us a visit in Camilla Cove

We spent a week in Camilla Cove hiking over the hills, filling our water tanks from a little stream, fishing for arctic char, observing polar bears, and watching old movies aboard *Cloud Nine*. The Canadian icebreaker, *Sir Wilfred Laurier,* was stationed about 200 miles south of us at Gjoa Haven and she was soon underway to come to the aid of the two boats in distress. By radio we followed the progress of the drift of the two boats northward toward us. Amazingly, one of them passed undamaged right through a group of small islands. When *Laurier* reached *Idlewild,* she was unable to tow her off the ice floe but by patiently directing the flow of her bow thruster against the floe, she eventually managed to get the boat to slide back into the water. *Laurier* then reentered the pack, which had loosened considerably, found *Fine Tolerance* and towed her out to safety. We had seen *Laurier's* helicopter and she had assured us by radio that she would see all four boats in safe water before she departed.

After a week, ice begins to invade our safe cove

On September 10th *Laurier* advised us that she had deposited the other two boats in open water and would be coming to assist us in getting out. We were to try to get out as far as we could into deeper water to accommodate *Laurier's* deeper draft. By this time ice had even invaded our little refuge. We managed to get out the entrance, but in 6 hours of butting and shoving we managed to go only an additional 200 yards or so through the ice. Meanwhile, *Laurier* very, very slowly eased toward us with a man on the bow taking careful soundings with a hand leadline and another pair of men in a small boat scouting for the deepest water. She even touched bottom once but kept coming until her bow was right up against us. As she backed out we were able to follow in her path until we reached open water. A masterful performance.

With barely enough water for her draft, the icebreaker,
Sir Wilfred Laurier, eases her bow to us and backs out

Our elation at being free was soon dampened when we were informed that ice was blocking our path of retreat via Bellot Strait or

Peel Sound and that we would have to follow *Laurier* south for about 20 miles where she would take us to a safe anchorage in Wrottesley Inlet. After dark she stopped and informed us that it was getting too shallow for her and that we were to go on ahead and find a suitable anchorage. By now it was pitch dark and snowing and a rising tail wind was blowing us down on a lee shore. By radar we groped around an island and into the Inlet where we could find only depths of about 350 feet. Eventually we found a wide spot with shallower water and got our anchors down in 75' of water. Daylight the next day revealed the high snow-covered mountains on all sides, heavy snow on our decks and a herd of a dozen musk oxen gazing at us from the shore. As the wind howled through the rigging, a more remote and forbidding location I never hope to see.   Only the knowledge that our icebreaker escort was waiting for us outside kept our spirits up.

Our utterly desolate anchorage in Wrottesley Inlet
with new ice beginning to form on the water

Early on the morning of our fourth day at anchor *Laurier* summoned all three boats to join her as soon as possible. *Fine Toler-*

ance was still disabled and tied to the ship with all three blades of her propeller missing, her rudder stock twisted and her hull badly dented. A strong easterly wind during the night had opened a wide lead along the shore and cleared the ice from Bellot Strait. A large Class A ice-breaker, *Louis St. Laurent*, which was equipped with powerful under-water blowers on each side to shove the broken ice aside, was also waiting for us to form up close behind the *Laurier.* Our little convoy of two icebreakers, one yacht in tow and three others in close forma-tion proceeded slowly through a mile or so of thick ice, then faster as we got into more open water. By dark we had reached Bellot Strait and managed to force our way through against the current which reached 6 knots in one place. By 11:00 PM we were anchored in Fort Ross at the end of an exciting and dramatic day.

The performance of he Canadian Coast Guard and the assis-tance they so freely gave us was truly impressive. It seems the mission of the men on the icebreakers was to see to it that all of the traffic in-cluding boats attempting to transit the Northwest Passage – there were eight of us – were to be helped safely out of the passage at season's end or at least left safely in a suitable harbor. Their friendliness and helpful attitude seemed to have no bounds and for that we were very grateful.

It was now September 14th and we faced a voyage of 3400 miles down the Atlantic to Norfolk, VA where Roger hoped to put the boat up for the winter. The forecast was not good as we got underway up Prince Regent Inlet against a strong northeasterly wind. By eve-ning, we hove-to to avoid ice floes in the dark and to ease the boat in the very rough seas. On our 4th day we reached the little Inuit village of Pond Inlet where we took on fuel and a few groceries then headed out to sea between spectacular snow covered mountains. After that, it was a long hard push against nearly constant headwinds with only a one day break when we took refuge in a little cove in Labrador to ride out a gale with 60 knot gusts and a very brief stop at St. Anthony, on the northern tip of Newfoundland, for fuel and food. The weather on the East Coast was not good because of a lingering disturbance caused by a late season hurricane. On October 12th, my 75th birthday, we ar-rived in Norfolk and moored at the impressive Norfolk Yacht and Country Club, a far different scene from what we had seen on our re-cent travels. Within a couple of days we had stripped the sails off the boat, packed our duffel bags and were on our way back to Marin County.

Rough going on our 3,400 mile retreat to Norfolk, Virginia

Almost everyone asks me if I would try it again. I usually respond that of course, it was a disappointment to have failed to get through the Passage and forfeit the bar-bragging rights that would have gone with it, but still, it had been a grand adventure. Considering the condition of the ice in the 2005 season, I think it all worked out just fine. It turned out that the gale we encountered on our way back up Prince Regent Inlet actually opened up the critical section of the passage for a couple of days, according to Peter Semotiuk, a ham radio operator in Cambridge Bay. If we had not been rescued and escorted out of the passage, it is *possible* that we could have gotten out of Camilla Cove and made it out into the open stretches of the NW Passage but having escaped the ice we would have then faced the world-class storms of the Bering Sea in late season. But to answer the question: Sure! I would sign on to try again in a heartbeat. Ironically, I checked the ice map for August 29, 2006 and was amazed to see that there was no ice at all in the NW Passage. I guess our timing was just a bit off.

Jane, Milly and me in Tiburon

EPILOGUE

At this writing, (2006) two years after our trip to Alaska, we still own *Misty* which means we have owned her for 10 years, a new record. Previously our longest ownership was 8 years. Perhaps we will keep her for some time to come since Jane gets upset whenever I mention getting a different boat. This applies particularly to any notion of getting a power boat. Her usual comment on such an idea is to say, "Yeah and just what do you plan to do when the motor quits?" She has a point. Anyway it is a moot question since we still hope to head north again on *Misty* one day on another cruise, hopefully to Alaska which I consider to be the finest and most interesting cruising area in the world.

Early in the year I fulfilled a promise to help my friend, Carl Seipel, on the first lap of the single-handed voyage he planned to make from San Francisco to New Zealand in hopes of revisiting some of the places he had enjoyed during his circumnavigation in *Fia* 30 years earlier. Carl had bought a bargain-priced Yankee 30 sailboat, renamed *Tootsie,* for the trip four years before and in the interim had steadily improved her with, among other things, a small diesel he purchased on e-Bay. I helped the program along in minor ways by building a spray dodger, recutting a jib (from the yacht club dumpster), making a storm trysail, awnings, and other things.

After a hectic week of preparations, we shoved off on February 23, 2006 from the San Francisco Yacht Club in dubious but acceptable weather. As we ran down the Coast in moderate westerly breezes with heavy overcast, I was surprised and Carl was delighted with how fast and easily she slipped through the water. Carl was so pleased that he said if he had known, he would have named her *Lightfoot.*

We got a very, very strange surprise the first night between Pigeon Point and Point Sur. I was on watch and heard a very low, steady tone like the low note of a diaphone. It was loud enough that Carl heard it from his bunk and asked me what was going on. I didn't know but I observed three, evenly spaced looms or columns of diffuse light on the horizon. They were far enough away so that I couldn't see the source of the light, meaning the light was possibly eight or more miles away, which was totally inconsistent with the loudness of the tone. As I was looking at the lights through the binoculars, I was amazed to see what I can only describe as "reverse tracer shells." Suddenly a stream of bright orange lights would appear then they would be sucked back into the light loom at extreme speed. This happened over and over from all three light sources for six or seven minutes. Suddenly the sound, the light looms and the "reverse tracers" stopped for about ten or fifteen minutes then reappeared farther astern with a repeat performance lasting about 5 minutes. I was sorry I didn't get Carl up to corroborate my story which I admit was pretty unbelievable. I can only assume it was either the military up to some of their ominous tricks or a UFO. I don't much believe in UFOs, but now I'm not so sure!

Tootsie departs from the SFYC harbor for Mexico

We rounded Point Conception in the morning of the second day to hear a dire forecast of a big approaching storm. We had intended to run between Santa Rosa Island and Santa Cruz Island, but instead changed course for Santa Barbara where we spent three days waiting for the storm to pass. A two day run took us to San Diego Bay where we spent a pleasant couple of days at the Coronado Yacht Club as a guest of my old shipmate, Jim Algert, doing last minute jobs, putting more stores aboard and getting our Mexican fishing license.

We arrived in Ensenada about midnight and anchored off the old sunken Catalina Island steamer which is now occupied by a mob of sea lions who bellow and bark all night. The next day Carl went ashore to try out the new Mexican entering procedure. The whole works is housed in a new little building right on the waterfront with separate windows for the harbormaster, customs, and immigration. There is even a mini-bank to pay the fees. The only thing missing is a Xerox machine to provide the multiple copies they want of everything, which means one must run all over town to find a copy shop whose machine is not broken or which is not closed for siesta.

While Carl was ashore I anchored *Tootsie* between pair of sailboats, a green cutter from Oregon and a black schooner from Washington. While waiting, I had the VHF on and began to hear an unbelievable stream of profanity, ranting and death threats (in English). Looking around with the binoculars, I soon figured out that the source of the outrage was the guy on the Oregon boat and it was being directed to the group on the Washington boat. Next I heard several pings and realized that the Oregon guy had a rifle and was shooting at them! It was pellet rifle, but still I didn't like being in the cross fire all that much. The next scene was even better when the antagonists got into their inflatable dinghies with outboards and engaged in a ramming battle. The Washington boat's dinghy, with another dinghy lashed alongside, was rammed by the Oregon dinghy at speed capsizing one dinghy, throwing two people into the water including the Oregon guy and sending his dinghy zooming round in circles with the motor at full throttle. It was total pandemonium. By a miracle, the Oregon guy managed to catch his dinghy and crawl aboard then retreat to his boat while hurling dire threats at his attackers ("You're goin' to diiie! You're goin' dowwn!"). Shortly thereafter the Mexican Navy showed up to board both yachts. I decided to change neighborhoods by reanchoring near an American schooner whose skipper informed me that the two boats had been in the harbor for nearly a whole year and had been fighting continuously!

We sailed the next day non-stop for La Paz with plenty of nice northwesterly wind. We were amazed at the way the little Yankee 30 could move. On our second day out of Ensenada we logged a 160 mile day. Not bad for a little 30 footer! On the 5th day we rounded Cabo San Lucas and headed up into the Sea of Cortez only to run into a stiff norther about 30 miles north of Cabo. We weren't going any-where in our little boat against it, so we hove-to for a couple of hours, changed our mind and started to run back to Cabo for a while then changed our mind again and battled our way up to Los Friailes Bay, about 40 miles north of Cabo. After a day at anchor, wondering how long the north wind would blow, I decided to head home and let Carl start practicing his solo sailing technique in preparation for his big trip to New Zealand.

I caught a ride to the beach and stuck out my thumb. My first ride on the dirt road was with a couple of elderly American desert rats in a jeep. My next ride was with a Mexican family in the back of their rattly old pickup. The third leg toward the highway was with a silent young Mexican who might have been some sort of cop. Finally I got a ride with another young Mexican in a van heading south toward the airport where he worked. He drove like a maniac, stopping twice to water the flowers at a couple of those little shrines they built to memo-rialize crash victims. When I asked what that was all about, he ex-plained they were for his relatives. I was afraid someone might have to build one for me, but we arrived safely at the airport and soon I was on a plane bound for home. It had been an interesting trip. I found out later that the wind had died on the evening of the day I left.

*   *   *   *

Like a running river, life goes on. On April 14, 2006 Jane and I celebrated our 50th wedding anniversary. Actually we celebrated it in June when Anne and Rob and their partners, Greg and Kendall, put on a splendid backyard party for us and a very large group of our friends along the banks of Gallinas Creek, almost on the spot where we built and launched *Sea Bear* nearly 20 years ago. Can years slip by so fast? Yes they can. Indeed they can.

Robert Va
679 Hawth
Tiburon, (

March

Librarian
Kentfield School

Dear Librarian,

This week I had lunch with a mutual friend
yachting figure in the East Bay named Hal
the cost of a number of copies of my recent
Memoir, with the request that they be given

 She said she had enjoyed the book so muc
interest to young people who, living near o
inspiration to seek adventure in the world (
would be a nice, if modest, memorial to ou
people of all ages the joys of boating.

Although I wrote the book with adults in r
age 12, seemed to enjoy the book very mu
Middle School who will do the same. We
on the shelf of the school library in hopes

Thank you.

Sincerely,

Robert Van Blaricom